ST LUKE
Theologian of Redemptive History

HELMUT FLENDER

ST LUKE
Theologian of Redemptive History

TRANSLATED BY
Reginald H. and Ilse Fuller

Fortress Press
Philadelphia

English Edition
First Published in 1967
by S.P.C.K., London

AMERICAN EDITION
First Published in 1967
by Fortress Press, Philadelphia
Library of Congress Catalog Card Number 67–18245

© (Translation)
Reginald H. and Ilse Fuller

Printed in Great Britain

IN MEMORY
OF MY BROTHER
KARL-FRIEDRICH FLENDER
1923–1944

Acknowledgements

Thanks are due to the following for permission to quote from copyright sources:

Faber & Faber Ltd and Harper & Row, Inc.: *Theology of St Luke*, by H. Conzelmann.

Nicholson & Watson Ltd: *From Tradition to Gospel*, by Martin Dibelius.

S.C.M. Press Ltd and Charles Scribner's Sons: *Theology of the New Testament*, by R. Bultmann.

Biblical quotations from the *Revised Standard Version* of the Bible, copyrighted 1946 and 1952 by the Division of Christian Education of the National Council of the Churches of Christ in the United States of America, are used by permission.

Contents

Foreword to the English Edition

The German original of this work was accepted as a dissertation by the Theological Faculty of the Friedrich-Alexander University (Erlangen-Nuremberg) in the summer of 1964. Professor Gerhard Friedrich served as my adviser. I am more at home in Systematic Theology, and so he was able to help me with constructive criticism during the early stages. I owe him a deep debt of gratitude—not least for the generous hospitality he showed me in his home. For financial assistance towards the original printing my heartfelt thanks are due to the Church of the Rhineland, Westphalia, Hesse-Nassau, and the Palatinate, and to Professor Beckmann who was instrumental in raising the funds.

The questions which guided this exegetical research into Luke–Acts arose out of practical work in teaching the Gospel to young workers. I have been much stimulated by my reading of English theological literature, and I am therefore particularly glad that my study of Lucan theology can be published in English so soon after the appearance of the German edition. With C. K. Barrett I believe "that the focus of New Testament studies is now moving to the Lucan writings", and I offer this work as a contribution to the problem of "the relation between history and theology" (*Luke the Historian in Recent Study*, Epworth Press, 1961, p. 50).

My thanks are due to Professor Ernst Wolf for accepting this work in the series *Beiträge zur evangelischen Theologie*, to Professor and Mrs R. H. Fuller for making the English translation, and to the S.P.C.K. for the interest they have taken in it.

Düsseldorf, May 1966   HELMUT FLENDER

Abbreviations

Introduction

The distinctiveness of Lucan theology has become increasingly apparent during the last few years through the study of the history of redaction.[1] Like Mark and Matthew, Luke does not merely transmit the tradition as it came to him. He is also a theologian, interpreting the Christian message for his own time. In this interpretation he is guided by a certain dogmatic understanding which proves him to be a theologian of the post-apostolic age.[2] The received tradition is built into a dogmatic framework with a resultant modification of its original meaning. This concentration upon contemporary theological witness is matched by an attrition of the tradition. The dogmatic scheme determines and alters the context of the traditional terms. The tradition becomes "material", items that have to be fitted into the theological scheme. That leads, for example, in the christological titles, to their "promiscuous" use. Luke can put them to an entirely different use from that for which they were originally intended.[3]

From all this it follows that exegesis cannot be confined to a study of the origins of the theological concepts in the history of religion. As an interpreter Luke writes out of a particular theological background. Therefore, in order to interpret his statements we must combine considerations of history and theology, taking

[1] Beginning with H. J. Cadbury, *The Making of Luke–Acts* 1958[2], but principally, H. Conzelmann, *The Theology of St. Luke*, 1960 (German edn, *Die Mitte der Zeit*, 1964[5]).

[2] There is complete agreement on this point among scholars. But their judgements and assessments of Lucan theology vary considerably.

[3] H. Conzelmann, op. cit., p. 171, n. 1; this is already true of the pre-Lucan tradition, as F. Hahn, *Christologische Hoheitstitel*, 1963, has clearly shown. On Luke's use of the christological titles to build up the pattern of Christ's earthly and heavenly modes of existence see pp. 42f. The indiscriminate use of the christological titles in Paul is demonstrated by W. Kramer, *Christ, Lord, Son of God* (SBT 50), 1966, p. 182 (cf. p. 150).

account of the fact that the historical tradition, in all its manifold variety, has been modified in the interests of a particular dogmatic scheme.

This raises another question. Does the tradition, thus formed, still retain any theological significance of its own? Once Luke's own distinctive theology has been recognized, there is a danger of its being allowed to overshadow the tradition itself.[1] What theological relevance does that tradition still possess? Luke uses early Christian texts as sources for his own Gospel. Yet he does not regard them merely as sources. They are also primarily testimony to Christ. He listens to them and applies them anew to his own situation. Thus he remains faithful to the kerygma enshrined in the tradition.[2] But he is faithful to the spirit rather than to the letter. Tradition is something that can be reshaped, and Luke deals with it very freely. For the transmission of tradition is something that occurs on the human level, within history. But on the spiritual plane he contrives to preserve the thread of continuity in the witness to Christ. He adapts his message to his own age. But it is the same Christ to whom he bears witness. It is this fidelity to the underlying spirit that gives him the human freedom with which he shapes it.

Regarded from this point of view, the Lucan writings appear unusually fruitful for the problem of hermeneutics. Here, within the canon, is an instance of a writer wrestling with the question of how to expound the Christian message in a new situation. Luke is not original here. In many ways he just carries on what Mark

[1] Cf. the warning against Haenchen's one-sided treatment of Lucan interpretation in his commentary on Acts, in R. Bultmann's "Zur Frage nach den Quellen der Apg.", *NT Essays* (in memory of T. W. Manson), 1959, pp. 68–80.

[2] That is shown by a comparison with Mark. See above, pp. 98ff (the hearing before the Sanhedrin); pp. 111ff (the apocalyptic discourse); pp. 146ff (sermon at Nazareth), etc.

Cf. J. Schniewind, "Zur Synoptiker-Exegese" in *ThR* NF 2 (1930), p. 142; G. Bornkamm, *Jesus of Nazareth*, 1960, p. 17; W. Marxsen, "Exegese und Verkündigung" in *ThEx* NF 59 (1957), pp. 8ff, regards the whole of the NT as "exegesis" (p. 9). He puts forward the thesis that "false exegesis" (in the sense of present-day scholarship) can nevertheless be legitimate proclamation for Luke's own age (p. 8). But how far may we classify Matthew and Luke as "interim solutions" between Mark and John (p. 47), and then dismiss them like Marxsen as outmoded, or, at the very least, as subject to correction in the light of Mark and John?

had started. Yet a synoptic comparison will give us a pretty clear view of the gulf between the theology of Mark and that of Luke.

Much work has already been done in this field. Previous essays, whether written *pro* or *contra*, are all alike in treating Luke as a theologian who adjusts himself pragmatically to given conditions in the post-apostolic age and who indeed has no other course open to him. This makes Luke appear as an *epigonē*, as one who has fallen from the heights of Pauline theology (maintained by Mark and recovered by John). With Luke theology becomes crystallized and salvation objectified. Luke stands on the fringes of the New Testament canon, or even outside of it, an example of "early Catholicism".[1] This makes the Lucan writings merely the source of Church history in the post-apostolic age.[2] Any significance for the present—that means any properly theological meaning—would at best be merely negative.[3]

This is the starting-point of the present essay. Its aim is to develop those structures of Lucan theology which have a claim to be taken seriously—over and above their purely historical and contemporary significance. As soon as we raise the question of the theological relevance of the Lucan writings, we are confronted with the fact that Luke lived in the post-apostolic age.

[1] The discussion was inaugurated by P. Vielhauer in 1950 in an essay entitled "On the Paulinism of Acts" (Eng. Tr. in *Studies in Luke–Acts*, ed. L. E. Keck and J. L. Martyn, 1966, pp. 33–50). See also R. Bultmann, *Theology of the New Testament*, 1955, pp. 116f. The thesis has been stated very trenchantly by E. Käsemann in his essay on "The Problem of the Historical Jesus" (Eng. Tr. in *Essays on New Testament Themes*, 1964, pp. 28f) (cf. the list of works on this theme in Haenchen, *Apostelgeschichte*, p. 46, n. 2); and more cautiously ibid. in 1961[13]; H. Conzelmann in *The Theology of St. Luke* assumes that Luke holds a full-blown conception of redemptive history. He is followed by E. Grässer, *Das Problem der Parousieverzögerung in den synoptischen Evangelien und in der Apg.*, 1960[2], pp. 178ff; W. Marxsen, *Der Evangelist Markus*, 1959[2], pp. 30f, 64ff, 95ff, 129ff; H. E. Tödt, *The Son of Man in the Synoptic Tradition*, 1965, pp. 94ff, 282f; G. Klein, *Die Zwölf Apostel*, 1961, thinks that the Lucan theology of redemptive history was produced in reaction to the gnostic crisis (pp. 213f).

[2] E. Käsemann, "Paulus und der Frühkatholizismus" in *ZThK* 60 (1963), p. 85 sees in the change after Paul an "historical necessity", which he calls "legitimate" because of the "necessity and embarrassment" of that period. This is how the Apostle Paul used to be justified at the turn of the century!

[3] So G. Harbsmeier, "Unsere Predigt im Spiegel der Apg" in *Ev Th*, 10 (1950–1), p. 365.

This means that his situation was much more like ours than the apostolic age (Paul), with its imminent expectation of the second coming. Like Luke, we live in an age which stretches out into an indefinite future. Like Luke we have to face up to the problem of living in this world. In view of our situation, so different from that of Paul's, we must allow Luke to ask us whether we understand correctly the way in which the Pauline message is relevant to us, written as it was with such entirely different presuppositions from our own.[1] We could have a "Paulinism" which is a loyal translation of Pauline terminology, but which in a very different situation reproduces the exact opposite of what Paul intended.

The basis of this whole dilemma seems to me to lie in the as yet unsolved problem of historism. Bultmann has hard words to say against this kind of historism, "which conceived early Christianity and with it the New Testament as a phenomenon within the closed continuum of world history linked together by cause and effect" and "is then no longer . . . interested in the question of truth". Against this view he enters the lists with the kerygma as "God's word addressing man as a questioning and promising word, a condemning and forgiving word".[2] In this way Bultmann can retain the contemporary relevance of the Biblical testimony. But he has to pay for it dearly. First, and inevitably, the New Testament message undergoes considerable reduction. Only Paul and John really fit into his scheme of things. The narrative portions of the New Testament have to be gauged by Paul and John. In place of interpretation, for the present they are compared with Paul and John by the standards

---

[1] This is where the dilemma of our contemporary theological situation becomes apparent. To-day we are once more aware that man is to a large degree determined by his social environment and that the important decisions in society are made not by the individual but by the group. Hence our contemporary world seeks for clarification in social and ethical problems. This is where Luke can help us. But we must let his theology stand on its own feet and not look at it through the spectacles of Pauline terminology. This is recognized by A. N. Wilder, "Kerygma, Eschatology and Social Ethics" in *The Background of the NT and its Eschatology* (in honour of C. H. Dodd), 1956, p. 516. He maintains that what we need is "kerygmatic social ethic". Unfortunately however, he develops his ethic solely in terms of Pauline theology (pp. 522ff).

[2] *Theology*, pp. 245, 244, 240.

of the history of religion.[1] On the other hand, Bultmann looses the New Testament testimony from its historical moorings. Since the kerygma only touches upon "the moment" in time and never the past, it can never become objective,[2] nor enter into the continuity of history.[3] The kerygma touches man in human structures which remain the same down the ages. The whole social realm in which human history unfolds remains excluded. The fact that God enters the transitoriness of the world is played down by existentialist interpretation and demythologizing. In this *a priori* framework the thought of Luke cannot be adequately grasped. Bultmann argues correctly that Luke "has surrendered the originally kerygmatic sense of the Jesus tradition and has historized it".[4]

But even those who set positive store by redemptive history cannot do justice to Luke's design. For redemptive history cannot but suggest to modern man the notion of a revelation history open to human observation just as much as any other history. The difference between statements of faith and reflection is obscured.[5] Of course faith bears witness that God's salvation enters history. This is the justification for speaking of redemptive history. But the observation of, and reflection upon, the past must not reduce divine salvation to the same level as human history. The qualitative difference between the action of God and that of man must be preserved. Otherwise we shall fall into historical pantheism. It is our task to show that Luke is conscious of this problem, and when we speak of "redemptive history" we are using the term only in a non-technical sense.[6]

Thus as we see it Luke has planned his Gospel on more

---

[1] Cf. Part III of Bultmann's *Theology* where his method is quite different from that of Parts I and II.

[2] Cf. Bultmann, ibid., pp. 240f.

[3] Cf. F. Lieb's discussion with H. Ott. in *EvTh* 15 a (1955), pp. 507ff (*Sophia und Historie*, 1962, pp. 321ff), especially the discussion about the independent reality of our corporeal life as willed by God, pp. 514ff (*Sophia*, pp. 329ff). On the debate over Bultmann's conception of the kerygma see P. Althaus, *Fact and Faith in the Kerygma of Today*, 1959, *passim*.

[4] Ibid., p. 117.

[5] Cf. K. G. Steck, *Die Idee der Heilsgeschichte*, ThSt 56, (1959), pp. 55f.

[6] We indicate this where necessary by quotation marks.

levels than Conzelmann has allowed us to see in his monograph *The Theology of St. Luke*. Although we have taken
over many detailed insights from Conzelmann we cannot
agree with his overall understanding of Luke's theology. He
lacks a clear grasp of the real presuppositions of Luke's thought,
and consequently forces it into the categories of modern
thought.[1]

The example of Conzelmann shows that we cannot understand
Lucan theology until we have discovered the framework of his
thought. Luke's peculiar way of thinking, it seems to us, expresses
itself especially in the way he puts his texts together. For this is
where the redactor has the chance to state his material. In Chapter
I of this work we shall examine Luke's "technique of composition", and we will try to develop some of the more noticeable
patterns in his thought. In this the examples chosen will be geared
to the subsequent parts of the work. In Chapter 2 we discuss
Luke's use of "secular language" and the missionary preaching in
Acts. His missionary sermons are determined by his Christology
(2A). Since Luke distinguishes between Christ's heavenly and
earthly modes of existence, he can give relative independence to
his presentation of the human life of Jesus. The situation of man
prior to faith receives special consideration. The language Luke
uses in addressing the outside world (2B) and the way he applies
the Christian message to the secular order (2C) are to be understood in the light of this Christology. Chapter 3 is an inquiry into
Luke's view of redemptive history. It begins with the thesis that
Luke's time scheme is that of Revelation 12. In heaven the final
victory is anticipated and the exaltation of Christ represents the
consummation of salvation in heaven (3A). This is what raises
the question about the continuation of history both in the Church
and in the world and how this continuation of history is to be
assessed theologically. In 3B, we shall try to show how Israel

[1] Here Conzelmann is always fully aware of the distance between then and
now; cf., for example, *St. Luke*, p. 36. But he makes no distinctions in his use of
the term *Heilsgeschichte*. Luke's statements are made at different levels (from the
kerygmatic "to-day" in Luke 4.18 to the historical note in Luke 3.1f). But
Conzelmann finds in them "no other view of history . . . than that implicit in
the view of redemptive history which prevails throughout Luke" (p. 168). Is
that the language of the first century or of the nineteenth?

provided a model both for the history of the world as well as for the earthly history of the Christian community. Finally, in 3C the actual presence of salvation in the gift of the Holy Spirit and in encounter with the exalted Christ will be discussed.

1

The Dialectical Structure of Luke-Acts

Luke–Acts contains a great many parallels and contrasts. These involve not only the juxtaposition of individual texts but also correspondences which run all through the work. R. Morgenthaler has made a detailed study of this subject.[1] In his investigation of the parallels in wording, sentences, and paragraphs, and of the overall composition, he concludes that the "law of two" is the characteristic feature of Lucan style.[2]

It is in shaping his material in accordance with this law that Luke's special ability as an editor lies. Morgenthaler's basic thesis is the "two-membered architectonic art of Luke".[3] Previously, L. Brun had demonstrated the "technique of composition in Luke's Gospel".[4] Similarly, Conzelmann finds it a "feature of Luke's account" that allusions to earlier passages occur without any direct reference to them.[5] In this deliberate shaping and composition of the material lies the special contribution of Luke as a redactor and the distinctive character of his Gospel. It is here that he betrays the patterns in which his theology is given expression. The literary form subserves the theological conception.[6] From the way he edits his materials we can infer a

[1] R. Morgenthaler, *Die lukanische Geschichtsschreibung als Zeugnis*, 2 vols, 1948, 1949.
[2] Ibid., I, 96.   [3] Op. cit., I, p. 195.
[4] L. Brun, *Zur Kompositionstechnik des Lukasevangeliums* (Symb. Osl. 9), 1930, pp. 38–50.
[5] Luke 4.13/22.3, 20.25/23.2; 13.35/19.38; 2.7/22.11; 2.14/19.38; 2.38/23.51 (*St. Luke*, pp. 75f, n. 4).
[6] Because our intention is thus limited we need not pursue any further the controverted literary problem of the doublets in Luke. Some have spoken, with special reference to the "great omission" of Mark 6.45—8.28, of Luke's "avoidance of doublets". So H. Schürmann, "Die Dublettenvermeidung in Lk.-Ev." in ZKTh 76 (1954), pp. 83ff; J. Jeremias, "Perikopenumstellungen bei Lukas?" in NTS 4 (1958), pp. 115ff; P. Wernle, *Die synoptische Frage*, 1899, p. 6;

distinctive systematic framework which we need to know before we can understand Lucan theology.[1]

In the following pages we shall put together selected units of material which are arranged in complementary, climactic, and antithetical parallelism, and so endeavour to lay bare the theological concerns which these patterns express.

A. COMPLEMENTARY PARALLELISM

(a) The compositional arrangement of a number of sayings comes out very clearly in the well-known contrast between Man and Woman. In Luke stories about a man are frequently paralleled by stories about a woman:[2] these parallels mostly occur in the

a different view is taken by W. Bussmann, Synoptische Studien I, 1925, p. 57; for a balanced view cf. W. Larfeld, Die nt.lichen Evangelien nach ihrer Eigenart und Abhängigkeit, 1925, pp. 321ff.

[1] By raising the question of the concepted horizon within which Luke writes we follow a very different methodological procedure from Conzelmann in his monograph, The Theology of St. Luke. Conzelmann would put Luke's distinctiveness into focus by first eliminating the prior development of the tradition (ibid., foreword to the third edn). Correct though this principle is from the traditio-historical point of view (its value has been demonstrated by Conzelmann in a whole series of discoveries), it is necessary to proceed with great caution in view of Luke's theological stance. This comes out only in a highly one-sided way when the pre-Lucan traditions are ignored (and therefore distorted). Take for instance the term μετάνοια (St. Luke, pp. 99ff). Repentance, according to Conzelmann, becomes in Luke the "condition of forgiveness" (p. 100). Where, however, he speaks of δοῦναι μετάνοιαν (Acts 5.31; 11.18), thus understanding repentance as a gift of salvation, Conzelmann believes the phrase to be a familiar one, the original meaning of which has been lost (p. 100). Here he overlooks Luke's predilection for dialectical contrasts. Luke places contradictory statements side by side, thus refracting the Christian message and preserving its mystery. It is a gift from heaven (Acts 5.31) and a decision to which a man is challenged (Acts 2.38; 3.19; Luke 3.8; 5.32; 13.3, 5). It is proclaimed, as a new reality of life (Acts 17.30; 20.21; 26.20). It follows the saving action of God and precedes its actualization as "repentance for the forgiveness of sins" (Luke 3.3; 24.47).

[2] Zacharias and Mary (the angelic annunciation: Luke 1.11–20/1.26–38; glory to God: 1.46–55/1.67–79), Simeon and Hannah (2.25–38), the widow of Sarepta and Naaman (4.25–8), the healing of the demoniac and Peter's mother-in-law (4.31–9; cf. Mark 1.21–31), the centurion of Capernaum and the widow of Nain (Luke 7.1–17), Simon the Pharisee and the woman who as a sinner (7.36–50), the man with the mustard seed and the woman with the leaven (13.18–21), the good Samaritan and Mary and Martha (10.29–42), the man with the 100 sheep and the woman with the ten pieces of silver (15.4–10), the importunate woman and the publican (18.1–14) or the friend at night (11.5–8), the women at the tomb

special Lucan material. Even if they were already arranged in this way in his source, the passages from Acts show that Luke has deliberately extended and developed this type of parallelism.

Luke expresses by this arrangement that man and woman stand together and side by side before God. They are equal in honour and grace, they are endowed with the same gifts and have the same responsibilities (cf. Gen. 1.27; Gal. 3.28).

(b) The parable of the good Samaritan and the story of the ruler are introduced by the same question, τί ποιήσας ζωὴν αἰώνιον κληρονομήσω (10.25; 18.18); and Jesus' reply is similar in both cases. He refers them to the law. In the first instance he asks the scribe a question (10.26). In the second he recites the law to the ruler (18.20). After this beginning, each narrative takes its own line. The discussion with the scribe ends with the question about the neighbour. The rich man is challenged to sell his goods and to follow Jesus. Thus Luke gives us two answers to the question of eternal life. The question turns upon God (following Jesus) and the neighbour (as the one who helps me and who needs my help).[1]

By means of this dialetic Luke gives the relationship to God and the relationship to the neighbour a relative independence, but at the same time relates them to each other by the question about eternal life. The change compared with Mark is made clear in another place, containing the twofold commandment of love to God and neighbour (Mark 12.28–34). Luke follows up this commandment with the parable of the good Samaritan and so anchors it firmly to the ethical sphere.[2]

---

and the Emmaus disciples (23.55—24.35), the sleeping men and the women at the mill in the last judgement (17.34f; cf. Matt. 24.40f), Ananias and Sapphira (Acts 5.1–11), Aeneas and Tabitha (Acts 9.32–42), Lydia the purple seller and the Philippian jailer (Acts 16.13–34), Dionysius and Damaris (Acts 17.34).

Cf. Cadbury, *The Making of Luke–Acts*, p. 234; A. Schlatter, *Das Evangelium des Lukas* 1960[2], p. 347; Morgenthaler, op. cit., I, pp. 104f.

[1] Cf. E. Fuchs, "Was heisst, 'Du sollst deinen Nächsten lieben wie dich selbst'?" in *ThBl* 11 (1932), pp. 129ff; G. Bornkamm, "Das Doppelgebot der Liebe" in *Nt.liche Studien für R. Bultmann*, 1957[2], pp. 85ff; W. Knox, *The Sources of the Synoptic Gospels* II, 1957, pp. 57f; further, K. Barth, *Church Dogmatics* I, 2, pp. 411ff, and the exposition of H. W. Bartsch, *Wachet zu jeder Zeit*, 1963, pp. 96ff, based on Barth, ibid.

[2] On this "social interpretation" see above, pp. 72f.

(c) The two versions of the ascension story (Luke 24.50–3; Acts 1.9–11) are presented in a similar way, as P. A. van Stempvoort has shown.[1] According to him Luke 24 refers to the inward relationship of the disciples to their master. Jesus appears to them for the last time in the form of a priest giving his blessing (cf. Ecclus. 50.20–2) and they worship before him.[2] Side by side with this doxological interpretation of the ascension we have the ecclesiological or historical interpretation in Acts.[3] *Proskunēsis* and *eulogia* are "an attitude of the inner circle of the church", but "this inner circle is destined to go out into the world";[4] in other words, the history of the Church must follow the Gospel. The second interpretation of the ascension is realistic.[5] The categories of space and time play a great part in Acts 1. It is one of Luke's most typical pieces of writing.[6]

Although it is helpful to point out the difference between the theological sayings of Luke 24.50ff and Acts 1.9ff, it is still a question whether van Stempvoort's exegesis agrees with Luke's intention. The story in the Gospel is in the first place a farewell scene (the blessing with the uplifted hands).[7] Luke wants to make it clear that "Jesus is not seen at all times by all believers in this position: even for the disciples it came to an end".[8] It signifies the end of Jesus' life on earth. From now on he will no longer be visible among his disciples.

The ascension of Jesus is only hinted at here in negative terms. He parted (διέστη) from them. But this parting does not make

---

[1] P. A. van Stempvoort, "The Interpretation of the Ascension in Luke and Acts", *NTS* 5 (1958–9), pp. 30ff. Stempvoort's treatment is put to positive use by E. Grässer, "Die Apg. in der Forschung der Gegenwart" in *ThR* NF 26 (1960), pp. 254f; C. K. Barrett, *Luke the Historian in Recent Study*, 1961, pp. 55ff; cf. also Haenchen, *Apg.* pp. 675f. This is a further argument against the theory that Luke 24.50–3 is an interpolation: cf. K. Lake, *The Beginnings of Christianity* V, 1933, pp. 3f; H. Sahlin, *Der Messias und das Gottesvolk*, 1945, pp. 1ff; Conzelmann, *St. Luke*, p. 94. P. Menoud in his "Remarques sur les Textes de l'ascension dans Luc–Actes" in *Nt. lichen Studien für R. Bultmann*, 1957², pp. 148ff has in the meantime changed his mind on the subject and now pleads for the Lucan origin of Luke 24.50ff and Acts 1.1ff ("Pendant quarante jours" in *Neotestamentica et Patristica*, 1962, p. 148, n. 1).

[2] Ibid, p. 35.   [3] Ibid., p. 39.   [4] Ibid., p. 37.
[5] Ibid., p. 41.   [6] Ibid., p. 42.
[7] E. Klostermann, *Das Lukasevangelium* 1929², p. 243.
[8] Schlatter, *Lukas*, p. 457.

the disciples sad. They return in "great joy". They remember Jesus as they saw him disappear, dispensing his blessing. Through their own εὐλογεῖν they remain on earth in touch with him in heaven. That is the way this story describes the end of Jesus' earthly life on earth. But this description, for all its reserve, expresses the certainty that there will be a new beginning as promised in 24.49.

The ascension story in Acts 1 is given quite a different slant. While the word "heaven" does not even occur in the first story, it is most striking that here the "ascending into heaven" is mentioned four times like a refrain,[1] and the words οὐρανός occurs four times.

v. 9 ". . . he was lifted up (ἐπήρθη) . . ."

v. 10 "While they were gazing into heaven as he went, . . ."

v. 11 ". . . looking into heaven. This Jesus who was taken up (ἀναλημφθείς) from you into heaven will come in the same way as you saw him go into heaven."

The two men "in white apparel" who interpret the event (cf. Luke 24.4) point to an "eschatological" situation. The connection with the return of Jesus is made clear. Jesus is the Lord of heaven who now sends out his apostles as witnesses (1.8) and will one day assume[2] his dominion visibly (an exact parallel to Luke 19.11–27).

Luke 24 views the "translation of Jesus from the earthly to the heavenly life"[3] from the human angle, while Acts 1 looks at it from above, in the light of the destiny of Lord of heaven.

---

[1] H. Schlier, "Jesu Himmelfahrt nach den Lukanischen Schriften" in *Besinnung auf das NT*, 1964, p. 237.

[2] Hahn, *Hoheitstitel*, p. 126ff, rightly distinguishes between "assumption" on the OT pattern and "exaltation" in the sense of enthronization in heavenly majesty, as expressed in Psalm 110.1. In my opinion he is also right in suggesting that Acts 1.9–11 is an ancient picture of an assumption looking forward to the parousia, which Luke has taken up and put to use (pp. 106f). But even if the "exaltation" played "no part in this ascension story" (pp. 126f, n. 4), this is no longer true of the way Luke regards it. Luke himself attaches particular significance to his juxtaposition of the heavenly enthronement and the parousia, (Acts 1.11), and the transference of functions from the returning Christ to the exalted One. In Hahn's terminology we may say that Luke 24 deals with the assumption of Jesus and Acts 1 with his exaltation.

[3] T. Zahn, *Das Evangelium des Lucas*, 1920³, ⁴, p. 397.

We shall discuss these two angles, the earthly and the heavenly existence of Jesus, further.[1]

(d) The two eschatological discourses of Jesus differ characteristically from each other. This also applies to the respective addresses. Luke 17.22–37 is concerned to teach the disciples, while 21.5–36 is part of Jesus' teaching in the Temple in Jerusalem and is addressed to the people.[2] This is specially remarkable since the apocalyptic discourse of Mark is "secret teaching of those close to him",[3] that is, just Peter, James, John, and Andrew (Mark 13.3). Wellhausen thinks the reason why the other disciples are not included is that "they had already asked the same question and received an answer which should have prevented them from raising it again" (17.22).[4] Conzelmann considers it a literary device of Luke to enable him to present what follows as a continuous discourse (Luke 18.1ff).[5]

But it is easy to explain the change of address from the contents of the discourses. They certainly do not express "the same teaching";[6] they regard the return of Jesus from entirely different points of view. According to Grundmann the emphasis in 17.22ff rests upon "the suddenness and unexpectedness with which the days of the Son of Man burst upon them", whereas 21.5ff speaks of "the time preceding this sudden and unforeseen end".[7]

Let us try to clarify the difference between these two texts further, starting with Luke 21.5.[8] The very introduction to the sayings, vv. 5–7, shows the difference in the situation as between Luke and Mark. The κατ' ἰδίαν of Mark 13.3 (cf. Matt. 24.3) is

---

[1] See below, pp. 37ff.
[2] Cf. Luke 20.1; 21.37f; on this Conzelmann, St. Luke, p. 125.
[3] M. Dibelius, From Tradition to Gospel, 1935, p. 260.
[4] J. Wellhausen, Das Evangelium Lucae, 1904, p. 116.
[5] Ibid., p. 123.   [6] Conzelmann, ibid., p. 123.
[7] W. Grundmann, Das Evangelium nach Lukas, 1961[2], p. 378.
[8] On the whole subject cf. (apart from the commentaries) F. Busch, Zum Verständnis der synoptischen Eschatologie, 1938; G. Harder, "Das eschatologische Geschichtsbild der sog. kleinen Apokalypse Mk 13", ThViat 4 (1952), pp. 71ff (on the latter see J. M. Robinson, The Problem of History in Mark, 1957, pp. 62f, n. 3); Conzelmann, St. Luke, pp. 125ff; followed by Marxsen, Evangelist, pp. 129ff and Grässer, Parousie-Verzögerung, pp. 152ff; see also W. G. Kümmel, Promise and Fulfilment (SBT 23), 1957, pp. 95ff.

omitted and thus the secret character of the speech vanishes. Since Luke knows of the κατ' ἰδίαν and uses it elsewhere to indicate teaching confined to the disciples (cf. Luke 10.23, the blessedness of the witnesses) we feel sure that Luke has a reason for making the change. The destruction of the Temple is no longer an eschatological secret but an event in the past and therefore an obvious fact. This world—so the discourse continues —is headed for the judgement of God which has already begun with the destruction of Jerusalem.[1] The succession of events already envisaged by Mark,[2] is further emphasized by Luke.[3] The history of the world (v. 26) is connected with the suffering of the faithful (vv. 12ff) and the judgement upon the Jews (vv. 20ff). Thus this discourse deals with the overall history of this world as terminated by the coming of the Son of Man.

Very different is the situation in the sayings of Jesus in 17.22ff. This is "esoteric" teaching addressed to the disciples. Luke brings out here the mysterious character of the return of Jesus which not everyone can comprehend. He transfers the esoteric aspects of Mark 13 to this passage. This consists of the present effects of the still future return of Christ.

The present relevance of the second coming is brought out by the theme of suddenness. Here there is no mention of signs except perhaps the suffering of the Son of Man (v. 25). The day of the Son of Man breaks suddenly into the ordinary life of eating, drinking, marrying, and trading (vv. 27f).[4] Imminent expectation is replaced by "a constant orientation towards the end".[5]

This emphasis on the present relevance of the last judgement

---

[1] See below, pp. 111ff.

[2] Kümmel, op. cit., pp. 46ff (in opposition to Busch).

[3] V. 9b: πρῶτον, οὐκ εὐθέως; vv. 10, 21, 37: τότε; v. 12: πρὸ δὲ τούτων πάντων; v. 24b: "until the times of the Gentiles are fulfilled". This takes into account the continuation of time. As Wellhausen, Lucas, p. 118, has it, Luke is bringing the prophecy up to date. On the problem of the "demythologizing" or dehistoricizing of eschatology (Conzelmann, St. Luke, p. 128), we shall have occasion to speak later (pp. 111ff).

[4] Luke has combined the Noah saying from Q (Matt. 24.37ff) with the Lot saying, which was originally combined not with the saying about the flood but with the logion about fleeing in haste (cf. Mark 13.15f and Luke 17.31f). In this way Luke underlines the sudden and unexpected character of the parousia (Harder, op. cit., pp. 83f).

[5] F. Hauck, Das Lukasevangelium, 1934, p. 173.

is combined with the singling out of each individual concerned. This is suggested by the saying about gaining and losing one's life (v. 33).[1] It noticeably interrupts the flow of thought, since v. 34 follows smoothly upon the warning of v. 32. The whole section vv. 33ff acquires a new meaning, referring no longer to the decision in the last judgement but to the acceptance or rejection of the individual.[2] Now 12.20 ("this night your soul is required of you") can be taken to mean the individual death of the faithful (v. 34) which is unpredictable.[3] "This night" in the context then means the day when the individual either loses his life or "gains it".[4]

Our analysis of Luke 17.22ff and 21.5 shows how Luke can relate the present and future aspects of the eschatological consummation. The course of history towards its end and the ever present end in the life of the individual are described in passages which complement each other.

(e) Further examples of the same phenomenon are the story of Cornelius (Acts 10f) and the account of the Apostolic Council (Acts 15). Both texts make the point that Gentiles can be accepted into the Church without conforming to the Jewish law and so mark an important phase in Luke's account of the history of the early Church.[5]

The Apostolic Council is the "great turning point, the transition from the earliest church to the church of the 'present day' ".[6] The time of the apostles' rule is over, Peter and the other apostles appear for the last time. The leadership of the

---

[1] The saying occurs at Mark 8.35 par. and in the Q form in Matt. 10.39 (cf. John 12.25). Luke—in contrast to 9.24—has put it into better Greek (Grundmann, ad loc).

[2] C. H. Dodd, *The Parables of the Kingdom*, 1953[13], p. 87.

[3] The question of the historical origin of the phrase "in this night" remains unaffected by this Lucan interpretation; cf. on this A. Strobel in *ZThK* 58 (1961), pp. 16ff.

[4] Cf. Luke 23.43, "Today you will be with me in paradise"; further, *The Gospel of Thomas*, Log. 61, "the one will die, the one will live".

[5] The basic treatment will be found in the two analyses of M. Dibelius, *Studies in the Acts of Apostles*, 1956, pp. 93ff ("The Conversion of Cornelius").

[6] H. Conzelmann, *Die Apostelgeschichte*, 1963, p. 81; cf. Haenchen *Apg.*, pp. 402f.

Church is taken over by James and the elders (cf. Acts 21.18).[1]

In the interpretation of this event it is remarkable that we are given no reason for the great change in the Church. In the speeches of Peter and James, which are the centre of the account, there is a back reference to the story of Cornelius.[2] The change is accounted for in purely historical terms, without recourse to the revelatory acting of God. There is mention of the divine election (15.7, 14) but Luke avoids describing God's action directly. He thus tells us that God and his action cannot be traced through history like that. We only hear of the actions of the Church leaders, who obey God's will as they have come to know it.

On the other hand, in the story of Cornelius there is only one individual—Peter—in the centre. He learnt the will of God in a normative "first vision" that Jews and Gentiles should eat together.[3] The divine initiative is strongly emphasized. In his trance Peter sees the heavens open and "something descending like a great sheet" (10.11). Both the picture and choice of language are strongly reminiscent of the baptism of Jesus (Luke 3.21b, 22a). Three times the heavenly voice asks Peter to eat. Then the vessel is "taken up" again into heaven (Acts 10.16).[4] Now while Peter is still perplexed with doubt, the Holy Spirit commands him to enter the house of Cornelius (v. 19). There he pronounces the truth which had just been revealed to him, that no man can be called common or unclean (v. 28). After Peter's sermon the receiving of the Holy Spirit sets seal to the divine truth of the event (v. 44) upon which follows Cornelius' baptism in the name of Jesus Christ (v. 47).

This "event is not regarded as an isolated incident of no importance; it is a decision which vitally concerns the whole Gentile world" (v. 45).[5] Acts 11. 1–8 connects this incident "with the whole church as represented by the church of Jerusalem".[6] Peter in his apology before those "of the circumcision"

---

[1] Haenchen, op. cit., p. 403.

[2] The phrase ἀφ' ἡμερῶν ἀρχαίων (Acts 15.7) gives the Cornelius story "fundamental significance" (Dibelius, op. cit., p. 95).

[3] Dibelius op. cit., pp. 117f; in the original legend Cornelius was the chief actor, op. cit. p. 121.

[4] ἀνελήμφθη, as in Acts 1.2, 11, 22, of Jesus' ascension.

[5] Haenchen, op. cit., p. 299 (on 10.45).   [6] Conzelmann, Apg., p. 62.

(11.2) repeats the whole story in great detail, thus showing its basic importance. This section is the connecting link with chapter 15.

Thus Luke succeeds in presenting the complexities of the redemptive events in a clear yet mysterious way. He narrates the mystery of the revelation and the divine instructions to the individual witnesses, placing side by side with them the measures taken by the Church's leaders in carrying out these instructions.[1]

(f) Let us examine further the pattern which Luke follows in drawing parallels between events which happen to the community and those which happen to individuals. First, we shall explore the connection between the destruction of Jerusalem and the crucifixion, then the connection between the ascension and the resurrection.

For Luke, the destruction of Jerusalem and the crucifixion are brought into a much closer connection than they are in Mark. As early as Luke 13.34 we are told that the prophets die "not only in, but through the agency of Jerusalem".[2] The passion story is framed by the account of Jesus weeping over Jerusalem (19.41ff) and his warning to the daughters of Jerusalem on the way to the cross (23.27ff). The saying about the green tree and the dry (23.31) makes the connection perfectly clear. The crucifixion makes the judgement over the Jews and their city inevitable.

Thus the crucifixion is brought into close connection with an event of general history, namely, the destruction of Jerusalem.[3] Yet "the change over to something which is unique",[4] the transposition into an individualistic key, is a striking feature of Luke's version of the passion. It is not "the completion of salvation, but . . . the history of a saintly man closely united with God".[5] Whereas Mark and Matthew portray the passion in

[1] E. Haenchen, "Judentum und Christentum in der Apg." in ZNW 54 (1963) speaks of a "whole series of miracles" in the Cornelius story (pp. 167f) and calls chapter 15 in comparison with it "jejune and pale" (p. 174).

[2] Conzelmann, St. Luke, p. 199; cf. also pp. 132ff; further, G. Braumann, "Die lk. Interpretation der Zerstörung Jerusalems" in Nov. Test. 6 (1963), p. 122.

[3] On this see pp. 111ff.   [4] Dibelius, Tradition, p. 203.

[5] Dibelius, Tradition, p. 201.

terms of redemptive history, in Luke it becomes the story of a martyrdom.[1]

These two observations complement one another. Luke replaces the treatment of the cross as an event of redemptive history with the destruction of Jerusalem as an act of divine judgement in history. It is the just punishment for the "judicial murder" accomplished by the Jews. Not until the city has fallen does the crucifixion become relevant to history. But this removal of the passion story from the level of history is not to be accounted for by "the literary needs of the historian".[2] It is for theological reasons that Luke avoids treating the crucifixion as a fact of general history. Had he treated it in this way he would have surrendered the eschatological meaning of mystery of the cross. The world, for which the cross betokens divine judgement, would then have been branded as inherently wicked and its character as creation would have been denied.[3] On the other hand, Luke's individual presentation gives him a chance to express the "eschatological character" of the cross-event as a kerygmatic message.[4]

(g) Let us test the relationship between *the exaltation and resurrection of Jesus* in a section of Peter's speech before the Sanhedrin in Acts 5.30f. There Peter testifies that God raised Jesus from the dead and exalted him to his right hand as "Leader and Saviour". According to Wilckens the statement about the exaltation in v. 31 is a second testimony, going further than the statement about the resurrection and clearly distinct from the latter.[5] The relationship between resurrection and exaltation in this passage is a twofold one. First, the raising of Jesus precedes his exaltation

---

[1] Dibelius, *Tradition*; we shall return to this subject below, pp. 52ff, hence our silence on it here.

[2] Dibelius, *Tradition*, p. 203.

[3] According to Conzelmann, *St. Luke*, p. 227, n. 2, Luke attempts no "demonstration of man's sinfulness", just as there is also a complete absence of any cosmological or speculative elements in Acts' conception of sin.

[4] The actual saving significance of the Cross will be discussed below, pp. 157ff.

[5] U. Wilckens, *Die Missionsreden der Apg.*, 1961, p. 152; for a different view see O. Bauernfeind, *Die Apostelgeschichte*, 1939, p. 94, and H. Braun "Zur Terminologie der Acta von der Auferstehung Jesu", in *ThLZ* 77 (1952), p. 533 (cf. *Ges. Studien*, 1962, pp. 173ff).

(v. 30). Thus it is an event of significance to Jesus himself. "It is God's vindication of him in view of his murder by the Jews."[1] Secondly, it is here stated that through the exaltation Jesus became ἀρχηγός. This word is to be interpreted in the light of Acts 3.15 and 26.23.[2] Jesus is "the first ever to be raised from the dead, whose raising thus initiates the general resurrection of the dead".[3]

Now it is remarkable that the determinative cause of the future resurrection of the individual Christian is not the resurrection of Jesus himself but his exaltation. It is because Jesus has been exalted to the right hand of God that he can be the leader or initiator of the resurrection of the dead.[4] Jesus' resurrection is here viewed from the angle of his new life with God in heaven (cf. Luke 23.43). In place of the shift of aeons which according to Paul was inaugurated with the resurrection of Jesus, the transition for Luke is from this world into the celestial world which exists concurrently. The resurrection of Jesus forfeits to the exaltation its cosmic character of introducing the world to come. For Paul resurrection and exaltation coincide while for Luke each has its own special function. The resurrection of Jesus is offered to the individual as the eschatological message of the new life in Christ,[5] while the exaltation is Jesus' entrance into the divine world.[6]

By interpreting the exaltation narrative in this way Luke escapes the danger of presuming a direct connection between the raising of Jesus and the general resurrection of the dead, which would prolong the eschatological reality of the resurrection into earthly time.

---

[1] Conzelmann, St. Luke, p. 205.

[2] Acts 26.23 speaks of the πρῶτος ἐξ ἀναστάσεως νεκρῶν, while in 3.15 Jesus is the ἀρχηγὸς τῆς ζωῆς. In both places the concentration is upon the new life of the faithful (Conzelmann, op. cit., pp. 205f; Wilckens op. cit., p. 174). It fits Luke's dialectic that in 5.31 Jesus becomes the ἀρχηγός through the ascension, whereas according to 3.15 he is already that at his death at the hands of the Jews.

[3] Wilckens, op. cit., p. 174.

[4] ἀρχηγός must therefore not be translated as "inaugurator" as in Heb. 12.2 (on this see Delling in TWNT I [E.T.], pp. 487f. Wilckens, op. cit., p. 175).

[5] On this see below, pp. 159ff.

[6] Long ago J. Weiss saw in this "change of the idea of the kingdom of God", the solution for our age, "which does not share the eschatological mood" (Die Predigt Jesu vom Reich Gottes, 1892, p. 67).

As we have now shown, Luke's narration exhibits a "complementary" structure. He sees various aspects in the story and considers each fact from every angle. He shows that real life is highly complex and cannot be reduced to a single denominator. To put it in modern terms, history cannot be treated objectively. For our present consideration the parallel between cosmic history and that of the individual is of paramount importance. It is a twofold aim that Luke achieves by his dialectic. On the one hand he preserves the real presence of the divine revelation without making it an objective, historical fact, while on the other hand he can describe the effect of the Christ event on the history (of the Church) without conferring on the latter a sacral character.

B. CLIMACTIC PARALLELISM

(a) Luke uses a pattern of climactic parallelism in order to bring out the relation between the old world and the new, between things that happen on earth and those which happen in heaven. Of course, he is fully aware of the differences—these will be discussed in greater detail in the next section—but he makes less of them, giving more weight to the analogy between the old and the new.

The difference between Mark and Luke on this matter comes out very clearly in their respective treatments of the question about fasting (Mark 2.18ff/Luke 5.33–9). Mark draws a distinction between the disciples of John (and the Pharisees) and the disciples of Jesus. The former are fasting, while the latter are celebrating a nuptial feast with their Lord. Jesus foretells the time when the bridegroom will be taken away and the disciples will fast again (v. 20).[1] The tension between fasting and rejoicing is described in the two appended parables. It is a tension between the old life and the new. Even Mark makes a point of the parallel between the old world and the new.

But while Mark gives more emphasis to the incompatibility

---

[1] Evidently v. 20 is a secondary interpolation. For R. Bultmann, *History of the Synoptic Tradition*, 1963, p. 19, the same is true of v. 19b.

between the old and the new, Luke reinterprets the twin parables with the addition of the proverb in Luke 5.39. Thus he gives it "an important interpretation; while the old and the new are incompatible, there may at the same time be a close parallel between them, though they are not to be confused with one another."[1] Luke thus concedes to the old world as represented by fasting[2] a certain significance of its own. It is a time of waiting. The enduring nature of the old is recognized, and with it the necessity of historical continuity (v. 39). But at the same time he preserves the absolute distinction between the new and decisive factor which Christ introduces. The cause of Christ is compared to a new garment which must not be torn (v. 36). Unlike Mark, Luke stresses the concern for the preservation of the new element.[3] For Luke, both aspects, the appreciation for the old and the emphasis on the totality of the new (a garment instead of a patch as in Mark) are not contradictory. The difficulty of interpreting in v. 39 together with vv. 36–8[4] is solved when we recognize the Lucan pattern of climactic arrangement.

(b) There is a striking "climactic parallelism between the stories of John and Jesus".[5] Brun has assembled the parallels in the Lucan infancy narratives:[6]

The annunciation of the birth, 1.5–25/1.26–38,
The naming of the child, 1.13/1.31,
Their future greatness, 1.15/1.32,
Their endowment with the Holy Spirit and with power, 1.17/1.35,
The appearance of the angel Gabriel, 1.19/1.26,
The pregnancy of Elizabeth, 1.24/1.36,
The canticles, 1.46ff and 1.67ff.

In this comparison the superiority of Jesus over John is immediately obvious: the supernatural birth of Jesus (1.35) and the

---

[1] Grundmann, *Lukas*, pp. 133f.
[2] In antiquity fasting was regarded as "an effective means for preparation for intercourse with the deity" (Behm, *TWNT* IV, pp. 927, 4f); cf. Acts 13.3, the sending out of missionaries; 14.53, the installation of elders.
[3] Maurer in *TWNT* VII, p. 961, 21ff.
[4] Cf. Seesemann in *TWNT* V, p. 714, 39ff.
[5] Grundmann, *Lukas*, p. 46.   [6] *Symb. Osl.* 9, 39.

name "Son of God" (1.35b) or "the Son of the Most High" (1.32). Jesus' superiority reaches its climax in the song of the angels at his birth (2.13f). Here the parallel between Jesus and the Baptist breaks down completely before the unique dignity of Jesus.

In Luke 3f the climactic parallelism between the Baptist and Jesus is continued. Each has a message (3.18; 4.18).[1] But Jesus is the Son of God (3.22) upon whom the Spirit of the Lord (4.18) rests. According to 7.33ff the Baptist is rejected in the same way as Jesus. And according to 7.29f all the people and the publicans justified God over the baptism of John while the Pharisees and scribes dismissed repentance with contempt.[2] On the other hand, John is the forerunner and as nothing in comparison with him whose coming he announces (3.16). He is a great figure in the old world but in the Kingdom of God the least is greater than he (7.28; cf. 16.16).[3]

Parallelism and decisive difference—such is the result of our survey. Obviously, Luke is very interested in showing that the Baptist stands shoulder to shoulder with Jesus, but at the same time they are poles apart.[4] The real importance of this dialectic will occupy us later.[5]

(c) There is also a clear parallel between the two missionary charges of Jesus (Luke 9f). The parallel structure of the discourses makes this quite clear. The message of the envoys is rejected—in 9.7–9 by Herod, in 10.13–15 by the unrepentant cities. Next we hear of the return of the disciples (9.10 and 10.17).[6] Following the first charge we get the miracle of the feeding (9.10–17) and

---

[1] The word εὐαγγελίζεσθαι is used by Luke in many different connections (on its use in Acts cf. R. Asting, *Die Verkündigung des Wortes im Urchristentum*, 1939, p. 337). In view of the Baptist's proclamation in Luke 3.6 ("all flesh shall see the salvation of God"), it is impossible to deny its redemptive significance in Luke 3.18 (Friedrich, *TWNT* II [E.T.] p. 719; for a different view see Bultmann, *Theology* I, p. 57; Conzelmann, *St. Luke*, p. 221). On the other hand it is clear that the εὐαγγελίζεσθαι of the Baptist is transcended by the proclamation of the kingdom of God (Luke 16.16).

[2] Bartsch, *Wachet*, pp. 83, 44.

[3] Cf. Friedrich in *TWNT* VI, p. 841, n. 367.

[4] Robinson (*Mark*, p. 22) claims that this double tendency is already discernible in Mark. But while Mark takes the Baptist into the fulfilment of time, Luke clearly demotes him from that position (Conzelmann, *St. Luke*, pp. 22ff).

[5] See below, pp. 152–62.   [6] Brun, op. cit., p. 45.

after the second the saying of Jesus about the fall of Satan (10.18). Yet it is obvious that the two missions follow the Lucan pattern of climactic parallelism. The number 70 (72) denotes all the nations of the world, seventy in Genesis 10, seventy-two in LXX.[1] The sending of the Seventy in 10.1ff prefigures the universal mission to the Gentiles. That is why the dimensions in the second speech are different from the first. It deals with peace on earth (10.5f three times, cf. 2.14) or the last judgement, which is on a cosmic scale (10.15). The precondition for this is the fall of Satan from heaven (10.18). That reduces the exorcisms of the disciples (10.17) to relative proportions. What happens on the celestial plane is decisive (10.20). The mission of the Twelve remains earth-bound and preliminary. The mission of the Seventy becomes the sign of the consummation in heaven.[2]

(d) Luke also includes in his pattern of climactic parallelism the relationship between the crowd and the disciples of Jesus. The first point to notice is the clear distinction between the two groups. The preaching to the crowd and the private teaching of the disciples have each their own special location.[3] The lake in Luke is no longer as in Mark the scene of Jesus' public appearances.[4] Note how Luke uses the situation of Mark 4.1 to introduce the story of the draught of fishes (Luke 5.1–3). Like the lake (cf. Luke 8.22ff) the mountain is also the place of the epiphany of Jesus to his disciples (Luke 6.12ff; 21.37ff; Acts 1.12).[5] The change of locale is clearly denoted each time. The call of the disciples by the lake (Luke 5.1ff) is followed by the healing of a

[1] Grundmann, Lukas, p. 207.

[2] Hence Jesus' doxology to the Father at the end of the second missionary charge and his beatitude pronounced upon the eyewitnesses (Luke 10.21–4). That Luke is consciously at work there is shown in the fact that in Matthew these two items occur in quite a different context. Cf. the contrast between Paul and the twelve apostles in Acts (see below, pp. 129f).

[3] According to Conzelmann Luke substitutes Mark's theory of the messianic secret with his peculiar pattern of "esoteric teaching, followed by public proclamation" ("Zur Lukas-Analyse" in ZThK 49 (1952), pp. 24f).

[4] Cf. Mark 4.1/Luke 8.4; Mark 2.13/Luke 5.27; Mark 6.31ff/Luke 9.10b; Conzelmann, St. Luke, pp. 27ff on the individual texts.

[5] Cf. Conzelmann, St. Luke, pp. 44ff; for a different view see W. Schmauch, "Der Ölberg" in ThLZ 77 (1952), p. 396. On the whole subject see R. H. Lightfoot, Locality and Doctrine in the Gospels, 1937.

leper in "one of the cities" (5.12). After the choice of the Twelve on the mountain (6.12ff) Jesus addresses a "large group of his disciples" on the plain (6.17). After the transfiguration on the mountain (9.28ff), the crowd meets him down below (9.37).[1]

These examples show clearly the distinct locations where the people and the disciples receive the word of Jesus. The special revelation (regarding the divine dignity and authority of Jesus) is confined to a particular location and so guarded against misunderstanding and profanation. The geographical location helps Luke to express the institutional aspect of the Christian revelation.[2]

Although this geographical separation of the disciples and the crowd is clear enough, there are several alterations of Mark which point in the opposite direction. Mark 4.11 distinguishes clearly between the two groups. The disciples ("you") are contrasted with those who "are outside". Luke 8.10, on the other hand, speaks of "others" in the kingdom. The antithesis is weakened. Similarly, in Mark 3.35 Jesus' relatives stand "outside" but his followers sit "around him" (v. 34). Luke preserves the word ἔξω (8.20). But Jesus' audience is not a closed circle but is left indefinite.[3] Luke is not content simply to contrast the two groups. Mark aims at a clear either/or decision while Luke transforms this contrast into a climactic parallelism between initial uncertainty and clear decision.

The locally symbolized separation between the crowd and the disciples is further relativized. In Luke 12 we find a double change of address. In 12.1 it is the disciples who are addressed. In 12.13, "one of the crowd" speaks. 12.20 is again addressed to the disciples, while in 12.54 Jesus turns once more to the crowd.[4] The contents of this chapter throw little light on the reason for this change.[5] The reason for it is shown in the interruption of the discourse in v. 41. Peter asks: "Are you telling this parable

---

[1] Cf. Conzelmann, "Zur Lk-Analyse," p. 24, n. 2.

[2] Again Luke's tendency to "social interpretation" is shown; see below, pp. 72f.

[3] Cf. Peter's confession, where the "human opinion" (Mark 8.27), as 8.33b and 7.7 show, is surely to be taken as a repudiation (E. Lohmeyer, Das Ev. des Mk., 1953[12], p. 162), Luke changes this to οἱ λοιποί (on this see below, pp. 46ff).

[4] Cf. Brun, op. cit., p. 46.

[5] Cf. Luke 8.16 and 11.37, where the same word is addressed once to the disciples, and on the other occasion to the people.

for us or for all?" Jesus answers, as so often in Luke,[1] with a parable, the parable of the faithful and unfaithful servants (12.42ff). With this—in a way similar to 13.23ff—the clear distinction between an inner and a wider circle is avoided. Jesus' words cause a separation of spirits, evinced in faithful or unfaithful service (cf. the parable). But this is not an automatic distinction. To be a disciple is not an inalienable right but a privilege to be constantly renewed in obedience. The division between the disciples and the people is not final but constantly re-established by hearing the word (or refusing to hear it). The same sequence can be found again within the Sermon on the Plain. After the introduction (Luke 6.17–19) a great multitude assembles to hear Jesus and to be healed (v. 17). An irresistible power goes forth from him and draws the people to him (v. 19). But he begins his actual discourse with a preamble to his disciples (v. 20), and in v. 27 it is stated emphatically that only those "who hear" are addressed. The purpose of this is to maintain the distinction between those in the crowd who are swayed by the miracles and the disciples who hear his word. This is what actually happens in the course of Jesus' preaching.[2] At the end of the sermon we read that he said all this in "the hearing of the people" (7.1). Here is the same absence of division between the people and the disciples as we find in 6.17.[3]

These examples show that Luke does not consider the crowd and the disciples as absolute contrasts. They are also ranged together. Only when Jesus addresses them is the distinction of the two groups made clear. On no account must the disciples be institutionalized into a "core group".[4]

(e) Luke also uses climactic parallelism to describe the rising crescendo in the rejection of Jesus' message. The two examinations

[1] Luke 12.13ff; 10.29ff; 13.23ff; 14.15ff.

[2] Note the direct speech in the Sermon on the Plain, contrasted with Matthew's Sermon on the Mount.

[3] This tension is unnoticed by Bartsch, *Wachet*, pp. 66ff, for whom the Sermon on the Plain, as contrasted with Matthew's Sermon on the Mount, is a "proclamation to the multitude" (p. 67). On the changes of the audience, cf. J. Jeremias, *The Parables of Jesus*, 1963[2], pp. 33ff.

[4] This tension between the people and the disciples recurs in Luke's doctrine of the Church (pp. 132ff).

of the apostles before the Sanhedrin are treated in this way (Acts 4.5–22; 5.17–42). The double report has led some to postulate different sources,[1] others to prove that according to rabbinic law custom required two successive trials.[2] Haenchen, however, has tried to show that it is Luke himself, inadequately informed by later reports, who is speaking here.[3] Whether Luke found two trials in his sources or whether he was personally responsible for both versions in Acts 4f, his own hand is in any case quite obvious.[4]

By his double report of the confrontation between the disciples and the Jewish authorities Luke succeeds in giving due weight to this important event. The crucial point (4.19; 5.29) that God must be obeyed rather than man can be stated twice over.

But there are also some very clear differences. The first version brings out the dilemma of the Sanhedrin in face of the Christian message. The healing of the impotent man (3.1ff) has already led the council to question the power (δύναμις) behind this miracle (4.7). The message of Peter amazes his hearers because the disciples are unlearned and ignorant men (4.13). They are at a loss what to say (4.14), and unable to reach a decision (4.16). So they try to get out of the affair by issuing unreasonable orders (4.18).[5]

During the second trial the hostility of the Sanhedrin comes out into the open (5.17ff). They come "enraged" and plan to kill the disciples (5.33). The Christian message now meets with strong resistance. It is important to notice that according to 5.17 it

[1] A. Harnack, The Acts of the Apostles, 1909, pp. 181ff.

[2] J. Jeremias, "Untersuchungen zum Quellenproblem der Apg." in ZNW 36 (1937), pp. 205ff. Cf. the survey of the history of criticism in Haenchen, Apg., p. 209 and B. Reicke, Glaube und Leben der Urgemeinde, 1957, pp. 56f, n. 1.

[3] Ibid., p. 212.

[4] B. Reicke, op. cit., pp. 55ff, assumes parallel traditions for the sections 2.42—4.31 and 4.32—5.42. Here he works out detailed correspondences between two sections. But in my opinion this very agreement argues rather for literary redaction. Different parallel traditions would surely exhibit stronger variations. That does not exclude the possibility that Luke has taken individual sections from his tradition. But the composition will be his own achievement. Reicke also discerns "a literary arrangement" on the part of Luke, of such a kind "that the tension is constantly increased" (op. cit., p. 113), and "the imprisonment of the apostles according to Tradition II appears to be more serious and threatening than the imprisonment in Tradition I" (ibid., p. 112).

[5] Cf. the sermon at Nazareth (Luke 4.16–30). There the first part leads to wonder and amazement on the part of the audience (v. 22), while in the second part they become angry with Jesus (v. 28) and seek to kill him (v. 29). See below, pp. 152ff.

is not the whole Sanhedrin which rejects the apostle's message. It is only the party of the Sadducees, which included the high priests. Consequently the front shifts. The acute hostility affects only one section of Judaism. The other party—the Pharisees, represented by Gamaliel who intervenes in the debate—hovers as it were on the edge of the Christian community (cf. Acts 22.3; 23.6ff). Gamaliel's speech carries the day. If you are unable to believe in Christ, at least you should not oppose the apostles but make room for the ways of God.[1]

Curiosity, amazement, and bewilderment in face of the words and deeds of the apostles prior to the real show-down—that is the tenor of the first version. The second version leads to the parting of the ways. Half of the Sanhedrin are determined to reject the message and proceed in open enmity against the apostles.[2] The other half represented here by the Pharisee Gamaliel remains open-minded on the question of what new action God will take in history.

In this pattern of climactic parallelism we have another peculiarity of Luke's composition. We shall meet it often later on, for example, in the two questions of Jesus in the confession of Peter (Luke 9.18ff), in the comparison between David and Jesus (Acts 2.34f; Luke 20.42ff), in the parallel between Paul and the Twelve, and in the relationship of Apollos and John's disciples to the Christian community (Acts 18.24–19.7). Luke puts side by side initial curiosity and faith in Christ as the Son of God (or rejection of him). The former is all right so far as it goes, but the latter is far and away superior.

C. ANTITHETICAL COMPARISON

We have seen in the foregoing section that there is an element of antithesis in the climactic parallelisms. Since the old world is

---

[1] For Gamaliel's "proof from history" see below 3B 2a.

[2] Acts 5.39b (ἐπείσθησαν δὲ αὐτῷ) restores the balance between their intention to kill (v. 33) and the subsequent punishment by whipping (v. 40). It is not that they followed Gamaliel's advice: they simply abandoned their intention to put the apostles to death (Haenchen, Apg., p. 208).

God's creation, the new world, for Luke, is analogous but superior to the old. Since the old world is fallen and under judgement[1] it stands in antithesis to the new world created by God in Christ. This must now be demonstrated.[2]

(a) Let us start by examining salvation and judgement in the work of Luke. As Simeon says to Mary, Jesus will be "the fall and rising of many in Israel" and a σημεῖον ἀντιλεγόμενον (Luke 2.34). The contrast comes out clearly in the Sermon on the Plain (cf. Matthew). The four beatitudes are followed by four woes exactly parallel in content (6.20–6). In three highlighted places in the Gospel we find the offer of salvation refused. In the sermon at Nazareth Jesus' words are not accepted (4.16f). The antithesis to this is Capernaum (4.31ff).[3] As he leaves for Jerusalem Jesus meets with rejection from the Samaritans (9.51ff). The acclamation of peace on the Mount of Olives (19.37f) stands in contrast to Jesus' weeping over Jerusalem for missing her peace (19.41ff). The two Jericho stories (19.41ff)[4] also come under the heading of salvation and judgement: salvation for the son of Abraham who welcomes Jesus (19.9) and judgement over the unrepentant Jews (19.27). V. 11a serves as a connecting link for the two pericopes.

The invitation to the kingdom of God in the parable of the great feast (Luke 14.16ff) is contrasted with the conditions of discipleship (14.25ff). The description of the situation in v. 25 (a large crowd following Jesus) brings out a double contrast. Individual invitations are refused and the crowd of followers is warned against illusions. The situation is similar in 13.18ff. The twin parables of the mustard seed and the leaven describe the universality of the kingdom of God. The tree which sheltered the birds is, according to Dodd, "a symbol for a great empire offering political protection to its subject-states". The birds symbolize

---

[1] According to Luke 4.6 the world is abandoned to Satan's power.

[2] The connection of Lucan dialectic with Greek thought needs special investigation. A marked predilection on the part of the Greeks for antithetical contrast is established by E. Norden, *Die antike Kunstprosa*, 1958⁵, p. 25.

[3] Conzelmann, *St. Luke*, pp. 38ff.

[4] Brun, op. cit., p. 48.

the influx of the Gentiles.[1] The leaven which the woman uses to ferment indicates by its vast quantity (39·4 litres) the "overflowing mass".[2] The antithesis to this universal range is the question (13.23): "Lord, will those who are served be few?"[3] The metaphors in the reply (13.25ff)—the closed door, exclusion from the kingdom of God, and the eschatological meal for those who come from all parts of the world—form a new contrast.[4]

(b) Corresponding to the message which betokens salvation and judgement, there is the receptivity and unreceptiveness of the hearers for the kingdom of God. What is a man's attitude to God's offer of salvation? Already in the two figures of the infancy narratives, Zacharias and Mary, we meet the differentiation.[5] Zacharias hesitates in doubt while Mary permits the renewing, creative word of God to take its course with her (Luke 1.38).

The contrast is singularly clear in the parable of the Pharisee and the publican (18.9–14). Here is a recurring motive in Luke. Simon the Pharisee stands side by side with the woman who is a sinner (7.36–50). The widow who entrusts her life into God's hand by giving her tiny gift ($\beta i o s$, v. 4) stands cheek by jowl (even in Mark) with the scribes who make their piety subservient to their reputation (20.45—21.4). The two sons in the parable in 15.11–32, as well as priest or Levite and Samaritan (10.29, 37), and the invited and uninvited guests at the great supper (14.15–24) are to be viewed in the same light. The Pharisee in 18.9ff is contrasted with the importunate widow of 18.1f.

Luke 18.15ff poses the question of who will enter the kingdom of God. Little children who have nothing of their own to give and so are completely dependent on others are contrasted with

---

[1] *Parables*, p. 190.   [2] Jeremias, *Parables*, p. 147.

[3] Wellhausen, *Lucas*, p. 74.

[4] W. Trilling, *Das wahre Israel*, 1964[3], p. 88, demonstrates the independence of the two logia, v. 28 and v. 29. In v. 28 the address is in the 2nd person, while v. 29 is a portrait in the 3rd person. The first is a threat, the second a word of promise, and both have affinities in content.

[5] It is certainly redactional, for Zacharias' question in 1.18 corresponds exactly to Mary's question in 1.34; not until the answer of Gabriel in 1.20 is the unbelief of Zacharias made known (cf. Judges 6.17f).

the rich (and powerful, an alteration compared with Mark) ruler. Similarly there is the contrast between the rich man and Lazarus (16.19–31) and between the two thieves at the crucifixion (23.29–43).

The responsibility of the disciple is emphasized in similar contrasts. The parable of the faithful and unfaithful servants (12.42ff) is followed by the saying about reward for service (12.47ff), with its distinction between the servant who knew the will of his master and the servant who did not. The parables of the sower (8.4ff) and the pounds (19.12) should also be mentioned in this connection.[1]

It is difficult to ascertain from the texts quoted, which come mostly from the special Lucan material, whether Luke found these contrasts already incorporated in the tradition. But his deliberate editing of the parallelism between the disciples and the kinsfolk of Jesus (8.9–21) is obvious when compared with Mark. In the interpretation of the parabolic discourse (8.9f) "what it means to be a disciple is described for the first time" and their "privilege in regard to the μυστήρια [note the plural] of the kingdom of God". But Jesus' relatives (8.19–21) have "no knowledge" of all this.[2] They are literally outside (cf. Mark 4.11), still behind the people (8.19). The ties of natural kinship do not guarantee proximity to Jesus. Only those who hear and keep the word of God can become disciples (8.21; cf. 11.27f).

Examples such as those quoted above run like a thread all through the Gospel. They show the emphasis Luke places on the decision which the message of Jesus evokes. The climactic parallelism between the old and the new is not reduced one-sidedly to the gradations of natural theology. Confrontation with Jesus does not entail a perfection or completion of the natural order. It is a life and death decision just like the word of God in the Old Testament (Deut. 30.19; 28.1ff).

(c) Closely connected with this is the contrast between the suffering and glorification of Jesus. The paradox that the *Kyrios*

---

[1] E. von Dobschütz, "Paarung und Dreiung in der ev. Überlieferung" in *Studien für G. Heinrici*, 1914, pp. 92ff.

[2] Conzelmann, *St. Luke*, p. 48.

destined for heavenly glory is at the same time condemned to suffering and death as a man is brought out with signal clarity in Luke. In the story of the walk to Emmaus this theme is described in summary terms: "Was it not necessary that the Christ should suffer these things and enter into his glory?" (Luke 24.26). The three passion predictions taken over from Mark follow this motif. The first (9.22ff) is linked to the confession of Peter (9.18) by minute changes in the syntax. The passion prediction in v. 22 is subordinated to the injunction to silence by means of a participial construction. "In place of the Messianic secret in Mark we have the passion secret in Luke."[1] This suffering of the Messiah is put in antithesis (by the δέ in v. 21) to the confession of Jesus as the Christ of God (τοῦ θεοῦ in v. 20 is a Lucan addition).

The second passion prediction (according to the Marcan reckoning) is preceded by the remark (peculiar to Luke) that they were all astonished at the majesty of God and marvelled at everything Jesus did (9.43). The third passion prediction is—by a change in the Marcan order—combined with the healing of the blind man of Jericho, so that the suffering Son of Man stands in contrast to the Son of David, who is greeted with so much enthusiasm.[2]

Luke adds two further passion predictions to the sayings about Jesus' heavenly glory. The story of the transfiguration (9.28f) is expanded by special Lucan material. In vv. 31f Moses and Elijah announce Jesus' "exodus" in Jerusalem. Secondly, the eschatological discourse (17.22ff), which speaks of the sudden appearance of the Son of Man on his day (v. 24), is furnished with a passion prediction (v. 25).[3]

The transfiguration story points ahead to the coming events in Jerusalem. The allusion to Jesus' agony on the Mount of Olives is obvious.[4] But side by side with this allusion to the suffering of Jesus the story of the entry into Jerusalem (or more accurately, into the Temple) contains another reference to the

---

[1] Grundmann, *Lukas*, p. 189.   [2] Brun, op. cit., p. 48.

[3] Hence Bultmann may well be right (*ThLZ* 72 (1947), pp. 271f), *contra* Kümmel (*Promise*, pp. 70f), in holding the verse to be a Lucan formation.

[4] Luke 22.40–6 (not Gethsemane): night scene (Klostermann on 9.31), the sleeping of the disciples, the heavenly apparition (Conzelmann, *St. Luke*, p. 81).

glory of Jesus (19.37f). The entry amidst the disciples' praise to
God is located on the Mount of Olives (v. 37a). Both the praise
and the agony take place on the Mount of Olives, and stand in
contrast with one another.

In 19.37 the disciples look back on the mighty works of Jesus.
This marks the close of an important section. From now on Jesus
performs no more miracles. The time for miracles is past and the
time for suffering begins.[1] So we can extend the thesis of this
section to the whole activity of Jesus. His miracles, which reflect
his heavenly glory, are contrasted with the "temptations" (22.28)
which he must endure at the behest of the Father's will.

The structure of Luke 4.1–15 exhibits the same kind of contrast
as those which run all through the Gospel. After the temptation
story (vv. 1–13) Luke, like Mark, records the beginning of the
Galilean ministry (v. 14). But to Mark he adds the point that as
Jesus teaches in the synagogue he "is glorified by all"
($\delta o \xi a \zeta \delta \mu \epsilon v o s$, v. 15). So he creates yet another antithesis.[2] The
conflict of Jesus with the power of Satan is contrasted with the
glory which is manifested on earth in his miracles ($\xi v \delta o \xi a$,
according to 13.17) and points to his final glorification.

In the last analysis, Luke's travel section exhibits this same
antithetical christological pattern. In Luke 9.51–6 and 13.31–3
there are programmatic references to the journey to Jerusalem.
Both notices are concerned with the crossing of the Galilean
border on the way to the city.[3] But while 13.31ff looks forward
to the death of Jesus ("it cannot be that a prophet should perish
away from Jerusalem"), 9.51 speaks of his "assumption". The

---

[1] Cf. Conzelmann, op. cit., pp. 76, 198.

[2] Brun, op. cit., p. 40.

[3] 9.51ff looks forward to the journey through Samaria, 13.31ff speaks of
attempts against him on the part of "Herod", the ruler of Galilee. The dupli-
cation of the saying in 13.32b, 33a has given rise to omissions (Wellhausen, *Lucas*,
p. 76; J. Blinzler, "Die literarische Eigenart des sog. Reiseberichts im Lk–Ev.
in *Synoptische Studien* (Wikenhauser Festschrift), 1953, pp. 45f). But the dupli-
cated logian is intelligible in the light of the Lucan antithesis: miracle (*doxa*)
and suffering. Jesus' activity first takes the form of exorcisms and healings, then
becomes the path to suffering and death. Both are appointed by God and for
fixed periods of time (to-day, to-morrow . . .), though these are not to be
measured by human standards (*contra* Conzelmann, op. cit., p. 197, n. 1, cf.
p. 68).

crucial question for our thesis is how we are to understand the word ἀνάλημψις.

We have to start from the premiss that 9.51a is Luke's own composition.[1] What does he mean by the "days of assumption"? If he said "day" as in Acts 2.1 we should naturally think of the day of the ascension (cf. Acts 1.2, 11, 22). But as he mentions "days" he seems to imply that Jesus' assumption embraces "the end of his whole course, including crucifixion, death, resurrection and ascension".[2] But that contradicts Luke's usage in other places, especially in Acts 1.11, where ἀναλαμβάνειν clearly refers to the exaltation of Jesus (cf. Acts 1.2, 22). How then are the "days" to be explained? Luke uses the term often in the Old Testament sense, meaning a period in future.[3] Like the "days of the Son of man" (Luke 17.22ff)[4] it could refer here to the time of Jesus' exaltation, the period of his heavenly reign which the Church is now experiencing. This period—continues v. 51a—will be consummated when Jesus enters into his heavenly glory.

This exegesis must be tested by a study of the context. How far the redactional work of Luke extends in 9.51–6 is a matter of dispute. Dibelius takes v. 51b as a doublet of v. 53b and concludes that Luke took the information from the body of the pericope and used it as an introductory framework.[5] Such borrowing seems unlikely to me because it leaves the phrase τὸ πρόσωπον αὐτοῦ in v. 51b unexplained, and it is this phrase which gives the sentence its special stamp.[6] It seems much more plausible to take vv. 51b, 52b, 53ff as a very ancient tradition governed by

---

[1] This point is generally agreed, in view of Acts 2.1; cf. Bultmann, *Tradition*, pp. 25f and supplementary note, p. 385; Dibelius, *Tradition*, pp. 47f; Schlatter, *Lukas*, pp. 269f; Conzelmann, *St. Luke*, p.66. Hence the traditio-historical origin of ἀνάλημψις does not decide the question; cf. Delling, *TWNT* IV, p. 9, 4ff, who quotes texts from late Jewish literature in order to connect the term to Jesus' death or assumption.

[2] Schlatter, *Lukas*, p. 270; so too K. H. Rengstorf, *Das Ev. nach Lk.* (NTD 3), 1962⁹, p. 129, and Grundmann, *Lukas*, p. 201, who compares it with the Johannine δοξασθῆναι.

[3] Luke 5.35; 17.22; 19.43; 21.6; see von Rad in *TWNT* II (E.T.), p. 946.

[4] See below, pp. 94ff.   [5] *Tradition*, p. 47.

[6] Rengstorf, op. cit., p. 129; otherwise G. Dalman, *The Words of Jesus*, 1909, p. 30; τὸ πρόσωπον στηρίζειν = to direct one's intention towards, is applied in the OT only in the sense of punishment (Zahn, *Lukas*, p. 397, n. 28); cf. Harder in *TWNT* VII, p. 654, 37ff.

the conception of a national and political messiahship of Jesus. This seems to be further indicated in Luke 9.11.[1] In an earlier stage of this tradition it may have referred to Elijah *redivivus* (cf. Mark 6.15/Luke 9.8). At any rate the desire expressed by the sons of Zebedee for fire to descend from heaven points in this direction.[2]

If this analysis of the history behind the tradition is correct, the Lucan redaction stands out clearly. By introducing the motif of the heavenly exaltation he removes the political associations in the traditional material before him. The destination is still Jerusalem—not, however, for the realization of an earthly kingdom but as the place of Jesus' heavenly exaltation.

The sending out of the advance party (v. 52a)—the second point clearly inserted by Luke[3]—proves this. Luke connects the journey to Jerusalem with the sending out of disciples (10.1ff) whose exorcisms are signs of the heavenly victory over Satan (10.17ff). This shows the journey to Jerusalem not only as a path to suffering but also as Jesus' triumphal procession to his heavenly exaltation.[4]

In this first part of our investigation we have concentrated upon the special features of Luke's presentation. We have seen that this is determined by a certain priority of theological concern. Luke shows no interest in the causal connection of events. On the contrary, he takes account of the non-objective character[5] of real life by presenting his material from several different points of view. Another observation is important for the further development of our thesis. Luke uses the form of climactic parallelism in order to place side by side what belongs both to the old and to the new world of God. This enables him to allow events in this world a relative autonomy and thus to bring out the human side more clearly. At the same time the human

---

[1] On this see Wellhausen, *Lucas*, p. 106; Grässer, *Parousieverzögerung*, p. 27, and (on Mark 11.10) p. 25.

[2] A. Schweitzer, *The Mystery of the Kingdom of God*, 1925, pp. 75ff.

[3] Wellhausen, *Lucas*, p. 46, refers to its connection with the mission in Luke 10.1ff; Dibelius, *Tradition*, p. 47.

[4] See below, pp. 72f, and, for the theological significance of the christological pattern of the suffering and glory of Jesus, pp. 157ff.

[5] E. Käsemann, *Essays on N.T. Themes*, 1964, pp. 48ff.

element is limited and overshadowed by the reality of heaven where the fate of this world is finally decided. The antithetical contrasts show Luke's awareness of the gulf between God and the sinful world standing under his judgement. That is why the glory of the Son of God must be hidden in the suffering and can only be accepted by the faith which overcomes the world. Readiness for this decision varies outside of the inner group of Jesus' disciples. While the people and the Pharisees are still undecided and open to the possibility of accepting the message of Christ, Jesus' kinsfolk, the people of Nazareth, and the Sadducees are completely closed to the message. By thus distinguishing between the various groups, Luke shows that even on the human level—that is, even before the decision of faith—various attitudes towards the Christ event are possible.

This pattern must be consistently maintained if it is true. So we now turn to the two themes which were of special concern to Luke in his age—the Christian message in the world, and "redemptive history".

2

The Christian Message in the World

Luke is regarded as the "historian" amongst the Evangelists. But opinions have changed over the nature and value of his writing of history. While E. Meyer classed Luke among the great historians like Polybius and Livy,[1] K. L. Schmidt had doubts about his historical credibility.[2] Dibelius called Luke "the first Christian historian",[3] but at the same time emphasized the difference between the purpose of Luke and of ancient history generally and the modern critical and scientific approach to history.[4] Conzelmann is of the same opinion. He shows (commenting on Luke 4.16-30) that Luke believed that redemptive history gave the clue to "correct" chronology. For him it is "as such of fundamental importance".[5]

I can only agree with Conzelmann. But we should avoid talking of Luke's "historization" of the Gospel message in the way which has been popular since Bultmann introduced the notion in his *Theology of the New Testament*.[6] This phrase suggests to the reader modern ideas quite unknown to the Bible or antiquity. Historization as we understand it nowadays means arranging events into a clearly organized system of cause and effect, in other words an immanentist view of history. As we have shown in Chapter 1, Luke never treats history in this objective sort of way.[7] Of course it is Luke's task as a post-apostolic writer to present the life of Jesus to his own age as a piece of past history.

[1] E. Meyer, *Ursprung und Anfänge des Christentums* I, 1962[2], p. 2.
[2] K. L. Schmidt, *Der Rahmen der Geschichte Jesu* 1964[2], 316; *RGG*[2] II, cols 1115f; *Der geschichtliche Wert des lk. Aufrisses der Geschichte Jesu* (*ThStKr* 91), 1918, pp. 277ff.
[3] *Studies in Acts*, pp. 123ff.   [4] Ibid., pp. 136f.
[5] *St. Luke*, p. 33.   [6] *Theology* II, p. 126; cf. pp. 116f.
[7] Cf. P. Schubert's criticism of Bultmann ("The Structure and Significance of Luke 24", *Nt.liche Studien für R. Bultmann*, 1957[2], p. 179, n. 26).

He is forced to give a chronological report in order to show that the life of Jesus like every human life is marked by a succession of events. We will answer the question of how Luke accomplished this task in three parts. First we shall consider the christology of Luke from this human angle. Secondly we shall deal with the apologetic aspect of the message, and finally with the penetration of the message into secular society.

A. CHRISTOLOGICAL PRESUPPOSITIONS

In order to understand the Lucan Christology we must first uncover the tradition in which he stands. Once more we come up against a dialectical pattern.

1. The Earthly and Heavenly Modes of Christ's Existence

(a) The contrast and parallelism between heavenly and earthly reality is not a Lucan peculiarity. It is on all fours with the world view of antiquity[1] and is taken for granted all through the New Testament.[2] This understanding of the world stamps a large part of New Testament Christology. It is especially clear in the ancient hymn in 1 Timothy 3.16.[3] The six lines of this

---

[1] Traub, *TWNT* V 513, 11ff; Sasse, op. cit., I, 677f; H. Bietenhard, *Die himmlische Welt im Urchristentum und Spätjudentum*, 1951, p. 13; Bietenhard works out the late Jewish conceptions of heaven in detail, but concludes by denying that they have any significance for the Christian message. For the Jewish apocalyptist "cosmology is . . . part of the 'apocalyptic kerygma' " (p. 255), but in the NT it has no place in the Christian message, which is not tied to any particular world view (256f). "Cosmology is not the object of the NT proclamation. . . . Therefore the world picture of the Bible can in principle be detached from its proclamation" (p. 259). By thus removing its spatial context and totally kerygmatizing the Christian message Bietenhard makes it quite unhistorical. We cannot take over the biblical world picture without reservation, but we can only hear the biblical message through this medium.

[2] On Paul cf., e.g., the essay of G. Friedrich, "ἁμαρτία οὐκ ἐλλογεῖται Rom. 5.13,", *ThLZ* 77 (1952), pp. 523ff, who sees in the passive ἐλλογεῖται a reference "to some activity in the heavenly world" (p. 523), and translates the word, as in Philem. 18, "to charge to one's account". Behind this phrase stands the "widespread oriental view that books are kept in heaven, in which all the deeds of men are entered" (p. 525).

[3] Not only the oldest reading Ὅς, which was later smoothed out, but also the poetical style (parallelism) show that the text is a quotation (J. Jeremias, *Die Briefe an Timotheus und Titus*, 1958[7, 8]; H. Conzelmann, *Die Pastoralbriefe*, 1955[3] ad loc.).

D

hymn describe a series of events in the upper and the lower world, following a chiastic pattern. "The two spheres are clearly presented in a local sense as the two halves of the cosmos, one above the other."[1] Although the first line mentions the incarnation, the emphasis lies on the exaltation.[2] This is described as justification in the Spirit, manifestation to the angels, and assumption into glory. This sequence may be following the prototype of the Egyptian enthronement ceremony.[3] The important consideration for us is that we no longer find a strictly chronological order in the successive events of redemptive history.[4] The Christ event is portrayed as a universal fact embracing heaven and earth. The intimate relation between the heavenly and earthly world is clearly expressed in the three pairs of antitheses.[5] In all six lines the verbs are in the passive. Each points implicitly to God as the source of each event, thus enhancing the impression that the whole process is a unity.

Alongside the triumphal procession of the exalted one through heaven the same happens on earth; "preached among the nations, believed on in the world".[6] The references to earthly events preserve the concrete character of the hymn, thus saving it from becoming mythological. Of course this does not alter the character of the hymn, "which abandons the chronological order completely in favour of a spatial pattern of 'below' and 'above' ".[7] In a moment we shall see how by contrast Luke's Christology combines the chronological course of history with simultaneous events in heaven.

---

[1] E. Schweizer, *Lordship and Discipleship* (SBT 28), 1961, p. 65.

[2] H. Windisch, "Zur Christologie der Pastoralbriefe", *ZNW* 34 (1935), p. 222, sees that here "the christological σάρξ–πνεῦμα doctrine is built into the incarnational Christology", because the theme of the hymn is the exaltation of Christ, which was originally meant to be taken in the sense of an adoptionist Christology (Ps. 2!) with nothing about pre-existence.

[3] Jeremias, ibid., pp. 22f.

[4] Schweizer, *Lordship*, p. 66.

[5] Schweizer shows in an illuminating way how the hymn fits in with the particular experience of the Hellenistic world, in which the unity of the cosmos is being constantly disrupted by powers of darkness. See ibid., 1962[2], pp. 146, 155.

[6] Schweizer, *Lordship*, p. 63.

[7] Schweizer, *Erniedrigung*, p. 182.

There is much in 1 Timothy 3.16 which echoes Luke–Acts.[1] We at once notice the terms ἀνελήμφθη (Acts 1.2, 11, 22) and δόξα. But the distinction between heaven and earth is Lucan too.[2] The mission to the Gentiles is the main theme of Luke. It is probable that the Christology of Luke is connected with the tradition in 1 Timothy 3.16. In this hymn the σάρξπνεῦμα antithesis serves as a bridge for a "Christology of two existences", which is discernible in several New Testament formulas.[3]

(b) As an example of these christological types we turn to the pre-Pauline confession in Romans 1.3f: ". . . who was descended from David according to the flesh and designated Son of God in power according to the Spirit of holiness by his resurrection from the dead . . .".[4] Whether the pair of words κατὰ σάρκα and κατὰ πνεῦμα belongs to the formula or has been added by Paul is disputed. Bultmann does not include it in his quotation of the formula.[5] But Schweizer points out how unlikely it would have been for Paul to have coined this phrase himself. The contrast σάρξ–πνεῦμα indicates in Paul the "antithesis between sinful man and his behaviour and the holy God and his acts".[6]

---

[1] Windisch, op. cit., shows the similarities between Acts and the Pastoral Epistles in the way they speak about the good conscience, good works, εὐσέβεια, in the biblicism of both authors, in the presentation of Christianity as Judaism freed of its limitations, and finally in the theological affinities between the two portraits of Paul.

[2] Luke 2.14; 14.7ff; 15.7, 10; 16.19ff etc.; cf. further, the theological pattern of Jesus' suffering and glory (see above, pp. 30ff).

[3] Windisch speaks of the agreement between the "παῖς–θεοῦ Christology" in the speeches in Acts and the christological tradition used in the Pastorals (op. cit. pp. 230f). This older tradition of which there are only occasional echoes in Paul (Rom. 1.3f) depicts the ἀρχαί of two modes of Christ's existence: his begetting from the seed of David and his installation as Son at the resurrection (cf. 2 Tim. 2.8, where the order is reversed). This "Christology of two existences" antedates the pre-existence Christology (op. cit. pp. 214–16). Cf. 1 Tim. 2.5, and above, p. 38, n. 2.

[4] The pre-Pauline character of Romans 1.3f is pretty generally recognized. The reasons for this view are given in E. Schweizer, "Rom. 1.3 und der Gegensatz von Fleisch und Geist vor und bei Paulus", in Neotestamentica (Essays in German and English), 1951–63, pp. 189ff; cf. O. Michel, Der Brief an die Römer, 1963[12], pp. 38f; Bultmann, Theology I, p. 49; bibliographical references in Hahn, Hoheitstitel, p. 251, n. 3.

[5] Schweizer, op. cit., p. 49; so too B. M. F. van Jersel, "Der Sohn" in den synopt. Jesusworten, 1961, p. 72.

[6] Schweizer, op. cit., pp. 189f.

This distinction, however, is obviously not present in the confessional formula.

Schweizer accordingly regards the formula in Romans 1.3 as analogous to 1 Timothy 3.16, both describing the earthly and heavenly spheres of Christ's existence. That is the way in which the community which shaped this phrase took up official Jewish Messianology and incorporated it into its exaltation Christology.[1] A new factor compared with 1 Timothy 3.16 is the arrangement of the antitheses in Romans 1.3f. In 1 Timothy 3.16 earthly and heavenly events form a single, universal process. But in the two parts of the formula in Romans 3.1f they stand in climactic parallelism. The historic existence of Jesus is described in terms of his Davidic descent. This in turn is visibly transcended by the exaltation of Jesus when he becomes the Son of God.[2] This makes the Davidic Sonship of Jesus strangely ambiguous. On the one hand it indicates the concrete place in history where Jesus lived his human life (among the Jewish people). On the other hand it merely marks the earthly origin of Jesus, while his real dignity as Son of God is founded upon the eschatological intervention of God, in the resurrection of Jesus from the dead.

(c) These considerations lead us to consider the synoptic pericope about Davidic sonship (Mark 12.35–7a, par.). The connection between this and the formula in Romans 1.3f has been emphasized by G. Bornkamm.[3] In its original meaning this tradition was obviously directed against a nationalistic form of the Messianic hope.[4] But what does it mean in Mark? He would hardly use it

---

[1] Schweizer, op. cit., p. 187.

[2] Michel, op. cit., p. 40, emphasizes that ὁρισθέντος is concerned with Christ's exaltation at his inauguration as Son.

[3] G. Bornkamm, Jesus of Nazareth, 1960, p. 190; idem (with G. Barth and H. J. Held) Tradition and Interpretation in Matthew, 1963, p. 33; cf. Conzelmann, RGG³, III, col. 630; Hahn, Hoheitstitel, pp. 113ff; 191f; 259ff.

[4] G. Friedrich, "Beobachtungen zur messianischen Hohepriestererwartung bei den Synoptikern", ZThK 53 (1956), p. 287; O. Cullmann, The Christology of the New Testament, 1963², pp. 132f; R. Otto, The Kingdom of God and the Son of Man, 1943², pp. 222; Grässer, Parousieverzögerung, p. 25, takes 12.35ff in connection with Mark 11.10. The "kingdom of our father David" there has an entirely Jewish-nationalistic meaning, which is corrected by Mark 12.1ff; 12.35ff; 13.2.

polemically against the title Son of David since he uses it else-where without hesitation.[1] If we agree with Bornkamm that the Davidic Sonship here, as in Romans 1.3f, indicates the earthly existence of Jesus, it still does not tell us what it meant for Mark. The paragraph closes with an open question (Mark 12.37a), which brings out the paradox that Christ is both Lord and Son. The question is significantly left unanswered (though the answer must be along the lines of Romans 1.3). Outwardly the Messianic secret remains intact. Only faith can supply the answer, which expresses the miracle of the two modes of Jesus' existence—earthly and heavenly.

The results of our discussion of 1 Timothy 3.16, Romans 1.3f, and Mark 12.35ff are as follows. There is an early christological tradition both before and after Paul, which is based on Hellenistic thought and which postulates two modes of existence for Jesus Christ, one earthly, the other heavenly. The parallel structure between 1 Timothy 3.16/Romans 1.3 and the theology of Luke on the one hand and the substantial agreement between Romans 1.3f and Mark 12.35ff, par. on the other suggest that the Christ-ology of Luke has to be understood along similar lines.

In what follows we will try to explain the peculiar nuances Luke gives to this general pattern. In doing so we shall, in line with our main concern in Chapter 2, concentrate especially on Luke's treatment of the humanity of Jesus.[2] In Chapter 3A the exaltation will be our primary concern.

2. Luke's Two Stage Christology

In Chapter 1 we noticed a shift in Luke's Christology as compared with Mark. The real mystery of the Son of God is for Luke the

---

[1] Bornkamm, ibid. (n. 26).

[2] The question of Jesus' humanity in the Gospels must not be equated with the modern problem of the historical Jesus. That question belongs to our age, and can easily act as a barrier to a proper understanding of the texts. A complex picture results from an inquiry into the particular theological understanding of the humanity of Jesus in Paul, Mark, Matthew, Luke, or John. When the question is posed in this way, following the testimony of the NT itself, the barren alternative, between the "that" and the "how" of the historical Jesus, is tran-scended, and leads to careful distinctions in interpretation (cf. Bultmann, *Theology* II, pp. 155ff).

passion of Jesus, and not, as in Mark, his whole existence as man.[1] That leaves untouched the question of the earthly part of Jesus' life, which is not determined by the passion—his words and deeds. Here Luke depicts Jesus in his unique, human manifestation, as he is visible to everybody—the people (Luke 7.16; 9.18f), the Pharisees (7.39; 13.31–3), the people of Nazareth (4.20), the Sanhedrin (22.67).[2]

Such a generalized presentation of Jesus is unavoidable for Luke because he must describe the man Jesus, who is for him the exalted, ever present Kyrios, in the past tense. The formula of Jesus' two modes of existence forms the background which saves the treatment of Jesus' earthly life from becoming mythological. The presence of God as it was experienced in Jesus must not become visible as a divine drama of salvation in the past. The two stage Christology also prevents the profaning of the divine mystery of Jesus through the presentation of his earthly life. Jesus remains the heavenly Lord even while on earth. This must now be demonstrated from the text of Luke.

(a) Luke took over the section about the Davidic sonship from Mark (Luke 20.41–4) with only minor alterations. This can hardly have been unintentional in view of the freedom with which he treats Mark elsewhere (cf. Mark 9.2ff and Luke 9.28ff etc.). This is an indication that he agrees with Mark's christological pattern. He does go further than Mark by omitting the οἱ γραμματεῖς in Mark 12.35b, thus generalizing the question: in what sense do people say (in the Church) that Christ is the Son of David (v. 41)? Here it becomes even more obvious than in Mark that the original

---

[1] See above, pp. 30ff on Luke 9.18ff.

[2] This does not exclude the possibility that for Luke Jesus is also Son of God in his words and works. But the difference is noticeable. If Jesus' glory lies concealed beneath its opposite, his suffering, it is simultaneously both veiled and visible in a parabolic way in his words and works. If the contrast between Jesus' suffering and glory exhibited an antithetical form, the relation of his words and works to his heavenly dignity is another instance of transcendent parallelism. In the first case the antithesis between the fallen world which Jesus endures, and the heavenly world is shown. In the second case we have the analogy between this world in its created form, which Jesus presents visibly for all, and the new creation of God in him, which is perceptible only to faith.

polemic has been turned into a dogmatic problem which was being canvassed in the Church.[1]

(b) The same christological structure is discernible in the message of the angel to Mary (Luke 1.26–38). Gabriel tells Mary that she will bear a son who shall be named Jesus (v. 31). Then his glory is foretold:

> He will be great, and will be called the Son of the Most High;
> and the Lord God will give to him the throne of his father David,
> and he will reign over the house of Jacob for ever;
> and of his kingdom there will be no end. (vv. 32f)

This is a comprehensive statement which cannot be improved upon within the limits of Israel's Messianic hopes. But because of Mary's objection (v. 34) the angel adds another prophecy:

> The Holy Spirit will come upon you
> and the power of the Most High will overshadow you;
> therefore the child to be born will be called holy[2],
> the Son of God. (v. 35)

Loisy pointed out the tensions between the two prophecies of the angel. According to v. 32 Jesus is Son of God "selon l'ordre de sa vocation", and there is no reference whatever to the virginal conception. After that, v. 35 has the effect of a "surcharge".[3]

Whether we are of opinion that the creative power of the Holy Ghost is a Hellenistic or an Old Testament concept,[4] we cannot overlook the tension between the two prophecies of the angel. It fits exactly into the pattern of climactic parallelism. Israel's hope for an *earthly* kingdom of the Son of David is transcended by the operation of the Holy Spirit, who is for Luke a *heavenly* power. It is difficult to say how far Luke himself has

[1] There is a commentary on the Lucan text in Acts 2.34f (see below, pp. 150ff). In Matt. 22.42 the question of Jesus, "What think ye of Christ?" is to an even further extent formulated as a title for the whole section.

[2] M. Dibelius, "Jungfrauensohn und Krippenkind," *Botschaft und Geschichte* I, 1953, p. 16.

[3] A. Loisy, *L'évangile selon Luc*, 1924, pp. 89f.

[4] The former is assumed by Loisy, op. cit.; E. Norden, *Die Geburt des Kindes*, 1924, pp. 76ff; H. Leisegang, *Pneuma Hagion*, 1922, p. 125; H. von Baer, *Der hlg. Geist in den Lukasschriften*, 1926, p. 125; the latter by Schweizer, *TWNT* VI, p. 399ff; according to Barrett, *The Holy Spirit in the Gospel Tradition*, 1954, p. 18, the concept is "at once Jewish and Hellenistic".

modified the material here.[1] In any case the pattern exhibited here conforms with Luke's Christology as the following texts will show.

(c) The Lucan version of the examination of Jesus before the Sanhedrin (22.66—23.1) shows a similar climax in christological statement. By omitting the saying about the temple Luke makes the trial a "compendium of Christology".[2] The structure of the pericope is noticeable. In contrast to Mark and Matthew he repeats the question, "Are you the Christ?" (v. 67)—"the Son of God?" (v. 70).[3] The two questions confront each other— separated by the statement about the exaltation of Jesus to the right hand of God. How do they differ? Hauck speaks of two decisive questions directed to Jesus. One refers to Messiahship in a political sense, the other to the religious element, his divine sonship.[4] Cullmann similarly points out the political associations of the title "Messiah". As he sees it, Jesus is deliberately correcting the High Priest's question "by substituting the 'Son of Man' for the 'Messiah' ".[5]

In fact it may be said that with these two questions two areas of consideration come into view which again correspond to the pattern of the two spheres of existence. Let us test this in

[1] The expression, "Son of God" in v. 35 is a constitutive part of this context, and forms the antithesis to "the Son of the Most High" (v. 32), which as 1.76 and the context dealing with the Son of David (in Luke's understanding) shows, is to be taken to mean "a man according to God's good pleasure". For a different view see Sahlin, Messias, pp. 124ff, who seeks to prove that υἱὸς θεοῦ is an interpolation.

[2] Conzelmann, St. Luke, pp. 84f, n. 3.

[3] Is this an earlier tradition? W. Bousset, Kyrios Christos, 1921², p. 55 regards Luke's separation as possibly "a more original tradition"; similarly Cullmann, op. cit., pp. 279f. J. Schniewind, Die Parallelperikopen bei Lk. und Joh., 1958², pp. 43f points out the agreement with John 10.24; 3.12; 8.45. Here Luke will be dependent on the Johannine tradition, since the linguistic usage (οὐ πιστεύειν, ἐρωτᾶν in the sense "ask") "is both in form and content specifically Johannine". Cf. also P. Winter, "Luke XXII 66b–71", StTh 9 (1955), pp. 112ff.

[4] Lukas ad loc.

[5] Op. cit., p. 120. Even those who, unlike Cullmann, do not presume a historical scene, will be able to accept his argument on this passage, but as Lucan theology. Cullmann works out the Lucan theology and then presents it as an account of history. That does not exclude the possibility that the problem of the political Messiah is a historical fact, as the false reaction of the disciples shows (ibid., pp. 123f). On the apologetic problem see below pp. 61f.

detail. It must be noted that Luke is not developing any static doctrine of the two "natures". He is not concerned with objective considerations but seeks to force an existential claim upon the reader.

To the question of the Sanhedrin: "Are you the Christ?" (v. 67) Jesus gives an "evasive" answer,[1] thus exposing the insincerity of the question and leaving the problem still in the air. If they are sincere they will be ready to answer it themselves (v. 68). The transition from v. 68 to v. 69 is abrupt. Vv. 67b–68 are a complete reply "in the nature of which there is nothing more to be said".[2] To this dialogue, already complete in essentials, Jesus adds the saying about the Son of Man sitting at the right hand of God (v. 69), in climactic antithesis. The transcendent majesty of Jesus is asserted "against all political misinterpretation".[3] If in retrospect the saying about the exaltation of Jesus to the right hand of God has an apologetic sound, it is also the premiss for the confession of his divine sonship (v. 70).[4] Because Jesus is the exalted one he is the Son of God.[5] Thus the Lucan οὖν in v. 70[6] refers the reader back to v. 69.

In his reply to the second question Jesus openly acknowledges his divine sonship. The situation is changed after the saying in v. 69. The narrow confines of the examination have been burst open. Now they "all" ask (including the reader of the Gospel) and are all expected to make their decision and confess the heavenly dignity of Jesus. The members of the Sanhedrin must make the confession involuntarily which includes us all: "What further testimony do we need? We have heard it ourselves from his own

[1] Klostermann, *Lukas*, ad loc. For a different view see Conzelmann, *Mitte*[5], p. 78; very emphatically Cullmann, op. cit., pp. 118f, who assumes even for the Marcan and Matthean version such an evasion on the part of Jesus to the "catch question" of the high priest.

[2] E. Hirsch, *Frühgeschichte des Evangeliums* II, 1941, p. 267.

[3] Rengstorf, *Lukas*, p. 259.

[4] Thus there is no antithesis here between the titles Son of Man and Son of God. On Luke 22.69, see below, pp. 98ff.

[5] This fits in with the Hellenistic understanding of sonship (see above, n. 1). On the title, Bultmann, *Theology* I, pp. 130ff. J. Bieneck, *Sohn Gottes als Christusbezeichnung der Synoptiker*, 1951, does not distinguish between the religio-historical and theological approach to the question, thus losing the chance of an effective critique of Bultmann.

[6] Cf. Luke 19.11; 13.18; Acts 2.33, 36 etc.

lips." Luke's ambiguous saying in v. 71 is an ingenious solution to the difficulty into which his composition has led him. In the course of the passion story he has to report the rejection of Jesus on the one hand, while on the other the christological structure aimed at the confession of faith by the reader requires that the self-confession of Jesus may also be accepted positively.

In Luke 22.66ff several typically Lucan statements are collected together:

1. The two modes of Jesus' existence are differentiated and stand in climactic parallelism to one another. The Sanhedrin only sees the Christ according to Jewish understanding, but the confession of the (exalted) Son of God is demanded of the reader.

2. The two stage Christology is exactly reflected here. The question: "Are you the Christ?" (in the Jewish sense of David's son) remains on the level of popular opinion, which regards Jesus as a prophet (7.16, 39; 9.8, 19). The question whether he is the Son of God is aimed at faith (as it is directed to the heavenly reality), which hears directly ("from his own lips") the voice of Jesus.

3. The section as a whole exhibits the same threefold pattern we are trying to work out in the course of this study:[1] (1) The level of human ambiguity is contrasted with (2) the level of heavenly consummation; (3) in living faith in Jesus as the Son of God the heavenly reality is present on earth.

(d) Up to this point we have been considering the two stage christological pattern. Now—still within the framework of this pattern—we shall concentrate on the special meaning Luke gives to the life of Jesus in the old world. The confession of Peter (Luke 9.18–22) will be a good starting point. Earlier on we discussed the dialectic between the Messianic glory and the suffering of Jesus.[2] Now we must concentrate on the two answers to Jesus' question (the crowd's opinion and disciples' confession). In general it appears that the crowd's opinion of Jesus (v. 19)

[1] Cf. the structure of Chapter 3 of this work.
[2] See above, pp. 30ff.

serves as the foil for Peter's confession of Jesus' Messiahship. On the other hand it has been rightly observed that v. 19 (cf. Mark 8.28) can be traced back to an independent tradition, since we find the same tradition in Luke 9.7-9 (Mark 6.14-16—Herod's judgement concerning Jesus).[1] Behind these "opinions of the crowd" may lie the original opinion of the (Jewish-Christian) circles, who saw in Jesus the return of Elijah or one of the prophets.[2] If this passage is, from the standpoint of the later stage of tradition, a polemic against such "earthly" conceptions of Messiahship—this is not the interpretation of Luke himself.

In Mark there are strong traces of the polemic. The opinion of "men" (Mark 8.27b) is certainly regarded as inadequate.[3] Yet it should be noted that this is not the opinion of Jesus' enemies.[4] The opinion of the people remains on the Old Testament level and so misses the dignity of Jesus as the Son of God. But it does not mean that they reject him.[5]

In Luke the tension between the positive statement and the negative framework is weakened. Luke replaces the word "men" by "crowd" ($\check{o}\chi\lambda o\iota$). This modifies Mark's derogatory judgement upon the opinion of the people. For in Luke $\check{o}\chi\lambda o\varsigma$ has no pejorative connotation. It is Jesus' followers who are still undecided.[6] The people are drawn irresistibly by Jesus' miracles (6.19) and marvel at the things they see (9.43b; 11.14). They even break out into praise to God (7.16; 13.7). Clearly Luke distinguishes the people ($\check{o}\chi\lambda o\varsigma$, $\lambda\alpha\acute{o}\varsigma$ or "all") from the leaders of the people.[7] While the leaders have already decided against Jesus, the people are still in sympathy with him although they have not yet recognized his heavenly dignity.[8]

[1] H. J. Ebeling, *Das Messiasgeheimnis und die Botschaft des Markus-Evangelisten*, 1939, pp. 215f; K. L. Schmidt, *Rahmen*, p. 174; Hahn, *Hoheitstitel*, p. 228.

[2] Perhaps also "the prophet" of Deut. 18.15; cf. "hear him" (from Deut. 18.15) with Luke 9.35b par.; further, John 1.21, 25; 6.14; 7.40.

[3] See above, p. 24, n. 3.   [4] Cf. on the contrary Luke 5.21; 11.15; 23.2.

[5] Cf. Ebeling, op. cit., p. 215.

[6] Meyer, *TWNT* VII, p. 586, 31f, calls it the "general public", which discusses the problem of Jesus' person, and argues over it.

[7] Here is another Johannine trait; cf. John 7.48f (Meyer, ibid., pp. 587ff).

[8] Luke 3.7 substitutes for the Pharisees and Sadducees (Mark 3.7) the $\check{o}\chi\lambda o\iota$ (cf. Luke 7.29f; Conzelmann, *St. Luke*, pp. 20f). In Luke 13.17 "all his adversaries" (i.e. the leaders of the synagogue and their henchmen) are ashamed; "the whole people" however rejoices over Jesus' glorious deeds.

Thus the opinion of the people has for Luke a relatively independent significance. It is certain that Peter's confession of Jesus' Messiahship in 9.20 represents the climax and goal of all Christian profession. Yet it is not unimportant how a man thinks of Jesus even before he makes a definite confession of faith. Jesus' dignity has a human, external side which is visible to all.[1] Luke takes up material from the synoptic tradition and uses it to describe the external manifestation of Jesus in terms quarried from the Old Testament. The three popular opinions cited in Luke 9.19 agree in using Old Testament types.

First, under this human aspect Jesus is seen in direct continuity with John the Baptist.[2] Luke intends this to represent a positive attitude to the human person of Jesus (Luke 20.1–8). There is a significant shift of interpretation compared with Mark 11.27–33. For Luke, the Baptist is not part of the gospel, that is, of the proclamation of the kingdom.[3] That is why the question about John's baptism is relegated to a position prior to the preaching of the gospel, as will be seen from the slight changes Luke has made in the text. He omits (v. 3) the ἕνα (Mark 11.29). For Mark it is "the one all-important question",[4] whereas Luke passes over it lightly. For Mark, everything turns on how men react to John the Baptist, whereas in Luke this is only a preliminary decision, one still within the Old Testament situation. At most, it expresses an open—or closed—mind towards the kingdom of God as it is present in Jesus. By refusing to answer Jesus' question (21b), the leaders of the people show their unreceptiveness to Jesus' message. So there is no point in answering the question about Jesus' (heavenly) authority (20.8).

In 20.6 John is called a "prophet"—which is exactly the

---

[1] E. Sjöberg, *Der verborgene Menschensohn in den Evangelien*, 1955, has emphasized "the contrast between the outward manifestation of the earthly Jesus, which was known to all, and the Messianic dignity which actually was his and which was confirmed by the resurrection" (quotation, p. 148). Also G. W. H. Lampe, "The Lucan Portrait of Christ", *NTS* 2 (1956), pp. 160ff, shows that in Luke the prophetic character of Jesus is strongly emphasized (cf. p. 168).

[2] On the relation of the Baptist to Jesus see above, pp. 21f.

[3] Conzelmann, op. cit., pp. 22f.

[4] E. Klostermann, *Das Markusevangelium*, 1950⁴, 119; ἕνα must be taken as equivalent to τινά (Blass-Debrunner, p. 247, 2; Klostermann, op. cit. on Mark 5.22).

popular estimate of him in 9.19. How does Luke use this title?[1] It is a favourite term, especially in the special Lucan material, to express outside opinion about Jesus. Further, when Jesus is talking to outsiders he employs it in reference to himself, often so as to veil his true claims. The best instance of the latter is in the saying that a prophet is without honour in his native city (Luke 4.24). After having declared himself to be the Messiah, anointed by the Holy Spirit (Luke 4.16ff), but still unrecognized as such, he speaks of what he is in a hidden way and only shows the outward side of his dignity. The case is similar when Jesus says that a prophet must die in Jerusalem (13.33). The audience here consists of the Pharisees, for they more than any other group were receptive to Jesus' message.[2] Schlatter, commenting on 13.33b, says "he does not use his royal name 'Christos' in conversation with the Pharisees. This would only aggravate the misunderstanding. But prophet, speaker of God-given words— that is a phrase not unacceptable to the Pharisees."[3] In the same way Simon the Pharisee sees only the prophet in Jesus (7.36–50). He has quite a definite idea of what can be expected of a prophet, v. 39. He is led to doubt Jesus' calling when Jesus fails to recognize that the woman is a well-known prostitute. Luke also uses the title "prophet" for the faith of the disciples prior to Easter. In Luke 24.19 Jesus is for the disciples an $\dot{\alpha}\nu\dot{\eta}\rho$ $\pi\rho o\phi\dot{\eta}\tau\eta s$ mighty in deed and word before God and all the people. This agrees with 7.16. When he raised the son of the widow of Nain the people praised God, saying: "A great prophet has arisen among us and God has visited his people."[4]

[1] In Luke sayings about Elijah are soft-pedalled: he even omits sayings referring to Elijah. The relation of Elijah to John the Baptist (Matt. 11.14) is suppressed at Luke 16.16. The "conversation during the descent" (Mark 9.9–13) is lacking. Mark 15.34–6 is left out, with its allusion to Elijah. This "disappearance of the Elijah typology" (Conzelmann, St. Luke, p. 88, cf. p. 25) is remarkable because it is Luke himself who has preserved more original Elijah traditions. In Luke 9.51ff, as well as in 7.11ff, it is clear that Elijah stories serve as the Vorlage. The assumption of Jesus in 24.50ff is reminiscent of 2 Kings 2. The term $\dot{\alpha}\pi o\kappa\alpha\tau\dot{\alpha}\sigma\tau\alpha\sigma\iota s$ in Acts 1.6 and 3.21 was connected with Elijah in late Judaism, following Malachi 3.22f LXX (Jeremias, TWNT [E.T.] II, pp. 933f). Cf. Luke 4.25f with 1 Kings 17.1f and Luke 22.43 with 1 Kings 19.5ff (Jeremias, ibid., pp. 934f).
[2] See above, pp. 25ff.   [3] Lukas, p. 332.
[4] On the passages quoted cf. Friedrich, TWNT VI p. 847, 23ff, who notes the breadth of meaning in the word "the prophet" and distinguishes between the

Now that we have reviewed Luke's use of the word prophet
let us return to the text in Luke 9.19. In verse 19b, Luke adds
τῶν ἀρχαίων ἀνέστη to his Marcan source. This makes Jesus a
figure comparable to John and Elijah. He changes the "ordinary
prophet" of Mark[1] into a "classical prophet". So Jesus is not
just any prophet. That would have been misunderstood in Hellenistic Christianity.[2] Rather, he belongs to the context of Old
Testament redemptive history. His humanity is not timeless,
as might be inferred from John 1.14, but bound up with
history.

With this positive interpretation of the opinion of the ὄχλοι
Luke 9.19 acquires a new shift of meaning in relation to the
whole pericope, 9.18–20, compared with Mark's. This verse is
no longer merely the foil for the confession of Peter. It is not that
the crowd misunderstands Jesus and sees only his outer human
side. The antithesis is still there in Luke. But at the same time the
two questions of Jesus form a climactic parallelism. The people
accept Jesus' real (prophetic= divine) humanity and so have not
yet arrived at the point of faith. The disciples, by contrast, confess
Jesus' real dignity as "Christ of God". The Lucan addition τοῦ
θεοῦ (v. 20) emphasizes this state of affairs. This double view of
the Christ event protects the confession of Christ from false
historization. From the historical point of view, that is in general
human terms, the popular opinion can only see that Jesus is a
prophet acting under the divine commission. Only the confession
of faith can penetrate the mystery of the Christ of God—in the
Lucan sense, that is as the Lord sitting at the right hand of God.

(e) Luke's concern to express Jesus' real humanity along with his
heavenly dignity is made clear in his composition of Luke

---

common type of OT prophet and the eschatological prophet (op. cit., pp. 842ff).

[1] Cf. Lohmeyer, Markus, p. 162, who, as far as Mark is concerned, rightly
infers from the different syntax of the two first names and the third saying that
the Evangelist understands them differently. Luke smooths it out (cf. Freidrich,
op. cit., p. 843, 25ff).

[2] The Greeks also know the prophet as "proclaimer" and "speaker" (Krämer,
TWNT VI, p. 783). He belongs to the personnel connected with the Delphic
oracle (pp. 786f) and according to Plato (Tim. 71e–72b) his function is to pass
critical judgement on "the words of the Pythia uttered in a state of frenzy" and
submit them to rational reflection (p. 788, 22ff).

3.21–38. The baptism and genealogy of Jesus "obviously stand side by side".[1] They thus form an illuminating example both for the composition of Luke and also for his pattern of the two spheres of existence. In the Lucan baptismal narrative the actual baptism is secondary—'Ιησοῦ βαπτισθέντος. The Baptist is not even mentioned.[2] The voice from heaven and the adoption of the Son of God occupy the centre of the stage. By contrast, the genealogy stands for Luke as a sign of the earthly descent of Jesus. We are told at the outset that "Jesus, when he began his ministry was about 30 years of age" (3.23).[3] This reference to the age of Jesus in v. 23a is followed immediately by the list of Jesus' ancestors. Originally, no doubt, the genealogy was intended to prove Jesus' Davidic descent. Now it is used to prove his humanity, like Luke 20.41–4 compared with Mark 12.35ff.[4] The succession of generations serves Luke to emphasize the historical rootage of Jesus' life.

Luke universalizes the genealogy more than Matthew, and extends it back to Adam. This links Jesus with the creation. It is emphasized by the addition of τοῦ θεοῦ in v. 38. Neither is this an "indirect testimony that Jesus is the Son of God" and thus "a link with baptismal narrative",[5] nor is his physical descent an "indication of his mission", implying that Jesus was "Son of God by physical descent as well".[6] Such interpretations obliterate the clear distinction Luke otherwise draws between the earthly and heavenly existence of Christ. Adam in v. 38 is man made in the image of God. His derivation from God points to this divine image (cf. Acts 17.26) and to the true humanity of Jesus which corresponds to this creation.[7] Luke does not conclude the

---

[1] Brun, op. cit., p. 40.

[2] Klostermann, *Lukas*, p. 55; Conzelmann, *St. Luke*, pp. 21, 180.

[3] E. Meyer, op. cit., I 50. This is not just an historical note, for the synchronization with temporal history has already been indicated in advance. It is particularly significant that it is not directly tied in with the beginning of Jesus' ministry (see below, pp. 122f).

[4] Cf. Hahn, *Hoheitstitel*, pp. 242ff.   [5] So Hahn, op. cit. p. 244.

[6] So Bartsch, *Wachet*, p. 55.

[7] For Luke Jesus' human life has a double significance. First it shows what true humanity is, as God created it to be. Secondly, it is a veiling of the divine Sonship, so that the people of Nazareth, who see in him only the son of Joseph (Luke 4.22), fail to see his true majesty (for a different view see G. Braumann, "Das Mittel der Zeit", *ZNW* 54 (1963), pp. 131f).

genealogy with Adam as sinner but points to his divine origin. If Jesus as the Son of God has a unique dignity (baptism), as true man he is comparable with others and can become an example to his own. More will be said about this in the following section.

(*f*) This theological pattern, with its equal emphasis on the earthly and heavenly life of Jesus, explains why Luke, as is well known, refers to Jesus as ὁ κύριος, thus exalting him to divine status, but at the same time lays special emphasis on his earthly character. The Lucan origin of the title ὁ κύριος is undeniable. For "it always occurs either in the special Lucan material or in the editorial changes to his sources".[1] The fifteen occurrences of the title in the Gospels do not, it is true, suggest any systematic use of it.[2] The "Master" approaches death (Luke 7.13) and Satan (13.15f) victoriously. He sends out his disciples (10.1) and engages in conversation with his followers (10.39; 17.5f etc.). In these contexts a uniform meaning of the word is undeniable. Luke is concerned with the one, ever present Lord, who in Acts and for Luke's own time is the exalted One.[3] But we have to guard against speaking of the "raising of the person of Jesus to the divine".[4] Luke does not intend by ὁ κύριος to make Jesus a divine epiphany

---

[1] Foerster, *TWNT* III p. 1092, 22f; note further the complete absence of κύριος from the old Syriac text (cf. K. Köhler, "Der κύριος 'Ιησοῦς in den Ev.n und der Spruch vom Herr-Herr sagen", *ThStKr* 28 (1915) pp. 475f, argues in favour of later redaction; for a different view see Hahn, *Hoheitstitel*, p. 89).

[2] Luke 7.13, 19; 10.1, 39, 41; 11.39; 12.42; 13.15; 16.8; 17.5, 6; 18.6; 19.8; 22.61a, b. Luke 19.31, 34 and 24.34 are excepted since the latter passage is about the Risen Christ, while the former is a parallel to Mark 11.3, where the absolute ὁ κύριος is used, which is exceptional in Mark. As a form of address, κύριε requires a separate treatment, since it may equally represent ordinary secular usage (Cullmann, *Christology*, p. 204). It is none the less worth noting that in Luke it appears chiefly in the special material (A. Schlatter, *Die beiden Schwerter, Lk.* 22.35–38, 1916, n. 1; F. Rehkopf, *Die lk. Sonderquelle*, 1959, pp. 58f, 99).

[3] On the use of κύριος in the Acts cf. J. C. O'Neill, "The Use of Kyrios in the Book of Acts", *SJT* 8 (1955), pp. 155ff; according to Hahn, op. cit., pp. 85, 89, Luke uses κύριος in reference to the authority of the earthly Lord, as Paul's use of ὁ κύριος shows (pp. 91ff). But although this may be true of the original tradition, I should hardly suppose there is any distinction between the earthly and exalted Lord in the use of κύριος, even in Paul (cf. 1 Cor. 9.1, "Have I not seen Jesus our Lord?"), to say nothing of Luke. So also H. W. Bartsch, "Wie redete die frühe Christenheit von J. Christus?", *Kirche in der Zeit* 19 (1964), pp. 60f.

[4] Bultmann, *Tradition*, p. 367.

veiled to unbelief but revealed to faith.[1] It remains an ambiguous term which may even be applied to the emperor (Acts 25.23). We see its parabolic sense above all in the use of ὁ κύριος in parables. The master who sets his servant over his other servants (Luke 12.42f, 45f), who invites guests to the feast (14.21, 23), and the unjust steward who is called to give an account of his steward-ship (16.3, 5), are, according to the picture-half of the parable, figures of everyday life. But there is no doubt he also represents God commissioning men, inviting them or giving them res-ponsibilities. Just as in these parables faith is the bridge between picture and reality, so too, faith is required in order to see in the earthly master the Lord exalted to God's right hand.[2]

The Lucan tendency to ambiguity comes out again in his description of Jesus' (exemplary) humanity. This can be illustrated in the prayer, suffering, and temptation of Jesus.

There is more emphasis on prayer in Luke than in any of the other synoptics. Jesus' baptism is accompanied by prayer (3.21). He goes up into the Mount of Transfiguration in order to pray (9.28). Before the call of the disciples he spends the night on the mount in prayer (6.12). Again before the confession of Peter he prays alone (9.18; cf. 5.16). It is Jesus' example that makes the disciples ask him to teach them to pray (11.1). Finally there is the agony on the Mount of Olives (22.31f) and the prayer at the crucifixion (23.34–46).[3] H. Greeven makes the point clearly:

---

[1] Similarly in Luke 5.8 the veiling remains unlifted. There is no reference to seeing God, as in Isa. 6.5. Peter "sees" a miracle capable of more than one interpretation.

[2] The question raised by Bousset in his *Kyrios Christos* about the origin of the title κύριος in the history of religion need not concern us here. There has recently been a revival of interest in this discussion. See Schweizer, *Erniedrigung*, pp. 77ff (cf. E. Schweizer, *Lordship and Discipleship*, (SBT 28) 1960, pp. 56ff), O'Neill, op. cit.; Cullmann, *Christology*, pp. 203ff; S. Schulz, "Maranatha und Kyrios Jesus", *ZNW* 53 (1962), pp. 125ff; W. Kramer, *Christ*, pp. 99ff; Hahn, op. cit., pp. 67ff.

[3] One thing is certain: the prayer life of Jesus is a "motif" of the evangelist (Bultmann, *Tradition*, p. 342). But this motif serves the theological intention of bearing witness to the humanity of Jesus. It is wrong to raise the direct question of its historicity, like E. von der Goltz, *Das Gebet in der ältesten Christenheit*, 1901, who leaves out of account those passages which he regards as historically worthless (p. 3). H. Greeven, *Gebet und Eschatologie im NT*, 1931, follows a more correct procedure. He sees clearly that no historical certainty can be derived

"The earliest church always appreciated the historical side of its exalted Lord, the time and the circumstances of his earthly life. The gospel narratives leave no doubt about this. Nothing could be more historical, real or earthly than the way Jesus prays in the synoptics."[1]

Luke depicts Jesus' suffering and death in terms of the suffering of the righteous man[2] who dies a martyr's death, thus incurring the same fate as Stephen.[3] Above all, the agony on the Mount of Olives is portrayed in this vein. Even in Mark "Jesus is portrayed as a martyr".[4] The highlight of the agony in Luke is "the appearance of the angel in answer to Jesus' prayer, together with a description of his wrestling in prayer (22.43f). Both these are typical experiences of a martyr."[5] The exemplary character of Jesus' prayer is strongly underlined by the call to prayer at the beginning and end of this section.[6] Dibelius points out the "change over to something which is unique" or "transposition into an individualistic key" in the Lucan version of the passion. The cry of the centurion at the foot of the cross draws special attention to this. This is not, as in Mark, the Gentiles' profession of faith in the Son of God (Mark 15.39). It declares that "a righteous man" has suffered (23.47), and the people return home shocked at his innocent suffering.[7]

Again in the temptation story, which Luke consciously links with the passion narrative (4.13/22.3), he depicts Jesus as the model of human victory over "temptations" (22.28—plural). Bartsch discerns even in Matthew a paraenetic intention. The signs of eschatological consummation in Mark (community in paradise

---

from the text, (pp. 13, 22, 36), but infers from the tradition that it was "the habit of Jesus to pray in silence to his Father" (p. 22). Cf. the excursus in Rengstorf, *Lukas*, pp. 251ff.

[1] Op. cit., p. 11.   [2] Cf. Luke 23.47, contrasted with Mark 15.39.
[3] Grundmann, *Lukas*, pp. 287f.   [4] Dibelius, *Botschaft* I, p. 265.
[5] Dibelius, *Tradition*, pp. 201f; his remark on the textual tradition, viz., that the omission of 22.43f leaves quite an inadequate account, is convincing (cf. *Botschaft* I, 269, n. 4).
[6] Dibelius, *Botschaft* I, p. 269.
[7] Dibelius, *Tradition*, p. 203; for further details see pp. 199–203. Cf. also H. W. Surkau, *Martyrien in jüdischer und frühchristlicher Zeit*, 1938; E. Lohse, "Lukas als Theologe der Heilsgeschichte" *EvTh* 14 (1954), p. 273; *Märtyrer und Gottesknecht*, 1955, pp. 187ff.

between man and beast, angels as representatives of the divine world, the desert as place of Yahweh's marriage with Israel as well as the satanic temptations) are replaced by a paraenetic dialogue. "It is intended for the community as an example or norm given by their Lord for their own behaviour."[1]

In Luke, however, it is in the prayers of Jesus, in his suffering and resistance to temptation, that his uniqueness comes out. In prayer, Jesus' unique relationship with God becomes a reality as nowhere else. His prayers may have been examples for the disciples (Luke 11.1), but that does not alter the fact that for Luke Jesus lives with his heavenly Father in a personal relationship which has no analogy, as the doxology in 10.21f shows. The same holds good for the temptation. Even if the humanity of Jesus is strongly emphasized here, Jesus' victory over the temptations remains the unique work of the Son of God (Luke 4.3, 9). Jesus is both "prototype" and example in temptation and only so does he enable Christians to overcome temptation in their own lives.[2]

Let it be said once more that only faith can recognize Jesus in his unique dignity and accept him. Faith is concerned with the one Lord, who as *Kyrios* is the man Jesus, and who as the man Jesus is the Son of God, victorious over Satan. The twofold christological pattern remains in the background and so prevents us from rationalizing the recognition of faith, from confounding Jesus' heavenly and earthly dignity and so making him a mythical demi-god.[3]

[1] *Wachet*, pp. 56f. A. Feuillet, "Le recit Lukanien de la tentation (Lc 4, 1–13)", *Bibl.* 40 (1959), pp. 613ff, has also pointed out the exemplary character of Jesus' temptation. Jesus appears as the new Adam, the prototype of every Christian in temptation, and in victory over it. This makes him the antitype of the first Adam, who fell when tempted in paradise, Luke 3.38 (pp. 624ff). Satan tempts Jesus less as Messiah than "comme un homme ordinaire" (p. 618). The temptation becomes the "modèle de tous les baptisées" (p. 620). The taking of Jesus up to the high mountain (v. 5) and the ministry of the angels (cf. Matt. 4.11) are omitted, since they are Messianic signs (p. 619).

[2] This tension is unnoticed by Feulliet in his essay quoted above, n. 1. Jeremias, *TWNT* (E.T.) I, p. 141 shifts the tension over to the other side, considering Luke's version to be shaped by the Pauline Adam/Christ typology. But whereas for Paul the *new* Adam is the man from heaven (1 Cor. 15.47), for Luke he is simultaneously the *true* man of this creation and the *new* man of the heavenly consummation. Cf. the identical threefold structure of Luke 3.21—4.13; 22.66–71 (see above pp. 44–6).

[3] Conzelmann has strongly emphasized the subordination of Christ to God (*St. Luke*, p. 173ff). The problem appears, however, in a different light when we

With this distinction between a reflective knowledge, for which the heavenly and the earthly are clearly differentiated, and the faith which accepts the one Lord already reigning, we have passed beyond the limits of this chapter. We will pursue this train of thought in a later part of this work, where we shall also deal with the unique meaning of Christ's passion.[1]

Here we were dealing mainly with the christological posture of Luke. Its framework is furnished by the Hellenistic scheme of the heavenly and earthly modes of Christ's existence. It enables the earthly life of Jesus to be given a relative autonomy, as a created life rooted in history. It has a double importance: on one hand Jesus as man stands in continuity with the Old Testament prophets. He gains acknowledgement even before he is known to be the Son of God. This attitude to Jesus forms the prelude to true faith. On the other hand Jesus is true Adam as God intended him to be at the creation. In this capacity he becomes the example of Christian life in the old aeon. In the light of this Christology, let us now examine Luke's understanding of the world.[2]

B. RESPONSIBLE WITNESS

1. *Apologetics and Kerygma*

The christological pattern of the earthly and the heavenly modes of Christ's existence gives shape to the witness of Luke as a whole. The gospel history has for Luke an earthly and a heavenly side.

---

observe the two modes of Christ's existence. That Christ in his *earthly* mode of existence is God's instrument (Acts 2.22) cannot be expressed theologically in any other way, if historical pantheism is to be avoided. On the contrary, in view of his heavenly mode of existence Conzelmann himself (in a comparison of Acts 15.36 with 13.5) says that these passages "show how God and Lord are interchangeable" (p. 220; cf. pp. 176, 188f, 216f, n. 2; similarly Haenchen, *Apg.*, p. 82).

[1] See below, pp. 138ff.

[2] In the tradition this brings about a peculiar backward shift. In the earlier stage of the tradition, the Davidic sonship of Jesus was divested of the Messianic character which had formerly characterized it and given a purely secular meaning, denoting the genuine humanity of Jesus. Luke however returns to these Jewish components of Messianology and puts them to a positive use, applying Jewish Christian traditions to express Jesus' prophetic dignity. Attention is called to Jesus as a prophet without making his real dignity as the exalted Lord accessible.

It is a visible and concrete fact on this earth and at the same time has a heavenly dimension. As Luke intends it, this order must actually be reversed. He does not, as we moderns do, start with history. For him the basic event is the exaltation of Christ, which gives him the perspective for the earthly history. This results in a twofold task. First, the Christ event has to be protected from earthly misinterpretation. Political or earth-bound Messianic notions have to be guarded against by *apologetic* means. Secondly even the saving significance of the Christ must be *attested*. That saving significance stands eternally through the exaltation of Christ into heaven. Both belong to each other. By guarding Jesus' Messianic mission from false interpretations and by exposing the way in which it differs from political dominion, Luke can make these human pictures serve as a parable for the heavenly glory of Jesus.

In this section we shall examine three pericopes (2.8–14; 19.11–44; 22.66—23.1). Then we shall seek to understand the prologue as "exoteric" language, and finally consider the Areopagus speech as an example of a sermon addressed to the outside world.

(a) In the nativity story (Luke 2) the reference to the imperial cult is clear.[1] The connection of the birth of Jesus with the Roman census, which is usually attributed to Luke himself,[2] has a dual purpose. First, it prevents a "misunderstanding of the Messiahship of Jesus". "Joseph's journey to Bethlehem signalizes his rejection of the Zealot way which opposes the imperial decree."[3] The sovereignty of the Roman Emperor is thus explicitly acknowledged. On the other hand it takes the most powerful man in the contemporary world to set in motion a train of events so far reaching as to excel all human might. This comes out clearly in the acclamation of the heavenly host.

The apologetic tendency comes out in three pointed phrases in the message of the angels. Decrees issued by the (divine)

[1] E. Lohmeyer, *Christuskult und Kaiserkult*, 1919, p. 30.
[2] Klostermann, *Lukas*, p. 29.
[3] Grundmann, *Lukas*, p. 80.

emperor constitute tidings of joy (εὐαγγέλια). They spell happiness and salvation for mankind. Birth announcements, comings of age, and still more the enthronement of the Emperor are εὐαγγέλια.[1] As Norden puts it, "The word εὐγγέλιον had long been used before the Lord, whose kingdom was not of this world, for prophecies about the world ruler."[2]

The title σωτήρ has similar associations. "But of course we should not take too one sided a view of the parallels in the Roman emperor worship."[3] The "belief in the *Soter* with all its ramifications" is in quite a different way concerned with the salvation of the world and mankind, whether it be the restoration of the social order by the Roman rulers, or the healing of physical and other external ills by Soter Asklepios, or redemption and eternal life through mystery deities.[4] According to Bousset σωτήρ "had become one of the terms from which even the Gentiles could get a glimpse of the superhuman, transcendent significance of Jesus".[5]

The word εἰρήνη is the third example, reminding us of the *Pax Romana*. Dibelius calls attention to the imperial inscriptions "which celebrate Augustus as the σωτήρ who ended the war under whose πρόνοια land and sea enjoy peace".[6] The Fourth Eclogue of Virgil is relevant in this connection. The birth of the divine child inaugurates a new era which fulfils man's yearning for the return of the peace of paradise. The child rules over a world at peace (*pacatum orbem*). This hope is realized[7] in the law and order guaranteed by the Pax Romana.[8] With Gressmann we can sum it all up by saying that the words σωτήρ, εὐαγγέλιον and εἰρήνη are "technical terms of Hellenistic thought" and "are derived from the courtly language of the imperial cultus".[9] At any rate this is where their analogies are to be found.[10]

The connection between the angelic message and the emperor cult has been disputed. Rengstorf sees no "attack on emperor worship".[10] Above all, Sahlin emphasizes the Old Testament

[1] Friedrich, *TWNT* II (E.T.), p. 724.
[2] *Geburt*, p. 157; cf. Bousset, *Kyrios*, p. 244.
[3] Bousset, op. cit., p. 241; cf. now also Foerster, *TWNT* VII, pp. 1010ff.
[4] Bousset, op. cit., p. 243.   [5] Ibid., p. 244.   [6] *Botschaft* I, 63.
[7] Virgil, *Bucolics*, Fourth Eclogue.   [8] Foerster, *TWNT* II (E.T.) p. 402.
[9] H. Gressmann, *Das Weihnachtsevangelium*, 1914, pp. 4, 20.
[10] *Lukas*, p. 41.

background throughout Luke's nativity story and calls attention to the "eschatological and Messianic overtones" of this section.[1] Similarly, Dibelius sees the limits of the parallel with the imperial cultus; "There is no mention of the cessation of war and strife. Rather it is something which God brings to pass among ἄνθρωποι εὐδοκίας."[2] He reminds us "that εἰρήνη is the equivalent of the Hebrew word *shalom*, which also means salvation, and in a Messianic prophecy must refer to the peace of the people of God (not of a war-ridden world)".[3]

All these questions are answered when viewed in the light of Luke's deliberate ambiguity. It is not merely an "attack on the emperor cult". It is equally concerned with the historical purpose of God for his people, which is achieved in the birth of Jesus. The Messianic prophecies are being fulfilled "to-day".[4] It is theologically irrelevant whether the title σωτήρ is "primarily the transfer to Jesus of an Old Testament divine attribute" and only secondarily derived from the Hellenistic cult,[5] or whether the title was taken over from Hellenism and interpreted in the light of the biblical tradition. This merging of various traditions is characteristic of Luke. He connects the Christ event with the powers of his time, gives it a context in the history of Israel, yet brings out the uniqueness and novelty in the exalted Christ—all this combined in a wonderful unity.

(*b*) Luke 19.11, the introduction to the parable of the pounds, is reckoned by the exegetes to be entirely the work of the

---

[1] *Messias*, pp. 230ff (quotation from p. 213).

[2] On the derivation of this expression from Qumran cf. C. H. Hunzinger, *ZNW* 44 (1953), pp. 85, 90; *ZNW* 49 (1958), pp. 129f.

[3] *Botschaft* I, p. 63.

[4] Cf. Sahlin, op. cit., p. 214, who argues that Luke has "an older written document lying before him, of a general religious character, i.e. a Proto-Luke which he has taken up and transformed into an apology for Paul" (p. 39). Sahlin's "Proto-Luke" extends from Luke 1.5 to Acts 15, while the Pauline sections, (15.35—28.31) are Lucan additions (p. 9). Thus Sahlin also sees the differences between apologetic and kerygmatic language in the Lucan writings and seeks to explain them from the history of the tradition by ascribing the kerygmatic language to Proto-Luke and the apologetic to Luke himself. Thus he indirectly confirms our exposition, which holds that Luke as a theologian brings the two types of language into a dialectic relationship.

[5] So Cullmann, *Christology*, p. 242; Foerster, *TWNT* VII, p. 1015, 30ff, sees in Luke's source the announcement of a saviour like one of the ancient judges of Israel.

Evangelist.[1] This does not exclude the possibility that he followed
a tradition about the expectation of the kingdom of God during
the entry into Jerusalem. The parallel to 9.51ff is unmistakable.[2]
The verse looks like an advance interpretation of the ensuing
parable: about the delay in the parousia.[3] But "as they heard
this" (v. 19.11) refers back to Luke 19.9f and is addressed to the
same audience who have just heard the words "To-day salvation
has come to this house."[4] To this, now, is added something else,
namely the following parable ($\pi\rho\sigma\theta\epsilon\iota s$). V.11 is not only an
introduction to the ensuing parable, but also serves to bracket
the promise of salvation in the Zacchaeus story with the call to
responsible action or the warning of divine judgement.[5] Thus
it is not correct to stop short at the apologetic aspect (although
that too is there). Luke's primary concern is the kerygmatic
aspect. It is still the day of salvation even if Jesus has been removed
into the invisible distance of heaven. The mission and responsibility of the community towards its Lord still holds good. The
parousia is not only postponed, but the present fulfilment of
salvation (v. 9) and the earthly mission (vv. 13b) change the
situation in "redemptive history".[6]

---

[1] On the way Lucan linguistic peculiarities are piled up here see Jeremias,
Parables, p. 99, n. 40.

[2] See above, pp. 34, n. 1.

[3] Jeremias, op. cit., p. 59; Conzelmann, *St. Luke*, p. 134, n. 1; Grässer, *Parousieverzögerung*, p. 118 n.

[4] Klosterman, *Lukas*, p. 185.

[5] Such transitions, which both separate and connect, are typically Lucan; cf.
Luke 3.15; 4.24; 14.15; 18.8b; 21.24c.

[6] Where the formal time scheme of immanent-historical observation, the
"purely historical" (Grässer), is the sole perspective of investigation, it raises the
problem which goes along with this time scheme, i.e. the delay in the parousia.
The *material* difference in the early Christian imminent expectation is then lost
sight of. For the imminent expectation has a different meaning for the Palestine
community from what it had for Paul. The Palestinian community expects the
return of Christ to be the turning point of world history, cf. the Q source with
the "apocalyptic enthusiasm of its Maranatha theology" (S. Schultz, "Maranatha",
p. 143). Paul on the other hand no longer ascribes any significance to the old
world, because he believes that the shift in the aeons has already occurred. Luke
takes up an entirely new position, combining the insights of both positions.
For him, as for Paul, the decisive element in the event of salvation has occurred,
but—in contrast to Paul—in heavenly reality, so that the old world and its
course still have a significance of their own. On the other hand Luke, like the
earliest Church, holds fast to the historical return of Christ, in which this world

This comes out even more clearly in the triumphal entry (Luke 19.28–38). Conzelmann has brought out the political intention behind this apologetic: "The acclamation at the entry loses all political significance in Luke; the concept of the Davidic Lordship is replaced by the simple title of King (the non-political sense of which is preserved) (19.38). Accordingly, the temple is the only goal of the Entry and the only place of Jesus' activity."[1] We may add: in exact parallel to 19.22ff (and to 22.67–9, see below), Jesus' reign is located in heaven. The phrase, "peace in heaven" (v. 38a) points back to the message of the angel in Luke 2.14. There the comparison was with the *Pax Romana*. Here the emphasis is on the absolute difference between this earthly peace and the peace of heaven.

This is the sense of the word "King" which Luke introduced into his Marcan source, replacing the expression "the kingdom of our father David that is coming". Jesus is a heavenly king, a king "not of this world" as in John.[2] The title "King" underlines the unique dignity of Jesus. The ground is being prepared for his altercation with Pilate (23.2f).[3] On the other hand, the claim of Jesus is made crystal clear to people outside in a word acceptable to the Hellenistic world.[4] Jesus' kingdom is established in "the name of the Lord". Thus it is a kingdom above all earthly kingdoms. But it cannot compete with them because it is of a different nature. It is obvious that here apologetics and evangelism are inseparably intertwined.

(c) Finally let us look once more at the examination of Jesus before the Sanhedrin (Luke 22.66—23.1).[5] We have already noticed the apologetic tendency in Luke (see above). The second reply

---

will be redeemed (Luke 21.28) and restored (Acts 3.21). Since salvation has already been consummated in heaven he is—unlike the Palestinian community—no longer tied down to an imminent end (Cf. Chapter III of this work).

[1] Op. cit., p. 139; cf. pp. 75f.

[2] John 18.36; cf. 6.15 and the parallel passage to Luke 19.38, viz. John 12.13, 15. The textual tradition in Luke 19.38a is not unambiguous. Yet the text offered by B fits in with the Lucan pattern: the king who comes (on earth) stands under the divine blessing (1st clause); therefore salvation and glory are already prepared in heaven (2nd clause).

[3] Conzelmann, op. cit., p. 198.

[4] Kleinknecht, *TWNT* I (E.T.), pp. 564f.   [5] See above, pp. 44ff.

of Jesus to the members of the Sanhedrin regarding the exaltation of the Son of Man to the right hand of God (22.69) acknowledges his superior heavenly dignity, thus guarding against a mis- understanding of his Messiahship. That is why Jesus cannot answer the question "Are you the Christ?" and be clearly under- stood. He actually claims to be χριστὸς κύριος (2.11).[1] His interrogators frame their question in national Messianic terms. They camouflage it in such a way as to involve Jesus in a political charge. Before this, Luke had given a similar twist to the story of the tribute money (20.19ff). In contrast to Mark and Matthew, it is not the Pharisees who challenge Jesus but the scribes and high priests, the group which also poses the question in 22.67 (again changed from Mark and Matthew).[2] Here is the first attempt to throw suspicion on Jesus in the eyes of the Roman authorities. In the trial before Pilate the question of paying tribute money to Caesar becomes the main charge (23.2). But the reader now knows that this accusation is sheer calumny.[3]

We will stop here. For further details of the political apologetic according to Luke the reader is referred to Conzelmann's work (see above, p. 61, n. 3). Our purpose here has been to give a few examples of the method Luke uses to combine apologetics and evangelism.

2. The Prologue

Let us begin with some of the characteristics of the much dis- cussed introduction to Luke's work. The polished Greek style differs considerably from the ensuing narrative (Luke 1.5ff).[4] The secular character of the language is very noticeable. "The same words could have introduced a work which has as its subject

---

[1] The christological title in v. 67 has a twofold meaning, depending on whether it is the questioner or the reader who hears it.

[2] There is another instance of Luke's thoroughgoing redaction in Luke 22.52. When Jesus is arrested (unlike Mark/Matthew) members of the Sanhedrin are in personal attendance. Schniewind, *Parallelperikopen*, pp. 35f, sees here the influence of Johannine tradition (cf. Mark 14.49 with John 18.20). These two explanations are not mutually exclusive.

[3] Conzelmann, op. cit., p. 140. On the political apologetic in Luke, cf. pp. 138-44.

[4] Dibelius, *Studies*, p. 65, n. 7.

some much discussed current event in secular history."[1] We miss such typically Lucan expressions as "proclaiming the kingdom of God" or the δεῖ, denoting that God's will must be done, the Holy Spirit who inspires the eye-witnesses and ministers of the Word, and not least the name of Jesus Christ itself, the κύριος about whom the Gospel is written.

Luke's intention seems quite obvious. "His ambition was to write his story in such a way that would impress even his cultured Greek readers."[2] He takes over the usage of his time, mentioning his predecessors in the field and the sources on which he based his work.[3]

But we cannot stop short with such practical considerations. We have reason to believe that the secular character of the Luke preface conceals a theological intention. Its linguistic affinities with the last part of Acts are noticeable.[4] Its similarities with the technical language of the legal profession have suggested an apologetic setting for Luke–Acts connected with Paul's trial in Rome.[5] We need not concern ourselves here any further with the literary problem, but noting the legal expressions can help us to pinpoint the special purpose of the Lucan phrases in the prologue. Luke is concerned to be what nowadays we should call "matter of fact". He uses language which is clear and comprehensible for everybody. Of course, as his Gospel shows, he knows the secret of the Christian faith. But that does not drive him to an esoteric position which says: "Here is something that can only be understood by a believer." He tries to find common ground with those outside the community. He does not water down the gospel message but points out its human exterior. The

---

[1] Dibelius, op. cit., p. 147.
[2] Bultmann, *Tradition*, p. 365; cf. Dibelius, op. cit., p. 88, 147.
[3] Cf. the parallels in Hellenistic literature as given by Cadbury, *Beginnings* II, pp. 489ff; on the prologue of Josephus, *Jewish War* cf. E. Lohse, "Lukas als Theologe der Heilsgeschichte", p. 257, n. 2.
[4] Agreement between the wording of the Prologue and the latter part of Acts: ἀπ' ἀρχῆς (Acts 26.4); ἄνωθεν (Acts 26.5) ἀκριβῶς (Acts 23.15; 24.22= ἀκριβέστερον); κράτιστος (Acts 23.26; 24.3; 26.25); ἐπιγινώσκω (Acts 22.24; 24.8; 23.28; 24.11); κατηχέω (Acts 21.21, 24); ἀσφάλεια (as an adjective, 21.34; 22.30); cf. H. J. Cadbury, "The Purpose Expressed in Luke's Preface", *The Expositor* 8, 21 (1921), pp. 431ff; Sahlin, *Messias*, pp. 39f.
[5] Sahlin, op. cit., pp. 40ff.

story of Jesus is not a myth but a real event, and the usual means of historical research can check it. This meets the need of the Greek reader for a consciously historical "picture in which the past *qua* past can be clearly understood".[1]

This is the sense in which we have to understand the emphasis on historical facticity in the prologue. It comes out quite clearly in the phrase "the things which have been accomplished among us". The word πρᾶγμα has quite a general and broad meaning, e.g. undertaking, concern, occurrence, situation, legal action.[2] This pale expression, which emphasizes the secular character of the narrative, has as its predicate "a longer and more sonorous word" (πεπληροφορημένον)[3] which in turn underlines the importance of these occurrences. The superlative importance of these happenings is further enunciated by other important sounding words (ἐπειδήπερ, ἀναταξεσθαι διήγησιν).[4] The introductory πολλοί points in the same direction.[5] Luke wants to create the impression that a great number of people have been involved in this earthshaking event.

Zahn connects the interpolated ἐν ἡμῖν with πράγματα and interprets it thus: "the whole range of facts appertaining to the Christian community, i.e. the history of Christianity".[6] In that case, as Cadbury notes, Luke 1.1–4 would be "the real preface to Acts as well as to the Gospel".[7] But Haenchen rightly points out that the preface is speaking of facts which others have already dealt with. This can only mean gospels, since at that time there were no Acts.[8] The perfect πεπληροφορημένων suggests completed events. But that applies only to the story of Jesus, not to

---

[1] G. Delling, *Das Zeitverständnis des NT*, 1940, p. 56; on the Greek conception of time, cf. T. Boman, *Hebrew Thought Compared with Greek*, 1960, pp. 123ff.

[2] Maurer, *TWNT* VI, p. 638.

[3] Cadbury, *Beginnings* II, p. 496.

[4] Cadbury, op. cit., pp. 492f, attributes it to the desire for rhetorical fullness.

[5] Cf. Acts 24.2, 10; Heb. 1.1; according to J. Bauer, "*ΠΟΛΛΟΙ*, Lk. 1.1," *Nov. Test.* 4 (1960), pp. 263ff, the word is a favourite introductory formula in Greek literature.

[6] *Lukas*, p. 48.

[7] Op. cit., p. 492; Zahn, op. cit., p. 50; Lohse, op. cit., p. 257, n. 3; Sahlin, op. cit., p. 9.

[8] E. Haenchen, "Das 'Wir' in der Apg. und das Itinerar". *ZThK* 58 (1961), p. 363.

the mission described in Acts. Acts is an open-ended book and points with the emphatic word in 28.31, ἀκωλύτως, to the uninterrupted spread of the gospel. We must thus understand ἐν ἡμῖν as emphasizing the human character of the story of Jesus. The facts dealt with have occurred on earth in our midst.[1]

The factualness of these events is proved beyond doubt by the unexceptionable tradition going back to the eye witnesses. Once the foundations have been ascertained ἀπ'ἀρχῆς Luke can build his own work on a firm basis. Words are piled up to explain the "accuracy" of his procedure. He has followed his sources right "from the beginning". He has collected "all" the narratives and put them in the right order. Thus he can present to his correspondent Theophilus a reliable understanding of the teaching in which he has been instructed.[2]

There is not a word to suggest that this so well-grounded story is intended to evoke faith (contrast John 20.31). True, the significance of these events in world history is repeatedly emphasized. But the secular style is kept up to the end. The addition in v. 3, "and the Holy Spirit", in some of the Latin MSS, shows that Luke's phraseology "struck his readers even in antiquity as too secular".[3] Only twice does he touch on the gospel with the ambiguous word λόγος (vv. 2, 4).[4] This refers to the news of Jesus Christ whose name, however, is still suppressed. Of the apostles there is no mention in the technical language of the

---

[1] The two ἡμῖν in vv. 1f need not include the same circle of persons. Luke includes himself in v. 1 with men (Christians) in general, in v. 2 with the Christians of his generation; otherwise G. Klein, "Lk. 1.1–4 als theologisches Programm", *Zeit und Geschichte*, 1964, pp. 198f.

[2] On ἀσφάλεια in connection with γνῶναι cf. Acts 2.36 (K. L. Schmidt, *TWNT* I [E.T.], p. 506); the position of the word at the end makes it emphatic (Cadbury, op. cit., p. 509).

[3] Zahn, op. cit., pp. 53f. We shall thus not find in the Prologue either the "dominant themes of Luke–Acts" (Lohse, op. cit., p. 258), nor a "theological programme" (Klein, see above, n. 1), nor must it be interpreted in terms of the Holy Spirit (U. Luck, "Kerygma, Tradition und Geschichte bei Lk.", *ZThK* 57 (1960), pp. 52ff). His arrangement in terms of aspects makes it possible for Luke to use completely secular terms here, without reducing the Christian message to a secular level.

[4] On the identity of the persons mentioned in v. 2 with the twelve apostles cf. Klein, op. cit., pp. 201ff.

community. They are only referred to in general terms as "eye witnesses and ministers of the world".[1]

Thus the story of Jesus is seen from different angles. The prologue highlights only the historical angle, which makes possible a close examination of the events according to secular methods of research. Alongside of this there remains without doubt the kerygmatic aspect of the story of Jesus, as is shown by the way the Gospel continues.[2] It is just this secular "exoteric" phraseology in the prologue which proves that Luke knows how to differentiate between secular historiography and evangelical witness. Even here Luke makes it clear that he does not draw a straight line from the salvation given in Christ to general history. The term "redemptive history" must be used very carefully when we are discussing Luke. It is certain that for Luke the "events which have been accomplished among us" are acts of salvation performed by God. But he has his own reasons for not saying this in so many words here. In the prologue Luke calls attention to the facticity of Jesus' history. That this is the act of God can no longer be proved as a fact. This side of Jesus' history is discernible only to faith. But that does not exclude the need for faith to be assured about the human side of that history. This attempt of Luke does not only apply to his own age, when the gospel was taken into the Greek world. It remains a fresh task for each succeeding era, with its changed understanding of the world.

3. The Speech on the Areopagus

Our task in this section is limited by the terms of our investigation. The question is, what theological justification has Luke for presenting the human external side of Christian preaching as he does in Acts 17.16–32? Is this sermon intended to open up to

---

[1] Cf. Luke 4.20; this does not exclude a *double entendre*. According to Acts 26.16 Paul is called "to serve and to bear witness". For the twofold meaning of witness in Luke see below, pp. 120ff.

[2] Of course the Christian reads Luke's prologue in the light of his knowledge of the Gospel, and takes the word λόγος to mean the Christian message, the things which have been accomplished to mean the acts of God (Lohse, op. cit., p. 261 and Luck, op. cit., p. 60, rightly call attention to the passive, which was used in Judaism as a circumlocution for the divine name), and the eye-witnesses and ministers to mean the apostles.

men the message of the eschatological salvation of Christ? Or does it involve a compromise with contemporary pagan religion and a concealment of the distinctive elements of the Christian message?

We will start by comparing the framework of the speech with the speech itself. Once more we run into Luke's method of putting contradictory sayings side by side. The contrasts are noticeable. According to 17.16, Paul is angry over the idolatry going on in the city. In 17.22, on the other hand, he begins by praising the Athenians for their fear of God.[1] By mentioning the previous preaching of Paul (vv. 17ff) Luke contrives to speak about the salvation accomplished by Jesus and his resurrection. For the reader this suggests the central theme of the sermon, while "with deliberately careful intention the name of Jesus is not mentioned in the speech itself".[2] But this reference to Jesus and his resurrection has a further purpose. It is no accident that the content of Paul's sermon is summed up by his audience, the Epicurean and Stoic philosophers. We learn in this way how the central message of the resurrection strikes those who are not prepared for it. It is inevitably misunderstood in pagan circles as a message of strange gods, of the god Jesus and the goddess Anastasis. On this background Paul's allusive and cryptic manner of speech becomes clear for the Christian reader. It is impressed upon him that the limitations in the audience's comprehension of the Christian sermon must be borne in mind.[3]

This framework creates the situation for the speech, which can only be understood in its concrete time and place. What then is the justification for its actual theology? First, the combination

[1] According to Dibelius, *Studies*, p. 66, the difference must not be exaggerated. That is right in so far as there is no real contradiction here. Rather they are "complementary" statements, in which "contact and contradiction" (R. Bultmann, *Glauben und Verstehen* II, 1958², pp. 177ff) stand side by side.

[2] Dibelius, *Studies*, p. 56, n. 90.

[3] That of course does not rule out an allusion to the trial of Socrates, who was also accused of introducing strange gods (Haenchen, *Apg.*, p. 465). Luke skilfully weaves several different motives together. Side by side with the reference to Socrates, who was unjustly condemned, he demonstrates the difficulties encountered by the Christian mission in the Hellenistic world. Hence also Luke's open admission of Paul's ambiguous success in Athens. If he had wished to extol the gospel as the supreme educational influence, the narrative, starting as it does, would be unintelligible.

of Old Testament and Hellenistic traditions must be noted. W. Nauck has analysed the speech with this in view.[1] That God, the creator of heaven and earth, does not live in temples is an Old Testament belief. The expression κόσμος on the other hand and the description of the temple as χειροποίητος is Hellenistic (v. 25).[2] V. 25b is an allusion to Genesis 2.7, "and he breathed into his nostrils the breath of life", while τὰ πάντα is Hellenistic.[3] The Hellenistic notion that God does not require anything serves "as an overture to the really important saying: God is the great giver. He who needs nothing himself gives everything to everybody."[4] V. 26 must be taken in connection with the creation story. Nauck recalls Genesis 1.28. The phrase "to live on all the face of the earth" reminds us of the commandment "to replenish the earth". The creation of *one* man is an Old Testament belief, the creation of the whole human race Hellenistic.[5] In v. 28 the Old Testament statement of man made in the image of God and the Hellenistic notion of man's affinity to God compete with one another.[6] This survey may suffice to bring out the "peculiar inter-weaving of Hellenistic and Jewish motifs".[7] Nauck's thesis is that Luke has taken up certain features of Jewish missionary practice (the sequence, creation–preservation–redemption), which had been subjected to Hellenistic influences long before Luke.[8] We have, however, to distinguish between the source of the tradition, and the theology which it is used to express. For the latter the point is irrelevant whether or not the speech on the Areopagus is derived from a Hellenistic–Stoic source with Old Testament additions or *vice versa*, a Jewish–Christian nucleus with Stoic embellishments.[9] Either explanation is perfectly feasible.[10] From a theological point of view the question

---

[1] W. Nauck, "Die Tradition und Komposition der Areopagrede", *ZThK* 53 (1956), pp. 11ff.

[2] Nauck, ibid., pp. 19f.   [3] Nauck, ibid., p. 23.

[4] Cf. Haenchen, *Apg.*[10], p. 462.

[5] Op. cit., p. 21. On the "philosophical" interpretation of v. 26 see W. Eltester, "Gott und die Natur in der Areopagrede", *Nt.liche Studien für R. Bultmann*, 1957[2], pp. 211ff.

[6] Cf. Haenchen, *Apg.*, p. 462.   [7] Nauck, ibid., p. 14.

[8] Op. cit. (motif pattern), pp. 31f.

[9] The formula is Nauck's, op. cit., p. 14.

[10] The latter is assumed by Nauck, op. cit., p. 22 for v. 28.

of origins does not matter, but only the intention of the author.

As we saw at the outset, the section 17.16–34 must be considered as a whole. The framework of the speech makes it unnecessary for us to look for a conclusion which would make the whole sermon Christian,[1] or to expect some soteriological statement in it.[2] It deals only with the exterior aspect of Christian teaching, the part of the message which can be universally understood. The really important question is whether this exterior aspect, the allusions to the creation story, is controlled by the central message, that is by Jesus Christ, or whether it represents a compromise with, and capitulation to, the world. Does Paul's sermon on the Areopagus open a way for Jesus Christ, or does it sidetrack the audience from the salvation wrought in him by inviting them to a "natural theology"?

Vielhauer takes the latter view. He correctly observes the "utterly different function" of natural theology in Romans 1 and Acts 17. But he overlooks Luke's dialectical approach discernible in the framework he gives to the Areopagus speech. Such superficial observations are bound to lead to the conclusion: "the natural knowledge of God needs only to be purified, corrected and enlarged, but its basic significance is not questioned."[3]

There is no idea of sin and grace there. The reason for this is that, "due to its kinship to God the human race is capable of a natural knowledge of God and of ethics (Acts 10.35) and has immediate access to God". "Pagan history, culture, and religion" are claimed as "the prehistory of Christianity".[4]

Let us take a few examples from the Areopagus speech and try to make Luke's intentions clear. It is well known that there was no altar in Athens dedicated to "an unknown God" but only to "unknown gods". "Presumably unknown gods were honoured

---

[1] Thus Dibelius, *Studies*, pp. 56f.

[2] Nauck, ibid., pp. 31f, rightly observes that the speech is meant, as the context shows (17.17f), to be understood in a soteriological sense. But he misses in it any "soteriological understanding of the work of creation" such as we find in the OT. Yet that would lead to a confusion of spheres, which is just what Luke wants to avoid. Faith in creation is for him the place where debate takes place with the outside world. The first article is the bulwark which protects the second article from distortion.

[3] "On the 'Paulinism' ", p. 36.   [4] Vielhauer, ibid.

F

in order that none should be overlooked."[1] This means that the change is due to Luke himself or to the tradition he has received from the early Church. What lies behind this change? The answer is both negative and positive. First, the inscription indicates an idea of God reduced to the barest minimum. That is especially clear when we compare it with 17.16. Paul addresses an idolatrous city concerning a god about whose character no statement can be made. He observes their idolatrous practices merely in a formal way and reduces it to the question of the true God. On the other hand the inscription on the altar makes one point clear: there is but *one* God. This agrees with the Old Testament belief in God. "In Paul's speech the writer takes it to mean the God of the Jews and Christians, though it certainly did not have that meaning in Athens."[2] Paul does not start out from some pagan doctrine of god. It is the external side of the biblical God accessible to all men that he presents.

All this is later expressed in terms of the Old Testament doctrine of creation. The Hellenistic motif of the self-sufficiency of God is thus taken up and corrected. It is taken up as a critique of Athenian idolatry and in order to emphasize God's transcendence over the world. At the same time, however, this self-sufficiency of God, his independence over the world, is corrected by the διδούς in v. 25, "he who needs nothing gives all men everything".[3]

The same happens in v. 28, which speaks of men's affinity with God. Whereas the emphasis on God's transcendence threatens to become deism, the danger here is pantheism. Paul uses this motif to emphasize the unique dignity of man. He is created by God and lives in relation to him. It is his task to feel after God and find him (v. 27). God will call him to account for this on the day of judgement (v. 31). The personal categories used here are so strong that any danger of pantheism is avoided.[4]

---

[1] Dibelius, op. cit., p. 81.   [2] K. Lake, *Beginnings* V, p. 245.
[3] Haenchen, *Apg.* (10th edn), p. 471.
[4] The use of εἰ ἄρα γε with the optative in v. 27 points to the openness of discovery. Such pessimism in respect to human potentialities is, according to B. Gärtner, *The Areopagus Speech and Natural Revelation*, 1955, p. 158, un-Stoic. Affinity with God must be the guarantee for the discovery of God.

By now Luke's aim is clear. Let us sum it up under three headings:

(1) Luke has to express the Christian message in the language of his readers. The complete misunderstanding of Paul's proclamation of the resurrection in v. 18 shows that in preaching the gospel everything turns on the way the audience understands it. Even Paul speaks the language of his day. But he "baptizes" pagan terms and uses them to express the reality of the *new* aeon.[1] Luke on the other hand engages the *old* world in a discussion on its own terms. He adopts pagan forms of thought, taking them up and correcting them from the biblical angle. Thus he achieves a flexible relationship between the old world and the Christian message.[2]

(2) In thus correcting pagan affirmations Luke starts from the knowledge that this world is God's creation and that its form can be renewed in the spirit of the gospel. Though Paul had emphasized the fallen state of the world, his theology of the cross must not be so generalized as to suggest that the world is inherently evil, thus ceasing to be God's creation. Luke does not deny the need of repentance (v. 30).[3] But that does not prevent him from looking at the world as a place which can be questioned as to whether it is open to God, as its creation implies, or closed to him.

[1] Cf. G. Bornkamm, "Gesetz und Natur (Rom. 2.14–16)", *Studien zu Antike und Christentum* (Ges. Aufsätze II), 1959, pp. 93ff.

[2] How little force there is in this relationship is shown by the conclusion of the speech. Right at the end (v. 31b) Paul speaks once more of the resurrection from the dead—and it is just this that evokes scorn and repudiation from many in the audience. Luke describes the situation in a matter of fact way (he must have experienced it often himself). Some reject the saving message, others remain undecided, a few become believers (on this pattern see below, pp. 152ff). It is significant that the scorn of the audience, which refuses to hear the Christian message, is occasioned not by the first part of the speech, but only by the reference to the resurrection of the dead. The speaker's apologetic remains on the level of his partner in the dialogue, whereas the proclamation of Christ must necessarily rise above this level, and looks for the free decision of faith.

[3] Note how differently the term "ignorance" is used in vv. 23b and 30. In the first case their ignorance related positively to the worship of God, in the second negatively to sin.

(3) This brings us to the question of how this understanding of the world is related to the Christian message. Paul himself expresses Christianity in the terms of his own day, the old aeon being overcome by the new. Luke on the other hand wants to transform the old aeon so as to make it receptive for that which is new in Christ. This means in practice that Luke introduces corrections from the Old Testament and—as we have shown—takes up elements from Jewish missionary practice. The Old Testament stratum remains clearly distinguished from the new element which comes in Christ. Man is challenged in the light of his responsibility towards the God who gave him life. The seriousness of this call to reponsibility is underlined by the prophecy of the judgement (v. 21) to be held by Jesus, who has been raised from the dead. The central, saving message of Jesus' resurrection is certainly subordinated to the prediction of judgement over the old world. But at the same time the *double entendre* in v. 31b[1] points to the salvation which comes from the risen Christ.

C. THE CHRISTIAN MESSAGE AND THE SECULAR ORDER

The post-apostolic community enters once more, in its historical course, upon a pre-Easter stage. Although it is conscious of the presence of its risen Lord, it is still moving forward towards his final revelation to all the world. For all the differences, its situation is similar to that of the Old Testament community in so far as it still awaits the final salvation (Luke 21.28). That is why the Gospels take the Christian reader along the way Jesus walked before Easter. They introduce him to the earthly life of Jesus, which leads to the cross and resurrection as future events.

Even Mark interprets the kerygma as past history.[2] That is why the "teaching" of Jesus plays such a pre-eminent part in

---

[1] On this see below, pp. 159ff.

[2] S. Schulz, "Die Bedeutung des Mk. für die Theologie des Urchristentums", *Stud. Ev.* II, 1964, p. 136.

Mark.[1] In his injunctions to the community Jesus becomes—in modern language—the proclaimer instead of the object of the proclamation. But the teaching of Jesus is "miraculous activity".[2] His divine sonship is hidden in his humanity, so that the people, and even his disciples, wonder about him (Mark 1.27; 4.41; cf. Luke 7.49).

Luke has built further upon Mark's initial suggestions.[3] In Luke the humanity of Jesus is given—in line with his Christology —a certain independence. The witness to Christ enters the world order, shows it to be God's creation and transforms it so as to make it open to the call of God. Just because the kerygma cannot be extended indefinitely into time, the post-apostolic community is obliged to offer a theological interpretation of man and history in order that it may hear the Christian message, which is ever new.

This relation between the Christian message and the world comes out best in the journey of Jesus to Jerusalem, in the table talk and in the pattern of question and answer. To these we will now turn.[4]

1. The Journey to Jerusalem

(a) We have already touched upon the christological themes in the "travel narrative". The journey to Jerusalem is the way to glorification and suffering.[5] But Jesus is not alone. His disciples accompany him on the journey and are bound through him into a community. Let us examine this point in greater detail.

---

[1] Mark 1.22; 4.1f; 6.2; 8.31; 12.35 etc.; cf. E. Schweizer, "Anmerkungen zur Theologie des Mk.", Neotestamentica, 1963, pp. 102ff; Rengstorf, TWNT II (E.T.), pp. 138ff.

[2] Schweizer, ibid., p. 103.   [3] S. Schulz, ibid., p. 143.

[4] The "social" interpretation to be demonstrated here is not to be confounded with a supernatural exposition of "facts of salvation". For Luke the social interpretation is always complementary to the individual's encounter with the word, a matter of which he is fully aware (see below, pp. 136ff).

[5] See above, pp. 30ff; we presume a theological understanding of the journey in Luke; cf. Conzelmann, St. Luke, pp. 53ff; J. Schreiber, "Die Christologie des Mk.-Ev.", ZThK, 58 (1961), p. 160, n. 4 (on Mark); for a different view, see J. Blinzler, "Die literarische Eigenart des sog. Reiseberichts im Lk.-Ev", Synopt. Studien (Wikenhauser-Festschrift) 1953, p. 35, n. 41.

Jesus leads his followers on the road to salvation, a road ending not in death but in eternal glory. This is what Acts means when it calls Jesus the ἀρχηγὸς τῆς ζωῆς (Acts 3.15; cf. 5.31), and when the disciples on the Mount of Transfiguration awake from sleep and behold the glory of Jesus (Luke 9.32). It is more difficult to see what the suffering of Jesus has to do with the disciples. According to Conzelmann the journey "expresses Jesus' awareness that he must suffer".[1] It "begins after the fact of the suffering has been disclosed, but not yet understood".[2] This failure of the disciples to grasp the "secret of Jesus' suffering" has a twofold significance for human existence. First, man's fear of suffering is taken seriously. As we go through life we do not meet with suffering as though it were a neat theological formula. It remains an enigma to natural man. In suffering he is "stupid and ignorant" like a beast before God (Ps. 73.22). This is how the Christian also starts out, just like the disciples before Easter. But unlike the disciples, the reader is called in his *post*-Easter situation to understand suffering as sent from God (δεῖ) and to accept it.[3]

The existential significance of Jesus for his disciples is further signified by the stereotyped picture of Jesus walking ahead of the group and having to turn around (στρέφειν) in order to speak to them.[4] Apart from this, Luke is the only Evangelist who actually describes the way to the cross (23.26–32). Jesus walks ahead and the crowd follow him. Simon of Cyrene carries the cross behind him (v. 26). The figurative meaning of this is plain enough.[5] The distance between Jesus walking ahead and men's relation to him as they walk upon the same way are equally shown in this picture. The way Jesus walks is unique, but his disciples may follow after him along it.

At the same time the journey to Jerusalem and the way to the

---

[1] Op. cit., p. 197.   [2] Ibid., p. 65.

[3] A. M. Ramsey, "The Narratives of the Passion", *Stud. Ev.* II, 1964, pp. 122ff, points out how often in Luke's version of the passion Jesus reaches out in sympathy for others, whereas in Mark he is much more isolated (Luke 22.31f, 61; 23.28ff, 34, 43 etc.). Thus Luke invites his readers to follow the Lord in his passion as the mark of the Christian life and to imitate it (pp. 130f).

[4] Luke 7.9 (to the people—the σαφετοῖς is an addition, cf. Matt. 8.10); 9.55 (to the disciples); 14.25 (to the people); 23.28 (to the women of Jerusalem).

[5] Cf. G. Bertram, *Die Leidensgeschichte Jesu und der Christuskult*, 1922, p. 73.

cross are very different. The way to the cross is not an extension of the journey. The destination of the journey is the temple in Jerusalem (Luke 19.45). It is an expression of the whole life of Christ in its uniqueness and concentration of purpose,[1] but also in its responsibility towards the world. This last point is especially emphasized in Luke.

(b) This is shown by the numerous sections of teaching material which occur in the travel narrative, without any direct connection with the actual journey to Jerusalem.[2] The love of neighbour (10.25ff), listening to Jesus' word (10.38f) and prayer (11.1f) are the three basics of Christian life.[3] Clearly, discipleship has priority over natural human relationships, as is shown in the words about discipleship (9.57ff; cf. 14.16ff).

This tension between the total commitment of discipleship and human responsibility comes out still more clearly in the collection of sayings in Luke 14.25–34. Nowhere else are the conditions of discipleship stated so forcibly (hatred for kith and kin, v. 26; readiness to carry the cross, v. 27; complete renunciation of possessions, v. 33).[4] In strange contrast we get the twin parables of the tower builders and the king going to war (vv. 28–32). They are hardly meant to illustrate the unconditional demands of discipleship.[5] For the unconditional following for which Jesus is calling here is originally based on his eschatological challenge.[6] There is no time for reflexion, either forward, to what may happen in the future (Mark 1.17, 20), or backward, to what has happened in the past (Luke 9.62). Yet the parables demand

[1] This is already true for Mark; cf. Schreiber, op. cit., pp. 160f, 171; Mark also portrays Jesus as going before and turning around. But he associates it only with the following of the Lord in his passion, and thus does not distinguish between the journey and way of the cross (Mark 8.33, Peter is to remain behind Jesus).

[2] B. Reicke, "Instruction and Discussion in the Travel Narrative", *Stud. Ev.* (TU 53), 1959, pp. 206ff.

[3] J. Schneider, "Zur Analyse des Lk. Reiseberichtes", *Synopt, Studien* (see above, p. 73, n. 5), p. 220.

[4] Cf. the toned down version in Matthew, 10.37 ("who does not love"); on the originality of the Lucan text see Bultmann, *Tradition*, p. 160.

[5] A. Jülicher, *Die Gleichnisreden Jesu* II, 1910, pp. 208, 211.

[6] E. Meyer, op. cit., I, p. 217, n. 2, sees the similarity between Luke 14.33 and 9.61f.

that men should look into the future and make an estimate of their present human resources. There is a tension between the eschatological challenge of Jesus and man's responsibility in history.[1]

This means that Luke limits the eschatological saying by inserting the twin parables.[2] If Jesus' eschatological challenge, which transcends time, is extended into time, it is misunderstood. To follow Jesus then turns into a task of the human will. Yet the twin parables impress upon us that to follow Jesus involves the utmost application of human strength. The future belongs to God alone. He demands unreserved confidence in the midst of suffering (v. 27), and the surrender of possessions (v. 33) without anxiety for the morrow. And yet within limits man does have a responsibility for this future. He has to plan and count the cost, and thus engage all his faculties. God has not created man to be the puppet of his will; God's will enhances the responsibility of the human will.

(c) The parable of the pounds (Luke 19.11–27) also deals with man's responsibility in the world. In comparing it with Matthew's version (Matt. 25.14–30) the first thing we notice is how Luke combines it with the story of the pretender to the throne. This imparts allegorical traits to the parable as a whole.[3] The

---

[1] Klostermann, *Lukas*, p. 154, sees rightly (*contra* Bultmann, *Tradition*, p. 160) that v. 33 is not the interpretation of the twin parables, but a return to the point at the end of vv. 26f, viz., a readiness for any sacrifice. The οὕτως οὖν is thus a Lucan addition, intended to connect the third saying about discipleship with the twin parables.

[2] Klostermann, op. cit., p. 153, rightly attributes the "striking γάρ" in v. 28 to Luke, and the secondary application of the verse to discipleship of Jesus in v. 33 (*contra* Jülicher, op. cit., pp. 208f).

[3] Whether this parable represents an independent parallel or not is disputed. Cf. Klostermann, ad loc. The editorial hand of Luke is unmistakable, but v. 27 can hardly be from his pen. Do we have here (as in 9.51 and 19.11) a fragment of some early political-messianic tradition, which Luke has connected with an event in temporal history? Because of Luke's transformation of his traditional material (on this, Grässer, *Parousieverzögerung*, p. 116) the question of the *Sitz im Leben Jesu* of this parable throws little light in Luke's own understanding of it; cf. Jeremias, *Parables*, p. 62; W. Michaelis, *Die Gleichnisse Jesu*, 1956³, p. 112; W. Foerster, "Das Gleichnis von den anvertrauten Pfunden", *Verbum Dei manet in aeternum*, 1953, p. 52; M. Zerwick, "Die Parabel vom Thronanwärter" *Bibl.*, 40 (1959), pp. 654ff; on the complicated history of its origin, cf. Hirsch, op. cit. II, pp. 161ff.

nobleman, who goes into a distant country to receive a kingdom and then returns, stands for Jesus, who went to heaven to be enthroned as Lord and then returns at the parousia.[1] In the ascension the picture of Jesus preceding his disciples is modified: Jesus ascends to his heavenly kingdom but his disciples remain behind and receive an earthly commission.

The injunction, "trade with these till I come (again)" (v. 13b), describes the task of the disciples between the ascension and the parousia. What does this command imply? We are inevitably reminded of Acts 1.6–8. While Jesus goes to heaven, the disciples are entrusted with a mission. In Luke 19.13 the work demanded of the disciples could easily be equated with missionary service.[2] But as I see it, it means primarily action in the world. The root πράγ– is already familiar from the prologue. The repetition of the word in v. 15b,[3] like the reserve which characterizes the whole parable,[4] shows that Luke wishes to emphasize the importance of secular activity. The motif of faithfulness in little things (v. 17) points in the same direction. As the unmistakable echo of 16.10 shows, this is meant to apply to the use of earthly goods.[5] The disciples have a responsibility to their master for future history. The community will have to give an account at the end of time when the master returns. It will have to answer for the state of the world. This responsibility accordingly cannot be limited to individual deeds of love, but extends to social and political life. Despite this the earthly tasks of the community are "very little" things. It would be wrong to set too much store by them. But these little things are the touchstone of faithfulness.

[1] Jülicher, op. cit., p. 486.

[2] B. Weiss, Die Evangelien des Mk. und Lk., 1901[9], ad loc. would support the view that it is the Holy Spirit which inspires them. Weiss observes that it is the pound of the two first servants themselves which creates the additional pounds (vv. 16, 18).

[3] Cf. also v. 23, where the saying about collecting the money with interest is used.

[4] This is where Luke differs from the Marcan version. In Mark this "pragmatic" trait is completely lacking.

[5] This explains why Luke does not speak of talents, but of "minae", though it is remarkable that the Lord pays out to his servants on his departure such a modest sum (according to Foerster, op. cit., p. 45, about $20), the purchase value of which would be the equivalent of $200 today.

The figure of the third servant (v. 20) makes it clear that the community must step out of its ghetto and engage bravely in the service of the world. The rewarding of the servants, as Luke treats it, points in the same direction. In Matthew the reward is to enter into the eternal joy of God (25.21b, 23b). It has been said that Luke keeps within the framework of the parable as regards the rewards, while Matthew goes beyond it.[1] But we must not forget that Luke has treated the parable all the way through as an allegory about Jesus and his disciples (the community). Thus the reward of ruling 10 (or 5) cities points to the fact that Christians are called on earth to responsibilities which extend to eternity, when they share the Lordship of Christ.[2] Responsible action is thus given a certain dignity; it is a parable of life in the new world of God.

(d) To prove one's worth in worldly life is demanded not as a single item, but is related to the Christian message, from which it receives its decisive criterion. Any worldly situation has to be tested to see whether it is open or closed for the message of salvation. Luke expresses this by the way he arranges material at the end of the journey to Jerusalem (18.9ff). In the parable of the Pharisee and the publican (ibid.) a contrast is drawn between pious self-justification and the sinner's reliance upon grace. Children are receptive for the kingdom of God (18.15ff), but not so the rich man (18.18f). The blind man of Jericho finds salvation but the rebellious citizens in the parable (19.12ff) incur judgement. With the last of these features the contrast reaches its climax. At the entry into Jerusalem the disciples acknowledge the coming of "peace in heaven and glory in the highest" (19.38b), while the city of Jerusalem remains unreceptive (19.41).

(e) This whole section is preceded by a question which, as it were, sets the theme: "When the Son of man comes will he find faith

---

[1] Wellhausen, *Lukas* 107; Jeremias, *Parables*, pp. 60f.

[2] Cf. Schlatter, *Lukas*, p. 406. It is worth noting that in very little of Luke does the idea of "faithfulness" remain eschatological. The Christian life has no value in itself, like the *politeia* in Origen and Eusebius of Caesarea (cf. H. Eger, "Kaiser und Kirche in der Geschichtstheologie Eusebs v. Caes.", *ZNW* 38 (1939), pp. 200f).

on earth?" (18.8b).[1] πίστις here obviously means man's receptivity for the coming Lord. This half verse not only serves as the title for what follows but also refers back to the preceding text. First, it concludes the eschatological sayings of Jesus in 17.22ff, then it points back to the collection of sayings about faith in 17.5ff. Let us examine Luke's treatment of faith in these passages, and see if we can find the same dialectic we have used elsewhere.

In answer to the apostles' plea for an increase of faith (17.5) Jesus describes faith as co-operation with the creative power of God, which surpasses all human measure.[2] Luke adds to this Q saying (cf. Matt. 17.20) the parable of the servant's reward, which is peculiar to himself (17.7–10). Earlier he had spoken of man's co-operation with God. Here he brings out the absolute superiority of God, in the picture of the master and slave. Viewed in connection with 17.5f, the parable warns us not to take faith as a human achievement. This is followed by the healing of the ten lepers (17.11–19), which continues the same thought.[3] Klostermann thinks that this story is "beyond doubt a variant of the healing of leper in 5.12ff".[4] But when we look at Luke 5.12ff it has a very different point. Obviously 17.11ff is not concerned with the healing for its own sake. It merely serves to introduce the following verses. So it would be wrong to ask about faith of the nine at the moment of their healing. The crux is whether faith continues *after* salvation. The nine do not persevere in faith. So Luke regards them as people who, though they have met Jesus, have not attained to salvation. By contrast the grateful Samaritan received the explicit assurance of salvation. His faith looks beyond the immediate moment and extends

---

[1] V. 8b is according to Bultmann, *Tradition*, p. 175, a secondary supplement to the secondary application of vv. 5–8. Jeremias, *Parables*, p. 155, n. 13, regards it as "an early Son of Man saying".

[2] That is to say, it is not a question of increasing the faith a man already has (Klostermann, *Lukas*, p. 171).

[3] On the special position of the pericope cf. Dibelius, *Tradition*, p. 58, n. 1; by means of the note about the journey in v. 11 Luke secures a transition from the discourse of Jesus to an incident. Since by vv. 20ff the discussion has lost any connection with time or to place, the insertion in vv. 11–20 is particularly striking and argues for a deliberate concern on the part of Luke.

[4] *Lukas*, p. 173.

into the future, as he shows by his expression of gratitude (v. 19).[1]

Thus Luke paints a complex picture of faith. He describes its superhuman power (17.6) while at the same time depicting it as a human attitude. Thus faith indicates the path on which the Christian follows his master. Faith experienced in the present becomes a thing of the past. Here there is no place for conceit. All we can say is that we are "unworthy servants" (17.10). Only God deserves the glory (17.18) in view of the help he has given (17.11ff). But the believer has a responsibility to the future too. What counts here is his readiness to meet the "Son of Man" (18.8b).[2] By bringing out the human side of faith, these stories fall into place in the travel narrative. They describe the Christian way of life in the world.[3]

Our interpretation of Jesus' journey to Jerusalem has resulted in the following points: with Christ the Christian is on his way through suffering and death to heavenly salvation. This "heavenly journey" is a concrete, clearly defined earthly path, upon which the Christian follows his Master. His following involves receptivity for the injunctions of Jesus as his risen Lord, and the acceptance of earthly responsibility under the Lord's commission. Unconditional surrender, regardless of human ties, and new involvement in the secular order co-exist in tension.

2. *The Table Scenes*

(a) Alongside the journey motif the hospitality accorded to Jesus is a characteristic of Luke. He treats the two motifs as parts of a single whole. In Jesus "God himself visits the people, hidden in the guise of the wanderer refreshing himself as a guest in their

[1] Cf. by contrast the coincidence of healing and salvation in the story of the blind man of Jericho (Luke 18.42).

[2] I.e., the disciples should remain in such a constant state of readiness that they do not notice how the time passes. That is how the passage is expounded by C. E. B. Cranfield, "The Parable of the Unjust Judge and the Eschatology of Luke–Acts", *SJT* 16 (1963), pp. 300f.

[3] Grässer, *Parousieverzögerung*, p. 38, sees rightly that Luke 18.8b represents "a typical problem for the church." But Luke's understanding of faith must not be interpreted onesidedly in terms of 18.8b (see above, p. 9, n. 1, on the term "repentance").

home". In the Emmaus story (Luke 24.13–35) this twofold motif of wanderer and guest comes out clearly.[1]

Here the christological aspect of the guest motif stands out clearly. In Jesus God visits his people, entering into fellowship with them (1.78). The people praise God for bringing back to life the widow's son at Nain: God has visited his people (7.16). Jerusalem on the other hand misses the *kairos* of this visit from God (19.44).

The visit occurs among sinners (5.27–38). Jesus' visit brings salvation to the house of Zacchaeus the tax collector (19.9). The Pharisees and scribes complain that Jesus receives sinners and eats with them (15.1f). Here we have the soteriological aspect of the guest motif. Fellowship with Jesus means forgiveness of sins and newness of life.

But we must go a step farther. The frequency of banquet scenes in Luke is striking. Apart from what Grundmann calls the "Lucan symposium" in Luke 14, the narrative of the Last Supper has undergone considerable expansion (22.14–38). Jesus visits with Simon the Pharisee (7.36–50), with Mary and Martha (10.38–42), and with still another Pharisee (11.37). The sharing of the meal is for Jesus a typical situation. It binds proclamation and faith closely to the questions of human community. The kerygma enters a particular social environment, opens it up to hear the gospel aright and transforms it into a parable of God's new creation. Let us proceed to analyse Luke 14.7–14 (24) and 22.31–8 and work out this social aspect of the gospel.

(b) The saying addressed to the *guests* about the order of precedence (vv. 7–11) touches upon a central problem of man's social life. Bultmann comments, "This is so typical of Wisdom, and so secular a rule of prudence, that we cannot help wondering how it ever came to be included among the sayings of Jesus."[2] According to Dibelius this warning was meant originally "as a parable intended to ward off false righteous claims before God".

[1] Grundmann, *Lukas*, pp. 27f; *idem*, "Fragen der Komposition des lk. 'Reiseberichtes'", *ZNW* 50 (1959), p. 253.
[2] *Tradition*, p. 104.

In Luke it was then transformed from "an eschatological warning" into "a rule of conduct at table".[1] This application of a
saying to social life is typically Lucan. He exposes the human side
of eschatology and places it in antithesis to the saying about the
Messianic banquet (vv. 15ff). Jesus is not just a social reformer
(as is shown by the following parable of the great supper, where
the divine invitation precedes all earthly affairs, however important they might be). But he is not other-wordly either. Jesus'
action takes away the sin of the world and at the same time gives
the world its due as the creation of God. The rule given here may
sound very ordinary—it has indeed this quite worldly exterior
—yet at the same time we can detect the hidden christological
core, as in Jesus' saying at the Last Supper: "I am among you as
one who serves" (Luke 22.27). The situation of the dinner party
prevents us from taking Jesus' saying as an individualistic piece
of ethical advice. He is not concerned with personal expediency
but with the right ordering of society.[2]

(c) The visible and invisible aspects of human behaviour are
brought out even more clearly in Jesus' word to his host about
the guests to be invited (vv. 12–14). Bultmann's judgement is
again pessimistic: "the saying is much more akin to the grudging
spirit of the last chapter of Eth. Enoch than to the preaching of
Jesus."[3] In Jesus' harsh criticism human calculation is brought
face to face with the gift of God's love which is meant to be
reflected in the behaviour of the disciples. Such selfless love is
the perfection of all human love, since love brooks no nicely
calculated "less or more".[4] Even natural man can perceive this.
But that this deed was done in conformity to God's love, a deed
of the "just" (v. 14), becomes visible only in the resurrection, in
the world of God. This is the theme of the following parable, in
which man's concern for real estate, cattle and family ties is seen
in the light of God's invitation.[5]

[1] *Tradition*, p. 248.   [2] In his instructions Jesus generally uses the plural.
[3] *Tradition*, p. 103.
[4] Schlatter, *Lukas*, pp. 334f; Grundmann, *Lukas*, p. 295.
[5] Cf. the agreement about the persons to be invited in v. 13 and v. 21 (Jeremias,
op. cit., pp. 44f).

(d) Similar to this antithesis between the divine invitation and the duties of secular society is the conclusion of Jesus' discourse at the Last Supper. For it ends with Jesus' intercessory prayer to God and his injunctions for the life of the community in the world (Luke 22.31–8). But here there is a different emphasis. Strife and temptation lie ahead.[1] No longer does Jesus visit people as their guest. Now he is preparing to take leave of his disciples. How are the disciples to behave after their master has gone on his way to the cross? There is the threat of the world's contempt and the longing for martyrdom, to do as Jesus did. Jesus gives this question a triple answer. First he promises his disciples (especially Peter) that he will pray for them.[2] Then he shows them how far they are from the commission which is his alone. Jesus goes to his death but the disciples are to go on living and to take care of their lives.[3] The end of Jesus is strongly emphasized. His life moves to a shameful end according to the mysterious will of God (v. 37a). But this end is for him alone (v. 37b: $\tau\grave{o}$ $\pi\epsilon\rho\grave{\iota}$ $\dot{\epsilon}\mu o\tilde{v}$).[4] The disciples must not imitate the unique way of Jesus. Their discipleship is no voluntary self-sacrifice.[5] They have a task to fulfil in the world.

For this task in the world the disciples need "secular" equipment. As well as scrip and purse, that is money and provisions,[6] they must have a sword—even more necessary than clothing.[7] The word is strongly highlighted by the way the sword is

[1] This introduces a contrast between the present passage and the peaceful conditions depicted in the missionary charge in 20.1ff (vv. 5f) and the end of Satan's power (10.18) (Schlatter, Lukas, p. 280). But this is no contradiction (Grundmann, Lukas, p. 406). Rather it is an accurate description of the ambiguous situation of the church in the midst of peace (Acts 9.31) and conflict (Acts 8.1). Hence we cannot say that Luke is contrasting "ideal period" and the "present with its tribulations" (Conzelmann, St. Luke, p. 82). True, Luke clearly distinguishes between the two states. But they do not simply succeed one another in time. That would be a onesided view. Even in the apostolic community there is peace (Acts 9.31).

[2] The aorist in vv. 31f suggests that Jesus' intercession for Peter is something unique. This suggests that the Lord's preservation of the community is no lasting condition, but realized again and again in every successive intervention.

[3] Schlatter, Lukas, p. 428.

[4] V. 37b serves to reinforce v. 37a; both occurrences of $\gamma\acute{a}\rho$ give the reason for v. 36 (Klostermann, Lukas, ad loc.).

[5] Martyrdom is for Luke something exceptional. He recognizes it, but limits it to extraordinary cases (Stephen, Paul).

[6] Schlatter, Lukas, p. 428.

[7] Cf. the climax in Luke 6.29 (Rengstorf, Lukas, p. 249).

compared with an outer garment (v. 36) and by the disciples'
reply (v. 38). How is this challenge to use the sword to be understood? In answering this question we must not lose sight of Luke
22.49ff. Jesus rejects the use of the sword at his arrest. This contradictory use of the word within the same chapter shows that Luke
confines the use of the sword to the protection of life and limb.[1]
Jesus' cause must on no account be defended with force. It is in
this ambiguous sense that the saying about the two swords in
v. 38 has to be expounded.[2] Jesus' reply remains uncertain;
while he expresses no direct rejection of force, he limits it and
warns them against the temptation of toying with the sword.[3]

Again it is clear that Luke is concerned to connect the Christian
message with social reform—whether in a parabolic description
of God's new creation in the community of Jesus (Luke 14) or as
patient endurance in the world of sin while being preserved by
the intercession of the Lord who is far away in heaven.

3. Question and Answer

(a) It is well known that Luke is inclined "to provide a situation
for detached fragments of tradition".[4] Already in Mark, and
even in the pre-canonical tradition,[5] words of Jesus are placed in
concrete situations. The process is carried further by Luke. It is
the special Lucan material in particular which comes in the form
of question and answer.[6] Luke wishes to stress that the words
and discourses of Jesus were spoken on particular occasions to
specific people who approached the Master with a doubt or a
question.[7]

There are several different ways of assessing this state of affairs.

---

[1] Conzelmann, op. cit., p. 81, gives a symbolic interpretation to the saying
about the sword "in connection with the Christian's daily battle against
temptation". But does such a spiritualization suit the concrete necessities of life,
like a purse, bag, or mantle?

[2] ἱκανόν ἐστιν=it is enough, it is a lot.

[3] For a survey of the various interpretations of this difficult saying see Rengstorf,
TWNT III (E.T.), pp. 295f.

[4] Dibelius, Formgeschichte des Evangeliums, 1959³, p. 159 (the passage is omitted
from the E.T., Tradition, p. 159).

[5] Mark 8.11f; 9.38–40; Matt. 8.19–22; 18.21f (Dibelius, ibid.).

[6] Grundmann, Lukas, p. 100.   [7] Lohse, EvTh, (1954), pp. 259f.

The motif of "question and request" is for Bultmann a literary phenomenon, a particular way of presenting the material.[1] For Dibelius it is a matter of style: the words of Jesus are clothed in the form of the *Chreia* in order to make them more "striking and impressive".[2] Lohse goes a step further and hints at theological reasons: "By providing the traditional words and sayings of Jesus with a framework, Luke gives the whole a narrative character and fits the logia tradition into the great historical outline. The words of the master are not timeless. They are themselves a part of history, as intelligible and trustworthy as the facts in the surrounding narrative."[3] We shall pursue this line of thought further and try to bring out the theological motivation behind Luke's dialogue style.[4]

(b) The ethical preaching of John the Baptist (Luke 3.10–14) is introduced by the question of the crowd: "What shall we do?" At first sight this looks like a straightforward literary introduction. But it indicates a definite human attitude towards the Baptist's preaching. It is one of expectation: they are receptive to his word. The importance of this attitude is stressed by the fact that the same question is put three times, each time by a different group of people. The tax collectors and the soldiers are given injunctions relevant to their specific situations. The preaching of the Baptist is thus related to a concrete audience. Human question and prophetic answer are closely intertwined.

Similarly with the disciples' request (11.1) to be taught how to pray. The occasion of the request is twofold: the example of Jesus impels them to explore the whole subject afresh; the prayer which John taught his disciples does not satisfy them.[5] In the

---

[1] *Tradition*, p. 336.
[2] Ibid., p. 160. On the chria cf. pp. 152ff.   [3] Ibid., pp. 259f.
[4] Mark already has the motif of question and answer (Mark 8.11–13; 12.28ff; 12.13ff; 12.18ff). Luke extends this motif further, adapting it to his own theology (cf. Dibelius, op. cit., pp. 161ff).
[5] We need not discuss here the historical background of this reference to the particular order of prayer observed by the Baptist's disciples. It is enough to note that the prayer requested by the disciples is something quite new, and not to be compared with the prayer of John's disciples. For Luke, John the Baptist is once again the representative of the old world (cf. Luke 5.33ff par.; see above, pp. 21f).

disciples' request the correct human attitude of receptivity for the Lord's prayer is characterized.

Similarly the apostles' request for an increase of faith (17.5) shows the only human attitude which befits the reception of the saving work of God. For "man cannot create his own faith. It is the gift of Jesus to his own."[1]

(c) If the previous examples show a readiness for the right reception of God's word, then the natural human attitude as such is somewhat ambiguous, as would be expected from fallen man. This ambiguity is obvious in the two beatitudes, Luke 11.27ff and 14.15. A woman compliments the mother of Jesus for her unique relationship to her son. That represents the outlook of natural man, who cannot see further than the physical and natural realm and so misses the new relationship with God which Jesus brings. The surprising thing is the reply of Jesus. Instead of rejecting the woman's infatuated ovation he corrects it.[2] True, everything depends upon a person's relationship with Jesus, but in such a way that in him God's word is encountered and becomes the real thing in life (Luke 1.45).

There is a similar correction of the man who said "Blessed is he who shall eat bread in the kingdom of God" (14.15). The beatitude is true as far as it goes. Whoever is permitted to eat bread in the kingdom of God is truly blessed. But this promise does not automatically come true. It depends on accepting the invitation God issues in this life through Jesus. In its Lucan form the parable of the great supper (vv. 16ff) insists on the priority of this invitation over all secular affairs.[3] Thus Jesus agrees with his fellow guest in v. 15, but makes the beatitude conditional upon present decision. Once again a human word and Jesus' answer are closely intertwined.

---

[1] Grundmann, Lukas, p. 333; cf. Schlatter, Lukas, p. 385.

[2] μενοῦν stands "in answers to emphasize or connect" = "rather, on the contrary" or "indeed, more than that", Arndt & Gingrich, Lexicon, p. 504.

[3] Involvement in the secular order is emphasized in vv. 18–20 far more than in Matt. 22.5. Luke certainly recognizes secular responsibilities (Luke 16.9; 19.13). But he does not canonize them. Instead he brings out unmistakably the absolute superiority of the kingdom of God.

Again the question of an individual in 13.23, "Lord, will those who are saved be few?" expresses a typically human attitude. Man draws comparisons. He learns about the world mainly from analogies. The company of the disciples is small (12.32). This leads to the conclusion that only few will be saved. But the argument does not hold in the world of God. In his reply Jesus does not indirectly repudiate the question, as though it were one that ought not to be asked at all. He simply ignores the question. Man is supposed to show concern for his salvation. In his reply he turns the question round. Instead of a general question about the number of the saved (which God only knows) he makes it an "existential" question about salvation. Jesus "aims his reply at the involvement and decision of his hearers".[1]

(d) For Luke the Old Testament-Jewish attitude is also a human position which must be corrected by the new reality which has come with Jesus. The inheritance over which Jesus is asked to arbitrate (Luke 12.13), the amazement he arouses by not washing before meals (11.38), the question of theodicy raised by Pilate's slaughter of the Galileans at the sacrifice (13.1), the complaints against Jesus for eating with sinners (15.1ff), the question about the date of the coming of the kingdom of God (17.20)—all these spring from the Jewish beliefs which are correct enough in themselves but have been rendered obsolete by Jesus' coming.[2] So Luke creates a dialogue situation, relating the old and the new world to each other. The new is not the abolition but the sublimation of the old.

(e) Let us review the material we have collected. Luke likes to introduce Jesus' words with a jolt (a question, a plea, or an explanation). This characterizes the human situation to which Jesus directs his word. The situation may be given shape by Jesus' answer, as in the case of the disciples' request for instruction

---

[1] Grundmann, Lukas, p. 285.
[2] The texts quoted here in (d) are all taken from the special Lucan material. For Luke 11.38 a comparison with Matt. (23.25) will clearly show the extension of meaning. But it is just as possible that Luke 17.20 is editorial (Bultmann, Tradition, p. 25).

in prayer (11.1). Usually, though, it indicates the natural understanding of man, which Jesus may accept, correct, or repudiate.

So we see a significant change in the preaching of the gospel.
In the texts we have examined, the word of God no longer
comes "vertically from above" as an eschatological summons
("kerygma" in the literal sense of the word), creating a distinctive
situation of its own ("Follow me", Mark 1.17–20; Luke 9.60).
Rather, it lights upon a situation which is already present on the
horizontal plane of history. It is a reply to questions which life
poses for the Christian. So the word enters the veil of history. It
not only calls the believer out of history but also becomes his
guide on his way through history. But this way through history,
this present situation, is in no way canonized (Luke 12.13f;
14.16ff). For Luke, the "desecularization" of man by the word and
the sanctification of the world as creation through the word
stand in a dialectical relation.

Let us review the ground covered in Chapter 2. How does Luke
witness to the Christian message in a time no longer dominated by
an expectation of the Lord but looking to a future in history?
We found throughout that Luke takes special account of the
relation between the Christian message and the world. In Luke's
Christology Jesus is seen not only as the (hidden) heavenly Lord
but also as the true man of this creation. Even as man (that is,
when he is called a prophet) he points non-believers to God and
serves as an example for his own. Accordingly the saving message
has an external and an inward aspect. First, it is apologetic. It
exhibits an evangelical responsibility for the outside world, and
guards against misrepresentations of the truth. Secondly, it is
the means of salvation. In the prologue and in Paul's speech on
the Areopagus this exterior aspect is more to the fore than anywhere else. In the prologue the intention is to insist on the reality
of Jesus' history. In the Areopagus speech the intention is to open
the pagan mind to the Christian message and to make that message
relevant to the contemporary world. Finally, Luke recognizes
that man has to live out his faith in this world. The journey to
Jerusalem, with its injunctions for Christian living in this world,
present the Christian life as one of discipleship. The table scenes

illustrate correct behaviour in social intercourse. It shows what that life is like when lived in fellowship with Christ in a fallen world alienated from God. In the dialogues, with their pattern of question and answer, the relation between secular life and the gospel is brought out clearly. Luke does not cut off this world from God. That would imply a one-sided, immanentist view of history. Though he is fully aware of the contrast between the fallen world and God, he insists that the world is open to God as he is revealed in Christ. In other words, Christ has restored the world to its original created state.

3

Jesus Christ and History

Luke is commonly regarded as the "theologian of redemptive history".[1] This view is quite widely accepted,[2] both by those who approve of his theology and by those who question it.[3] But, as we have discovered, it is almost impossible to give in capsule form an account of Luke's "theory of redemptive history".[4] Again and again we run into dialectical patterns which view incidents or truths from different aspects and on various levels. If Luke can distinguish between Christ's earthly and heavenly modes of existence, it is doubtful whether one can speak of any "continuity between redemptive history in Israel and in Christianity".[5] Be that as it may, Luke's theology is far more complex than the standard works of the day suggest. Bultmann's judgement that Christ "in the thought of Acts becomes the beginning of a new history of salvation",[6] is one

[1] Lohse, *EvTh* 1954, pp. 256ff.

[2] Cf. the survey in W. G. Kümmel, *Introduction to the New Testament*, pp. 100ff.

[3] Cf. O. Cullmann, "Parousieverzögerung und Urchristentum", *ThLZ* 83 (1958), pp. 1ff; Wilckens, *Missionsreden*, pp. 194f, speaks of a considerable agreement in the *description* of Lucan theology "from Käsemann to Cullmann", contrasted with the utmost lack of unanimity in their evaluation of it.

[4] Wilckens, op. cit., p. 203.   [5] Wilckens, op. cit., p. 204.

[6] *Theology* II, p. 117: on the subject see Vielhauer, "Paulinism", esp. pp. 45ff. E. Fuchs sees in Paul "the end of history" (*Zur Frage nach dem historischen Jesus* (Ges. Aufs. II), 1960, pp. 79ff). His concept of history is, however, developed in a one-sided way from the Pauline doctrine of the law. For him "history is to be understood as the product of sinful man's efforts . . ., to achieve life for himself" (p. 91). It is concerned with "the whole fate of man in time in bondage to time, in which man transmits his efforts to achieve life because he seeks to transcend himself" (p. 92, n. 18). History "as secularity, as life in the flesh and after the flesh" is "the product of sinful man's hunger for life" (p. 95). In view of this reduction of history to the demonic we must ask whether it is not equally true that history is permanently characterized as the place where God acts so (cf. Robinson, *Problem of History*, esp. pp. 54ff). Luke goes further than Mark. Recognizing as he does the continuation of time, he also takes account of those elements in history which it owes to creation.

that calls for modification. As we have seen in Chapter 2, Luke does not indulge in wholesale historization in a positivistic way. And, as we shall show later, he does not treat church history in supernatural or sacral terms.

The age in which he lived confronted Luke with a threefold task as a historian. First, he had to preserve the unique character of the Christ event in on-going history. Secondly, there was the problem of historical continuity between Israel and the Church. Thirdly, there was the problem of how to describe the presence of salvation in the Christian community as it passes through time. The ensuing discussion will be determined by these three questions. First we must speak of Christ's exaltation as the consummation of salvation in heaven, then of the Church's continuity with Old Testament and Jewish history, and finally of the presence of the heavenly salvation in the community.

A. THE EXALTATION OF CHRIST: THE CONSUMMATION OF SALVATION IN HEAVEN

1. The Exaltation and Parousia of Jesus Christ

(a) In the first place, it is necessary to stress the close connection between Christ's parousia and his exaltation. Only so can we grasp the importance Luke attaches to the exaltation. Functions previously assigned to Christ at the parousia are transferred to the exaltation. Thus in the earliest tradition the entry into Jerusalem included overtones of the parousia. It was in fact "the type of the parousia".[1] But in Luke's hands it becomes the type of Christ's Lordship in heaven. In a veiled kind of way this is expressed in the parable in Luke 19.12ff. The introduction to the parable in v. 11 is an explicit statement of the purpose of the ensuing narrative. As they approached Jerusalem, Jesus' followers were expecting the kingdom of God to appear at any moment.

[1] This is how Conzelmann, St. Luke, p. 75, describes it, appealing to Matthew 23.39 as the clue to Matthew's version of the triumphal entry.

So Jesus tells them a parable about a nobleman going to a distant land to receive a kingdom, with the intention of returning later (v. 12). Thus the parable serves as an allegory of the exaltation.[1]

The entry itself is shaped in a similar way. The disciples acclaim Jesus because of his mighty works (v. 37). That, at least, is what everyone can see. The entry is like the triumphal procession of a general returning victorious from battle. But that battle is first of all decided in heaven. It is the exaltation of Christ that establishes peace (v. 38). The disciples can enjoy this peace, whereas Jerusalem misses it (v. 42). The "king who comes in the name of the Lord"—that is, Jesus now entering into Jerusalem, is the heavenly Lord whose presence the community enjoys.[2]

We must now go into detail. First, the triumphal entry is a fulfilment of the prediction in Luke 13.35, that the temple will be left desolate until the coming of the Lord. For the quotation from Psalm 118.26, "Blessed is he that cometh in the name of the Lord", is repeated almost word for word. This gives a kind of symbolic fulfilment to Jesus's prediction in 13.35 that his disciples would not see him again until that time.[3] For the "seeing" which is promised in 13.35 has an eschatological character.[4] The disciples "see" the peace of heaven (v. 38b) symbolized in the miracles of Jesus (v. 37).

The geography of the entry is particularly emphasized.[5] It may well be that the description of the descent from the Mount of Olives was based on the testimony of an eyewitness familiar with the locality.[6] All the same, Luke has deliberately shaped the scene there.[7] Again, the entry into the temple points forward to the exaltation. It is even significant that Jesus does not enter the city[8] but goes straight to the temple. He cleanses it because he is going to teach there during his stay in Jerusalem (19.47;

[1] See above, pp. 76ff.

[2] On the relation of Jesus' journey to, and entry into, Jerusalem to his exaltation, cf. J. H. Davies, "The Purpose of the Central Section of St. Luke's Gospel", *Stud. Ev.* II, 1964, pp. 164ff.

[3] Similarly Jesus' lament over Jerusalem (13.34f) points forward to his prediction of the city's destruction (19.41ff).

[4] Cf. Luke 10.23; 17.22.   [5] Klostermann, *Lukas*, p. 189.

[6] Rengstorf, *Lukas*, p. 218.   [7] On the Mount of Olives see above, pp. 30ff.

[8] In Mark 11.11 εἰς Ἱεροσόλυμα is omitted.

20.21; 21.37f).[1] Then he enters the temple as "king",[2] thus showing that his kingdom is "not of this world".[3] For it is the house of God (v. 46, "my house") which he occupies as king. There God grants him the royal prerogative of teaching with authority. There is a connecting thread which runs through Jesus' mighty works, the disciples' acclamation about "peace on earth and glory in the highest" (v. 38b) and Jesus' teaching in the house of God. Earlier, he had manifested his heavenly authority in his miracles. Now he shows it at Jerusalem in his teaching in the temple.[4] It must be remembered that the temple was the final destination of the journey to Jerusalem.[5] Just as the journey was starting, Luke spoke of the "assumption" that was awaiting Jesus. And, as we have already noted, the journey to Jerusalem was meant as a kind of triumphal procession to his exaltation in heaven.[6] His occupation of the temple is a kind of symbolic anticipation of his enthronement in heaven.

(b) The story of the ascension (Acts 1.9ff) contains unmistakable echoes of the parousia terminology.[7] The angels, who interpret the scene, significantly link the ascension with the second coming. He will come again in the same way as he ascended into heaven (v. 11). The picture of the cloud and the Lord's coming recall the classic parousia text, Daniel 7.13. Thus the use of this text in the prediction of Christ's return shows that the exaltation and parousia meant roughly the same thing in early Christian thought.[8] For Daniel 7.13 "in its original meaning says nothing

---

[1] Conzelmann, ibid., pp. 76ff.

[2] In the quotation in v. 38a ὁ βασιλεύς is interpolated. In place of this Mark 11.10 speaks of "the coming kingdom of our father David".

[3] John 18.36; see above, p. 59.

[4] Conzelmann, op. cit., p. 198, also sees in v. 38b a connection with "the future exaltation" and in the teaching of Jesus in the temple "the form in which Christ manifests his kingship on earth".

[5] Cf. Christ's entry into the heavenly sanctuary in Hebrews. Luke, however, knows nothing of the "Jerusalem which is above". The Christian's own "journey to heaven" is accomplished by following Jesus on earth. But his journey ends in the heavenly glory like the way of Jesus.

[6] See above, pp. 30ff.   [7] See above, pp. 11ff.

[8] This is shown by the way Matthew 28.18 closely follows Daniel 7.13f LXX (H. W. Bartsch, "Zum Problem der Parousieverzögerung bei den Synoptikern", EvTh 19 (1959), pp. 127ff).

about the Son of man coming to earth",[1] but speaks of his enthronement in heaven.[2] This, in effect, is exactly what happened at the exaltation. The ascension, as Luke sees it, is a kind of anticipation of the parousia in heaven.[3]

(c) This close link between the two events explains the curious oscillation between the singular and the plural in the phrase, "day(s) of the Son of man" in the parousia discourse (Luke 17.22ff).[4] Luke has inserted the Q saying about the appearance of the Son of Man like lightning in a quite definite theological context. To begin with, v. 25 forms the antithesis of the appearance of the Son of Man in glory to the whole world. "First", it says, the Son of man must suffer. There is no question of an immediate parousia. Before Jesus appears in glory he must undergo humilation, for such is the divine decree. Thus in his composition Luke has included not only the exaltation but also the second coming in his dialectic of glory and suffering.[5]

In the second place, Luke has inserted an introductory link (v. 22) before the Q saying in vv. 23f.[6] This is puzzling. What

---

[1] Haenchen, *Apg.*, 117, n. 7.   [2] Schweizer, *Erniedrigung*, pp. 35f.

[3] For Conzelmann, *St. Luke*, p. 204, n. 1, the ascension of Jesus is the act of exaltation and the penultimate stage of Jesus' course in the sequence of redemptive history, with the parousia still to come. But the heavenly event, which Conzelmann himself describes as a "timeless conception" (p. 104) must not be "historized" in this way. For Luke exaltation and parousia are identical. Jesus' goal is achieved with his exaltation. The parousia is the manifestation on earth of the Lordship into which Jesus has entered in heaven. For faith this Lordship is already present, though invisible; at his visible return faith is consummated in the redemption of the body (Luke 19.38; 21.28).

[4] Vv. 24, 30, singular; vv. 22, 26, plural. Evidently Luke has combined different traditions here. Behind the expression "days of the Son of man" there may lie the traditional rabbinic conception of the "days of the Messiah" as the period immediately preceding the Messianic age (Strack-Billerbeck, II, p. 237; IV, pp. 816ff). What matters for us is the theological evaluation which Luke has given to these traditions.

[5] See above, pp. 30ff. The affinity of this passage with the transfiguration story, which has undergone similar modification, is clear.

[6] The saying about desiring to see one of the days of the Son of man may be an early tradition (Grässer, op. cit., p. 35). All the same, the Lucan modification is easily discernible. "The awkward juxtaposition of ἡμέραι and αἱ ἡμέραι τοῦ υἱοῦ τοῦ ἀνθρώπου marks the verse as a connecting link. In addition we have Luke's preference for the OT turn of phrase, 'days will come' (Luke 19.43; 21.6; 23.29", Kümmel, *Promise*, p. 38).

does he mean by "the days of the Son of man"? Does it mean Jesus' lifetime on earth?[1] Or is it a day "in the glorious Messianic age"?[2] The situation is complicated still further by v. 26, where the days of the Son of Man are compared to the days of Noah.[3] If these two passages are interpreted in the light of each other, it would seem that the "days of the Son of man" must refer to the exaltation of Jesus. There are two points in favour of this interpretation. First, the plural "days" denotes a period of time, not a single occurrence.[4] Secondly, the term undoubtedly has an eschatological connotation. This is deeply rooted in the tradition,[5] and it is unlikely that Luke would have used it here in any different sense. Finally, the plural "days" recalls the saying about the *days* of Jesus' assumption in Luke 9.51. Here is another parallel which makes it likely that a reference to the exaltation of Jesus is intended.

This then seems to be the clue to the curious correspondence between "day" and "days" of the Son of Man in this passage.[6] Theologically, that is as eschatological events, the exaltation and the return belong together. By drawing a distinction between "day" and "days" Luke makes it clear that the two events differ only in a formal sense, in terms of terrestrial chronology. In

[1] So Conzelmann, *St. Luke*, p. 105, n. 3; E. Schweizer, *Neotestamentica*, p. 88.

[2] Klostermann, *Lukas*, p. 175.

[3] It is assumed by many that the expression bears different senses in vv. 22 and 26. So P. Vielhauer, "Gottesreich und Menschensohn in der Verkündigung Jesu," *Festschrift für G. Dehn*, 1957, p. 57; Dodd, *Parables*, p. 108; Kümmel, *Promise*, p. 29. But can we credit Luke with changing the meaning of such an important expression from Jesus' earthly life to his parousia (or *vice versa*)?

[4] This accords with OT usage (von Rad, *TWNT* II [E.T.], 946f). The exact procedure followed here by Luke is shown by the change of "on that day" (Mark 2.20) to "in those days" (Luke 5.35). According to Conzelmann, *St. Luke*, p. 124, the expression "days" indicates that the eschaton is no longer imagined as a single event, but "as a succession of events distinct from one another" (on this see above, p. 94, n. 3). Cf. also Tödt, *Son of Man*, p. 105.

[5] On the eschatological use cf. Kümmel, *Promise*, pp. 36ff. The expression "to see" in v. 22 also points in the same direction. The days of the Son of man denote then not a fixed period of time, but a heavenly "time" which is contemporaneous with the earthly world. The days in question can thus include the time of Jesus' life under its eschatological aspect (cf. Luke 10.23).

[6] The day of the flood in v. 27 corresponds to the days of Noah in v. 26, the destruction of Sodom in v. 29 to the days of Lot in v. 28. The days of the Son of man in vv. 22, 26 stand in exactly the same relation to the day of the Son of man.

effect they mean the same thing. In other words, within the period covered by the exaltation, the return of Jesus is a particular moment in history, a "day", on which that which is already consummated in heaven will be realized on earth.[1]

(d) Our exegesis of Luke 17.22ff is borne out by the way it tallies with the controverted statement about the "restoration of all things" in Acts 3.30f. This text is usually applied to the parousia.[2] But there is little support for this interpretation in the actual text. The terms employed are quite different from the other primitive Christian statements about the return of Jesus.[3] True, the passage occurs in a context dealing with the end of the world. But the word used for Jesus' descent to earth is usually applied to his earthly mission ($\dot{a}\pi o\sigma\tau\epsilon i\lambda\eta$). This suggests the presence of an earlier tradition.[4] In fact v. 20 may be a "fragment of eschatological speculation centred upon Elijah".[5] Such a view of the Messianic consummation and of the assumption of the Messiah into heaven[6] may well have been transmitted in Baptist circles.[7] In that case, how then did Luke understand it—quite apart from the contemporary polemic involved in the transference of John the Baptist's rôle in salvation to Jesus?[8]

The import of Luke's statement can best be grasped by taking a look at the composition of Acts 1—3. The parallelism between the first two speeches of Peter is obvious.[9] It is brought out

---

[1] Compare "the days of the assumption" (Luke 9.51), followed by the "day of Pentecost" (Acts 2.1). That is to say, it is in the period of time covered by the exaltation of Jesus that the event of the outpouring of the Spirit will occur (see below, pp. 140f). A formal parallel occurs in the quotation from Joel in Acts 2.17ff. In v. 17 Luke substitutes for the $\mu\epsilon\tau\dot{a}$ $\tau a\hat{v}\tau a$ from Joel 3.1 the words $\dot{\epsilon}\nu$ $\tau a\hat{\iota}s$ $\dot{\epsilon}\sigma\chi\dot{a}\tau a\iota s$ $\dot{\eta}\mu\dot{\epsilon}\rho a\iota s$ with the result that the days of the giving of the Spirit are contrasted with the "day of the Lord", which is still to come. The B text has lost sight of this point and restored the text of Joel.

[2] E.g., Haenchen and Conzelmann, ad loc.

[3] Echoes of Daniel 7.13f are absent; cf. what Luke says elsewhere about the return of Christ (Luke 17.24; 21.27).

[4] O. Bauernfeind, "Tradition und Komposition in dem Apokatastasisspruch Apg. 3, 20f", Abraham unser Vater, 1963, p. 16.

[5] Wilckens, op. cit., p. 153, following Bauernfeind, Apg., pp. 66ff.

[6] Hahn, Hoheitstitel, pp. 184ff.   [7] Bauernfeind, op. cit., p. 17.

[8] Thus Bauernfeind, op. cit., pp. 17ff.

[9] F. J. Foakes Jackson, The Acts of the Apostles, 1960⁹, p. 30.

already in Acts 1.5ff, in the saying about the baptism with the Holy Spirit which Christ is to perform and in the disciples' question about the final consummation.[1] Peter's first speech is preceded by the outpouring of the Spirit (2.1ff), his second speech by the healing of the lame man in the name of Jesus (3.1ff). On each occasion the scriptural quotation and the kerygma is followed by a call to repentance (2.38; 3.19), which in turn leads to the assurance that this salvation is offered to Israel ("you", 2.39; 3.25f). Where the call to repentance is obeyed the gift of the Spirit is promised (2.38), but, in 3.20, the coming of times of refreshment and the sending of the Messiah Jesus.

Both of these events, according to Jewish tradition, are expected at the end of time. The gift of the Spirit, according to Acts 2, is a present experience for the community. Does it not therefore follow that the promise given in 3.20 is meant for the present too? If so, then—for Luke at any rate—those who repent will encounter the exalted Christ, the glorified servant, as Peter says at the beginning of his speech (v. 13).[2] This encounter with Christ will bring them "times of refreshing".[3] This is equivalent to the peace on earth promised at the nativity (Luke 2.14) and realized in heaven (Luke 19.38), but also present in the community (Acts 9.31). This time of salvation would then be an anticipation of the "restoration of all things" which is to happen at the end of time (Acts 3.21). In that case, a single event in the traditional expectation has been split up, just as the prophecy from Joel in Acts 2.17ff has been split up into the "last days", now present in the outpouring of the Spirit, and the "day of the Lord" which is still to come.[4]

[1] Bauernfeind, op. cit., p. 18, n. 2.
[2] On the connection of v. 13 with the exaltation of Jesus cf. Wilckens, op. cit., pp. 38f.
[3] A. Wikenhauser, Die Apostelgeschichte, 1961[4], p. 61.
[4] See above, p. 96, n. 1. This exposition clears up the difficulties in the text. The saying about Moses in Deuteronomy 18 no longer requires an awkward transition from the parousia to the earthly life of Jesus (Bultmann, Theology II, p. 115). The whole section is concerned with Israel's acceptance of its Messiah, who restores men to life by his miraculous healings (the speech is preceded by the healing of the impotent man "in the name of Jesus"), and whose word is to be heard (vv. 22f). The "these days" which the prophets have proclaimed (v. 24), like the days of the Son of Man, are to be understood as a period of time in the present (on this

If the above exegesis is correct, we have here another instance of the close connection between the exaltation and second coming. We fail to appreciate Luke's theological achievement if we think that all he did was to postpone the parousia to a later date and substitute the exaltation instead of it. Luke does not think in this formal kind of way, as we do with our modern view of history. He shapes the form—as we have seen in Chapter 2—in accordance with the content. He transfers theological statements previously associated with the parousia to the exaltation. That which is heavenly in a future sense is also heavenly in a transcendent sense. This is how he keeps up the tension between present and future in the eschatological realization of salvation, which the apostolic age had expressed in terms of an imminent expectation.[1] Now that the intimate connection between exaltation and parousia is clear, it is time to examine the connection between the exaltation and Old Testament redemptive history.

2. The Exaltation of Christ:
the Goal of Old Testament Redemptive History

It is necessary at this point to go back to the examination of Jesus before the Sanhedrin (Luke 22.66—23.1).[2] Here we find the clearest statement about the connection between the exaltation and Israel's redemptive history. The famous verse, Luke 22.69, must now be analysed in detail.

We will start with the Marcan text, Mark 14.62. There Jesus admits his Messiahship in language which combines Psalm 110.1

---

problem cf. Wilckens, op. cit., p. 43). Repentance is not focused on the parousia, but on the present encounter with the exalted Christ. The ὅπως ἄν here (with Conzelmann, Apg., p. 34) is not to be taken in a causal sense, as accelerating the parousia as in 2 Peter 3.12. Repentance and conversion prepare for the parousia, they do not bring it about.

[1] Luke 12.35ff portrays the second coming as the return of Jesus from the heavenly feast. But according to v. 37b the Lord comes to serve his own. By the use of Johannine terminology (cf. John 13.4) the text is applied to present encounter with Christ (in the Lord's Supper?). The exalted Lord "comes" again and again to his own, until he comes at the end of the ages for the redemption of the body (Luke 21.28).

[2] See above, pp. 44ff and pp. 61f.

with Daniel 7.13.[1] What is the connection between these two biblical quotations? As Grässer sees it, Mark 14.62 is speaking of "two events distinct both in timing and in subject matter . . . session and (καί) return".[2] Like Bousset,[3] Grässer regards this verse as "a clear statement of Christian faith: he sitteth on the right hand of God, from whence he shall come to judge the quick and the dead". So, he concludes, "Behind the combination of Daniel 7.13 and Psalm 110.1 there lies a theological intention. It is a deliberate attempt to insert an interim stage between the exaltation of Christ and his parousia."[4]

There can of course be no doubt that the two events are to be distinguished. As Mark sees it, Jesus is now seated at the right hand of God, while his coming on the clouds is still in the future. But this is what makes the combination of the two events by means of a καί so striking. They are placed on the same level. It bears out our thesis that the exaltation and parousia belong closely together in meaning, even in Mark.[5] The two events are connected by the inauguration of Jesus' reign in heaven. This is assumed in both quotations. Like the exaltation, the parousia is an eschatological event. What is consummated in heaven will assuredly be realized on earth. Psalm 110.1 interprets Daniel 7.13 in terms of a realized eschatology, but without changing its theological content. Christ, now enthroned in heaven, keeps alive the expectation of his coming on earth. That the continuation of human history involves a postponement of the imminent expectation need not be denied. Yet the introduction of the exaltation motif does not mean a reduction of the eschatology, but its transformation.

But there is still another problem. What does Jesus' reply mean in the context of the trial? The point of the story for Mark is obvious. There is no question that the Messiahship of Jesus is inaugurated when he is rejected by the Jews in the person of their supreme authority. They refuse to accept their Messiah

---

[1] Lohmeyer, *Markus*, ad loc.   [2] *Parousieverzögerung*, p. 174.
[3] *Kyrios*, p. 37.   [4] Op. cit., 174.
[5] H. Baltensweiler, *Die Verklärung Jesu*, 1959, p. 116, finds the same combination of exaltation and parousia in the Marcan version of the transfiguration story.

who had been sent to them by God. Thus they bring the story of their election to an end. They have no more future in which to hope for the fulfilment of salvation. The only future left for them is to see the exalted Christ returning as their judge while he comes as Saviour for those who believe in him. The enthronement of Jesus is portrayed on the background of the condemnation the Jews have brought upon themselves. The Christ event brings Israel's history to an end so far as its saving significance is concerned.[1] But this end is at the same time a fulfilment. For with Jesus' enthronement the purpose of God has reached its goal.

In Matthew's version of our text the finale of Israel's redemptive history is given even greater prominence. Before the combined quotation Matthew 26.64 inserts an adversative $\pi\lambda\dot{\eta}\nu$ and an $\dot{\alpha}\pi'$ $\ddot{\alpha}\rho\tau\iota$. This creates a greater caesura between the claims of Jesus and the prophecy of the coming of the Son of Man. Matthew "is concerned with the irrevocable, definitive, conclusively final ending which was fixed by the attitude of the Sanhedrin in this episode".[2]

All this is equally true of Luke's version. With the rejection of the Christ, Israel's redemptive history is at an end. A new era is inaugurated, an era characterized by the reign of Christ in heaven. This is a common assertion, but Luke gives it a significant interpretation by means of three changes in the text. In place of Matthew's additional phrase $\dot{\alpha}\pi'$ $\ddot{\alpha}\rho\tau\iota$ he has $\dot{\alpha}\pi\dot{o}$ $\tauο\tilde{\upsilon}$ $\nu\tilde{\upsilon}\nu$. The quotation from Daniel 7.13 is omitted. The $\ddot{o}\psi\epsilon\sigma\theta\epsilon$ is replaced by $\ddot{\epsilon}\sigma\tau\alpha\iota$.[3]

What is the connection between Luke's $\dot{\alpha}\pi\dot{o}$ $\tauο\tilde{\upsilon}$ $\nu\tilde{\upsilon}\nu$ and Matthew's $\dot{\alpha}\pi'$ $\ddot{\alpha}\rho\tau\iota$? Is it no more than an improvement of the Greek?[4] Or are the two versions entirely independent?[5] Tödt thinks it is quite "clear": the $\dot{\alpha}\pi\dot{o}$ $\tauο\tilde{\upsilon}$ $\nu\tilde{\upsilon}\nu$ indicates that "the new period of the history of salvation, the period of the Church"

[1] Cf. Mark 15.38; the rending of the curtain is "the advance sign of the divine wrath and judgement", Klostermann, Markus, p. 167.

[2] Tödt, Son of Man, pp. 82ff. The above quotation is on p. 84. Cf. Bornkamm, Tradition in Matthew, p. 33; R. Hummel, Die Auseinandersetzung zwischen Kirche und Judentum im Mt.–Ev., 1963, pp. 140ff.

[3] The addition of $\tauο\tilde{\upsilon}$ $\theta\epsilon ο\tilde{\upsilon}$ to $\delta\dot{\upsilon}\nu\alpha\mu\iota s$ helps to elucidate this for the reader of Luke (Grundmann, Lukas, p. 420).

[4] E. Norden, Die antike Kunstprosa, p. 486, n. 3.

[5] Conzelmann, St. Luke, pp. 84f, n. 3, who, however, does not offer any exegetical proof, but deduces it from his interpretation of Lucan theology.

has dawned, "in which the Son of Man is exalted to God's right hand as Lord of the community (cf. Acts 7.36). The parousia appears to have withdrawn into remoteness."[1] But there is not a trace of all this in the text. The νῦν in v. 69 clearly refers to the Son Man's *sessio ad dexteram* rather than to the period of the Church. The two things cannot be merged into a single temporal scheme. A comparison of this passage with other places in Luke where the same phrase occurs will show that he means the dawning of a new period of a quite different kind.[2]

Luke 22.69 also marks a "decisive shift from one period to another".[3] The period now dawning is that of Christ's reign in heaven. Luke is here following the usage of the LXX, where the same term is frequently employed, as in the familiar formula of the Psalter, "from henceforth and for ever more".[4] The ἀπὸ τοῦ νῦν preserves a *via media* between an unbiblical *nunc aeternum*[5] (which the Pauline or Johannine νῦν might suggest), and a linear sequence of similar periods, which Luke combines by means of ἀπὸ τότε (Luke 16.16). The beginning in time is clearly emphasized, thus excluding a timeless interpretation of the νῦν. Yet the difference in quality between the new period and the one immediately preceding it is brought out by the clearly marked boundary between the two.[6] Hence ἀπὸ τοῦ νῦν in Luke 22.69 must be interpreted strictly in line with ἀπ' ἄρτι in Matthew 22.64.[7] It marks the dawn of the last times inaugurated by the reign of Christ, which Luke, to be sure, experiences in a different way from Matthew and Mark.

Why does he omit the phrase, "and coming on the clouds of heaven"? It cannot be simply due to the delay in the parousia.[8] Luke is fully aware of the coming of the Son of man (21.27; 18.8b; 17.24, 26, 30).[9] Why then did he omit it here and not

[1] Luke 1.48 (period of salvation); 5.10 (period of missionary work); 12.52 (period of decision in face of imminent judgement); 22.18 (period of the absence of Christ in heaven).
[2] Luke 1.48 (the time of salvation); 5.10 (the time of missionary activity); 22.18 (the time of Christ's absence in heaven); Acts 18.6 (the time of the Gentiles).
[3] Stählin, *TWNT* IV, p. 1106, 9ff. [4] Stählin, op. cit., p. 1100, 19ff.
[5] Stählin, op. cit., 1105, n. 43. [6] Stählin, ibid., p. 1104, 13ff.
[7] So too Kümmel, *Promise*, p. 50, n. 102. [8] Grässer, op. cit., p. 176.
[9] Cf. Tödt, *Son of Man*, p. 102; H. K. McArthur, "Mark 14, 62", *NTS* 4 (1957–8), pp. 156ff; Bartsch, *Wachet*, pp. 106ff.

H

elsewhere? The exegesis of the Marcan text which we have offered above provides a clue. The suggestion contained there is developed further in Luke. All the emphasis is shifted to the exaltation, which in Luke now bears the theological weight which in Mark and Matthew is placed upon the parousia. The development of the text from Mark to Luke shows that the real problem exercising the community was not the continuation of time, but the certainty of Christ's final victory. At first, this certainty was closely bound up with the imminent return. Luke shows that the community is able to live in the certainty of the heavenly victory of Jesus. Since it is only his heavenly reign that matters (and not the earthly pilgrimage of the community towards the end of the world) he can drop all reference to the second coming.

The fact of the matter is, Luke *had* to omit it, because the heavenly reign of Jesus is invisible. Were it otherwise, it would be subject to human control, and thus forfeit its eschatological character (Romans 8.24). That is why he had to alter Mark's (and Matthew's) "you will see". The reign of Christ becomes visible only at the end of time, with the coming of the kingdom of God (22.18). Until that happens, the community goes on yearning to "see" the reign of the Son of Man (17.22). This seeing, which is still a future hope (cf. 21.27), serves to underline the temporary nature of the present situation. Luke can never regard it as a "permanent condition".[1]

As we see from Luke 22.69, the exaltation of Christ is the end of Old Testament history. Negatively, it is so because Israel rejects him. Positively, because it is the fulfilment of salvation for those who accept Israel's Messiah.[2] The universal significance of this fulfilment will be our next topic of discussion.

3. *The Exaltation of Christ:*
   the Universal Consummation of Salvation

(a) The exaltation of Christ is more than the end of Old Testament redemptive history. It is, as Luke sees it, the transcendental

---

[1] Grässer, op. cit., p. 176.
[2] See above, pp. 46ff, for the exposition of Luke 22.70f.

fulfilment of the Old Testament prophecies. With the reign of Christ, salvation ceases to be confined to a particular nation in history, and now extends to the whole cosmos. This is the point of the saying (peculiar to Luke) about the fall of Satan (Luke 10.18), where the victory is described as already consummated in heaven. The imperfect ἐθεώρουν leaves no doubt that the victory has already been won. The tense is particularly noticeable in view of the present tense earlier in v. 17, which speaks of the power the disciples had exercised over the demons. What has happened in heaven is prior to what the disciples have achieved. The saying recalls Acts 12.7ff, where there is another reference to the victory over Satan in heaven, contemporaneous with the battle going on on earth. An event which is nearing completion on earth is proleptically complete in heaven. There can be no doubt that Luke himself shares this view.[1] In its position in the second missionary charge this cosmic event points at the same time to the universal significance of the Christ event.[2]

(b) Again, the saying about peace in heaven (Luke 19.38) recalls Revelation 12.10. According to Foerster,[3] "the remarkable saying" asserts "that εἰρήνη (the same as σωτηρία in Revelation) is present and is fashioned in heaven". Accordingly the word must also be understood in the light of the Hebrew shalom (well-being, prosperity).[4] G. von Rad points out the connection between shalom and m'nucha in Deuteronomy, where it describes "the rest and pacification in the land of promise".[5] Luke may well have seen a typological parallel between Jesus' journey to Jerusalem and Israel's wandering through the desert to the promised land. If so, "peace in heaven" will correspond to the peace enjoyed in the land of Canaan (Joshua 1.13, 15; 21.44, etc.; Psalm 95.11).[6]

[1] J. Weiss, Die Predigt Jesu, p. 38, ascribes it to Luke's Jewish-Christian Lucan source.
[2] See above, pp. 22f.   [3] TWNT II (E.T.), p. 413.
[4] L. Köhler, Old Testament Theology, 1957, p. 240, n. 21.
[5] TWNT II (E.T.), p. 404; see further: "Es ist noch eine Ruhe vorhanden dem Volke Gottes", Ges. Studien zum AT, 1958, pp. 101ff.
[6] J. Mánek, "The New Exodus in the Books of Luke", Nov. Test. 2 (1957), pp. 8ff, works out a whole series of parallels with Israel's exodus from Egypt. He regards Israel's entry into the promised land as a type of the ascension in Acts 1.10 (p. 19).

If this exegesis is correct, we have here another case where an Old Testament prophecy has been raised to a cosmic level.

(c) Victory in heaven and peace on earth describe the reign of Christ, as is further shown by the treatment of the exaltation in Peter's speeches in Acts.[1] Acts 2.33–6 forms the climax and finale of the Pentecost sermon. It describes the triple effect of Christ's exaltation. It is the *sine qua non* of the outpouring of the Spirit. It gives Jesus a supremacy over David (who did not ascend into heaven). And it provides the ground of Jesus' pre-eminence as κύριος and χριστός.

In Luke the exaltation and the outpouring of the Spirit form a single whole. The gift of the Spirit takes for granted the consummation of salvation in heaven. Being thus riveted to the exalted Christ, it is preserved from a false immanentist interpretation. The transcendence of the Holy Spirit over the world and man is thus assured.[2] The second exaltation saying in vv. 34f is strongly reminiscent of Mark 12.35f. The fact that David did not ascend into heaven again stresses the exaltation of Jesus. Jesus' assumption is the paramount advantage he enjoys over David. It is the "eschatological" factor, the characteristic mark of temporal fulfilment. Again, the Old Testament promise that the Messiah would come from the Davidic line is transcended by the heavenly dignity of Christ.

At the end of this speech (Acts 2.36) Peter tells the whole house of Israel that "God has made him both Lord and Christ, this Jesus, whom you crucified". Whether the formula κύριος καὶ χριστός comes from Luke himself,[3] or from his tradition,[4] it fits in perfectly with Luke's theology. Jesus is the Christ to whom the Old Testament prophecy points. Through his heavenly exaltation he becomes the Lord (Kyrios), the one who reigns at the right hand of God (2.34f) and whose sway extends over the whole world.[5] As is indicated by the phrase ἐποίησεν ὁ θεός,

---

[1] Acts 2.33; 3.20f; 5.31; cf. Wilckens, *Missionsreden*, pp. 150ff.
[2] On the relation of the exalted Lord to the Holy Spirit, see above, pp. 18ff.
[3] So Wilckens, op. cit., p. 173; Conzelmann, *St. Luke*, p. 171, n. 2.
[4] So Hahn, *Hoheitstitel*, p. 116.
[5] Cf. the formulas χριστὸς κύριος (Luke 2.11) and χριστὸς βασιλεύς (Luke 23.2).

Jesus' translation to his reign in heaven is an already accomplished fact.[1]

(d) The passage about the exaltation in Acts 5.31 makes a similar point. In Acts 2.33 the exaltation was the necessary prelude to the outpouring of the Spirit. In Acts 5.31 the exaltation empowers Jesus to grant to Israel repentance and forgiveness of sins. For Jesus is exalted as ἀρχηγός and σωτήρ to the right hand of God, a statement which recalls the phrase κύριος καὶ χριστός interpreted above (Acts 2.36). The agent of salvation who confers forgiveness of sins is also the ἀρχηγός to eternal life (cf. 3.5). Here is another prerogative in which Jesus excels over David (2.29).[2] Once again, the horizons of Old Testament prophecy are widened by the exaltation of Jesus. Note also that the gifts of salvation are associated with the exalted Christ. Never does Luke allow them to be "historized" and so forfeit their eschatological character.[3] But this exposes him to a new danger. It suggests that at his exaltation Jesus leaves this earthly world to its own devices, and confines salvation to the devout individual. This however is ruled out by the saying about the "restoration of all things" (3.21), to which we must now return.

(e) The difference between the way Acts 3.21, and 2.33f, 5.31, speak of the exaltation, is striking. There is no reference here to

---

[1] The act of God must not be pressed into our formal time scheme, as though Jesus were first man and is now the exalted Son of God. This then raises the question whether v. 36 applies to the whole christological event (so Wilckens, op. cit., p. 173) or only to the exaltation (so Hahn, op. cit., p. 191). But Luke regards Jesus dialectically as both earthly and heavenly. On this view Jesus is Lord and Christ even in his earthly life, as the Gospel clearly shows. On the other hand through the intervention of God in the history of this world he is "made Lord". These two statements stand unmistakably side by side.

[2] In this climactic parallelism, however, the historical connection with the OT remains firm. Israel is named as the recipient of repentance and forgiveness of sins (cf. 13.23). Here Israel is the same as the λαός in Luke 2.11 (on this see below, pp. 132ff). The Hellenistic parallels to ἀρχηγός and σωτήρ are shown by W. Grundmann, "Das Problem des hellenistischen Christentums innerhalb der Jerusalemer Gemeinde", ZNW 38 (1939), pp. 65ff; but on the Jewish origin of the term σωτήρ cf. Foerster, TWNT VII, p. 1015, 30ff.

[3] See above, pp. 18ff.

Psalm 110.1.[1] Jesus' sojourn in heaven is entirely subordinated to the period of the restoration of all things. The earth is not left to itself after the exaltation. The consummation of salvation in heaven does not rule out the renewal of the earth at the end of time. The fulfilment of the Old Testament prophecies does not mean that they become completely spiritualized. God does not abandon what he "spoke by the mouth of his holy prophets from of old" (v. 21b; cf. Luke 1.70). The miracles of Jesus and those which he performs through others prefigure already here and now the new divine world. And so it will continue until ($\check{\alpha}\chi\rho\iota$ v. 21)[2] the exaltation of Christ and the renewal of the world eventually coincide.

We now have a clear idea of the fundamental importance that the exaltation of Christ had for Luke's theology. In it the parousia becomes as it were a reality in heaven, the already completed event of salvation. It marks the end of Israel's redemptive history and the cosmic shift of the aeons.[3] In the exaltation the Old Testament prophecies of the Messiah's reign come to rest, and yet they are transcended at the heavenly level.[4] Riveted as it is to the exalted Lord, the eschatological salvation is kept free from human control, thus avoiding a false sacralization of history. One result of all this is to raise anew the question of the actual continuation of history (of the world and the Church) after the exaltation of Christ. What place does this have in Luke's theology?

---

[1] Wilckens, op. cit., p. 152.

[2] Cf. the $\pi\rho\iota\nu$ in the Joel quotation, Acts 2.20.

[3] Here Luke differs from Matthew (and Mark), for whom the exaltation of Jesus does not bring the shift of the aeons. This will not come until the $\sigma\upsilon\nu\tau\epsilon\lambda\epsilon\iota\alpha$ $\tau\upsilon\hat{\upsilon}$ $\alpha\iota\hat{\omega}\nu\upsilon\varsigma$ (Matt. 13.39f, 49; 24.3; 28.30) and the parousia. But the exaltation does bring to an end the period of Jesus' humiliation and opens up the mission to the Gentiles (cf. Hummel, op. cit., p. 140; G. Bornkamm, "Der Auferstandene und der Irdische, Matt. 28.16–20", Zeit und Geschichte, 1964, pp. 171ff).

[4] Therefore Luke has on the one hand a continuity between the OT and NT in his Promise–Fulfilment pattern. But on the other hand the heavenly fulfilment achieved in Christ bursts the OT framework wide open. Hence the OT must be understood anew in the light of the Christ event. On the mutual relation of OT and NT cf. G. von Rad, Old Testament Theology II, 1965, pp. 319ff; H. Conzelmann, "Fragen an G. von Rad", EvTh, 24 (1964), pp. 113ff (on this cf. the review of E. Wolf, op. cit., pp. 165ff, and von Rad's reply, pp. 388ff).

B. ISRAEL AND THE CHURCH

1. *Jerusalem: the Place of Salvation and Judgement*

In the Lucan writings, Jerusalem, and its temple in particular, are highlighted in a remarkable way. This occurs "much more strongly than in the other Synoptics".[1] The Gospel begins and ends in the temple (1.5ff; 24.63). Morgenthaler identifies four scenes in Luke which provide a framework for the whole Gospel.[2] With this framework Luke combines a clear cut theological conception. Jerusalem is the scene where redemptive history is fulfilled. The divine salvation is planted firmly in a definite place in history, which prevents it from evaporating into a timeless idea and preserves the humanity of the divine revelation. For to be man means to be tied to a particular place in history.

It is for this reason that Jesus has to die in Jerusalem (Luke 13.33). The disciples must stay in Jerusalem to receive the power of the Holy Spirit (24.49; Acts 1.4), and to become witnesses, "beginning from Jerusalem" (24.47; cf. Acts 1.8). The risen Lord appears either in Jerusalem or in its neighbourhood (Luke 24.13, 18, 33, 52). It is in Jerusalem that the community assembles, "in the temple as the place which belongs to the people of God, the true Israel" (Acts 2.46; 3.1–3, 8; 5.20f, 25, 42). The reins of leadership in the fast-growing Church are kept "in the hands of the authorities in Jerusalem" (8.14–25; 11.2, 22; 12.25; 13.13).[3] Even Paul has to go up to Jerusalem to receive accreditation (9.27f; 15.2, 22).[4]

Luke draws further distinctions between various places in Jerusalem. He distinguishes between the city and the temple in the story of the triumphal entry and in Jesus' stay there before his death.[5] There is also a distinction between the people and their leaders. The people listen to Jesus in the temple (Luke 20.1), coming there early in the morning to hear him (21.38). They hang upon his words (19.48) and are shocked at his death (23.48).

[1] Lohse, *TWNT* VII, p. 330, 8; on what follows cf. pp. 330f.
[2] Op. cit. I, pp. 163ff; Luke 1.5—4.13; 19.45—24.53; Acts 1.4—7.60; 21.18—26.32.
[3] Lohse, op. cit., pp. 334f.   [4] See below, pp. 117f.
[5] Conzelmann, *St. Luke*, pp. 75ff.

Contrasted with them there are the "principal men of the people", the high priests and scribes who plot to murder Jesus (19.47b).[1]

Linked with the motif of the people listening to Jesus in the temple is the preaching of the apostles in Jerusalem (Acts 3.11f). The people are not responsible for the crucifixion (they did it "in ignorance", Acts 3.17). There is still time for them to repent and accept the Christ of Israel. It is similar with the Pharisees and Sadducees. The Pharisees disappear from the passion narrative.[2] They are thus exonerated from any guilt over the crucifixion. They represent that group among the Jewish leaders which is receptive to the Christian message. Gamaliel is a particular case in point (Acts 5.34ff).[3]

But there is another aspect to Jerusalem, and for this the distinctions noted above pave the way. Jerusalem rejects her Messiah and so becomes the scene of judgement. She brings upon herself her own destruction (13.34f). For it was there that Jesus, as the One sent by God, suffers a prophet's fate and meets his death (Luke 13.33). The acclamation from Psalm 118 in Luke 13.35, which occurs again at the triumphal entry (19.38), means fulfilment for the disciples in their jubilation, but judgement for Jerusalem because of its rejection of Jesus. That is why the passion, which follows the entry, is framed by two scenes which point to the impending judgement upon the Jews. One is the scene of Jesus weeping over the city (19.41–4), the other is the people weeping for Jesus (23.27–31).[4] The highlight of Jesus' great discourse in the temple (21.5ff) is when he says that the destruction of Jerusalem will represent the wrath of God over his disobedient people, as the scriptures had foretold (vv. 20–4).[5] The life of Paul as Luke describes it in Acts is the story of how the centre of the Christian community shifted from Jerusalem to Rome. It was God's will that this should happen (Acts 23.11).

---

[1] See above, pp. 46ff for ὄχλος.   [2] Conzelmann, *St. Luke*, p. 78.
[3] See above, pp. 25ff.   [4] Conzelmann, *St. Luke*, p. 133.
[5] The "Woe to the women with child", Luke 21.23 and the beatitude of the childless, 23.39, form a climactic parallelism and elevate the threat of judgement to the nth degree. Not a word is said about the new spiritual Israel in 23.29 (cf. W. Käser, "Exegetische und theologische Erwägungen zur Seligpreisung der Kinderlosen Lc 23, 29b", *ZNW* 54 (1963), pp. 240ff).

This double view of Jerusalem, which runs all through Luke–Acts, is obvious. It is the clue to Luke's interpretation of history after Christ. In the next section we will try to show how Israel's history, as fulfilled history, is incorporated into the Christian community. This sets the latter in the context of earthly history. Yet Israel's history still continues. It is the history of judgement, and provides the pattern for God's judgement over the fallen world as a whole.

2. Judaism: the Model of God's dealings with the World

What attitude should the Christian take towards the Jews? This was a problem for Luke the Gentile Christian, as it was for the Church in his time. Unlike Matthew, he is not living in a state of acute conflict with the Jewish synagogue.[1] The danger for Luke is that Jesus' judgement on the Jews, which the tradition contained, might be used by the Gentile reader for his own self-justification. That Luke realizes this danger can be seen from the way he treats the story of the centurion at Capernaum as compared with Matthew. He omits (Luke 7.1–10) the statement that the Gentiles will be accepted and the "sons of the kingdom" cast out (Matt. 8.11f), and transfers it to a different context in chapter 13, which we shall discuss a little later.[2]

Luke escapes this danger by applying the judgement pronounced over the Jews to the Christian community. He also depicts the fate of the Jews as a curtain raiser to the last judgement, so that it serves as a warning for all. This can be demonstrated from Luke 13 and 21.20–4.

(a) Luke 13 is given over entirely to the question of Jerusalem and the Jews. In the "call of repentance to the Jews" (vv. 1–9),[3] the points are shifted at the beginning. In a typically Lucan way[4]

---

[1] On this see Hummel, *Auseinandersetzung*.

[2] E. Schweizer, *Church Order in the New Testament* (SBT 32), 1959, pp. 65f, n. 239.

[3] Rengstorf, *Lukas*, p. 168; there is no need to go here into the question of the historical background of Luke 13.1; cf. O. Cullmann, *The State in the NT*, 1956, p. 14; J. Blinzler, "Die Niedermetzelung von Galiläern", *Nov. Test.* 2 (1957), p. 24ff.

[4] See above, pp. 84ff.

there is introduced a discussion of the problem of theodicy from the point of view of natural man. In his reply, Jesus shifts the question from the theoretical level and brings it home to the individual: "Unless you repent, you will all likewise perish." The warning is repeated almost *verbatim* after the passage about the collapse of the tower of Siloam. The repetition drives the point home (vv. 3, 5). The word "all" can be extended indefinitely. For Jesus, it means the Jewish people, but for Luke's readers it means everyone who hears this word. And it gives added point to the parable of the fig tree which follows. To bear fruit is something not only that Israel has to do, but the Christian community too. The fact that God's final judgement of Israel has already taken place in its destruction serves to reinforce the threat of judgement as a reality for all.

The next two pericopes, the healing of the bent woman (vv. 10–17) and the twin parables of the mustard and the leaven (vv. 18–21), continue the theme of accepting or rejecting salvation. They prepare the way for the question in v. 23, "Lord, will those who are saved be few?" This is a Lucan formation,[1] and provides the clue to the verses that follow. The question is framed in general terms, and applies to everyone. There is thus no excuse for allowing the sayings in vv. 28ff to administer to self-righteous pride (expulsion from the kingdom of God, and salvation for others from all over the world). It could have been taken that way in its original position in the story of the centurion at Capernaum. Of Matthew's "sons of the kingdom" (Matthew 8.12) not a word is said. "You" in v. 28 means the reader himself.

The theme is continued in the prophecy over Jerusalem, the city which kills its prophets (vv. 34f). It is quite likely that in an earlier stage of the tradition vv. 34f followed immediately after vv. 28–30.[2] If vv. 34f come after vv. 28, 30, the latter must refer to the Jews only. But that is just what Luke wants to avoid. It explains why he inserts vv. 31–3, the Pharisees' warning to Jesus to beware of Herod. This interrupts Jesus' discourse. After he has read the saying about Jerusalem's guilt in putting Jesus to death (v. 33), the reader no longer thinks that vv. 34f are

---

[1] Dibelius, *Tradition*, p. 162.   [2] Hirsch, *Frühgeschichte* II, pp. 132f.

addressed to himself. Thus the warning directly expressed in vv. 23ff is underlined. The destruction of Jerusalem, which the reader knows all about, serves as a dire warning. Thus these anti-Jewish sayings become doubly relevant. They serve as a direct warning to the Church in Luke's own day. And indirectly they set the fate of Jews before the community as an example of the way in which the judgements of God are accomplished.

(b) Our observations on Luke 13 are borne out in Luke 21.5ff, and help to deepen our understanding of the much-discussed Lucan version of the Little Apocalypse. We shall concentrate upon the prediction of the destruction of Jerusalem (vv. 20–4) and the place it has in the apocalypse as a whole.

First, let us take a look at the Marcan version. As we already noted when we were dealing with Mark 14.62, Mark connects the parousia, which for him still lay in the future, with an event which was already a present reality, namely, the enthronement of Jesus.[1] His procedure is similar in chapter 13. The great tribulation, which the community is undergoing at the present time, is not yet the End itself.[2] But so closely are the two connected, that the End is bound to follow the tribulation (v. 24). So from Mark's point of view the community is already living in the last days, even if the End is still to come. The scales have been tipped. "We are already at the beginning of the end."[3]

Conzelmann similarly thinks there is a caesura at v. 24.[4] As he sees it, "Mark has deliberately dissected two interrelated but clearly differentiated series of events which lie in the future", in the final epoch of world history (the great tribulation, which is a continuation of previous history, though of greater intensity) and the final cosmic catastrophe, which takes on supernatural forms. In the earlier series of events man is summoned to play his part, but in the latter series there is nothing more that he can do. All that remains is the gathering together of the elect.

[1] See above, pp. 98ff.
[2] V. 7; in v. 24 the time of the tribulation is clearly distinguished from the events of the End.
[3] Marxsen, *Evangelist Markus*, p. 128.
[4] H. Conzelmann, "Geschichte und Eschaton nach Mc 13", *ZNW* 50 (1959), p. 219.

For Conzelmann, this division in the final epoch of time is "the key to the whole process".[1] Thus Mark "prepares the way for the final denouement, and clears the ground for his successors to incorporate this period into a larger view of history".[2]

This is just what Luke has done. He "removes the eschatology from history and from all else that happens on the plane of history". This, as Conzelmann sees it, is what has happened to the destruction of Jerusalem and its temple. In Luke 21.20-4 the evangelist presents "a polemical excursus about matters which are mistakenly included among the eschatological events".[3] Hence the "abrupt caesura" between vv. 24 and 25, which gives a qualitative difference to the events before and after it. "The former events are historical, the latter supernatural and apocalyptic."[4]

But there is something suspicious about this "elimination of the connection between the parousia hope and the destruction of Jerusalem".[5] Why did not Luke simply omit the destruction of Jerusalem altogether? After all, for him it lay in the past, while the apocalypse was directed entirely to the future. It is not enough to say it was simply due to Luke's fidelity to the tradition. After all, he omits whole pericopes elsewhere.[6] In any case, he could have contented himself with the allusion in 19.41-4. But perhaps it is the other way round. Perhaps Luke deliberately intends to connect together events which in the actual course of history are separated, the one past and the other future, and does so because he writes from the perspective of faith. If that is the case, Luke has gone even further than Mark. Mark gave an eschatological colouring to what was present in his own day. But Luke sees what has happened in the past in terms of eschatological fulfilment. In this it is like the crucifixion which for him was an event of the past, just as it was for Mark.

To prove our thesis, let us begin with Luke 21.25, "And there will be signs . . ." The deep incision Conzelmann detects here

[1] Ibid., p. 215.
[2] Ibid., p. 221.   [3] St. Luke, p. 128.
[4] Die Mitte der Zeit (German Edn 1962) p. 134. (cf. St. Luke, p. 134. n. 1).
[5] Marxsen, op. cit., p. 134.   [6] E.g. Mark 9.9-13; 10.35-45; 10.1-12.

is by no means obvious in the text. By inserting καί as a connecting particle, Luke moves from the destruction of Jerusalem to the events of the End. Note the difference in Mark 13.24, where the adversative ἀλλά and the note of time, μετὰ τὴν θλίψιν ἐκείνην, make a clear break. This is typical of Mark's concern to separate the present and the future. Mark's purpose is to make it clear that the Church in his day is not yet living in the future he expects. In Luke the situation is quite different. For him the destruction of Jerusalem has already taken place, and is not to be confounded with the events which mark the end of history. He would be a bad theologian if he produced, as if it were special spiritual insight, what everyone already knows. What he wants to do is to preserve the eschatological connection between the destruction of Jerusalem and the end of the world. This connection is threatened with a split into past and future by natural thinking, which always puts its own present into the centre of the picture. Luke is interpreting Mark in the light of his own contemporary situation, a perfectly legitimate procedure, which in fact enables him to preserve spiritual continuity with his predecessor.

Marxsen thinks that the phrase "until the times of the Gentiles are fulfilled" (v. 24b) is meant to separate the section which precedes from the one which follows.[1] The reason for this break, he thinks, is that Luke wishes to introduce into v. 24b an allusion "to the situation at the moment of writing".[2] Once, however, we rid ourselves of any such formal time scheme, we arrive at the opposite conclusion. The phrase in question actually serves as a bridge between the destruction of Jerusalem (which is caused by the Gentiles, v. 24a) and the universal last judgement which is to come upon the Gentiles.[3] Here are two widely separated periods, presented as a substantial unity.

This bears out our exegesis of Luke 13. The fate of Jerusalem is an anticipation of the last judgement. The same fate which befell Jerusalem will, on a much vaster, cosmic scale, embracing the whole world, overtake the Gentiles—when their time is fulfilled (v. 26). The Church too lives between these two judgements of God, past and future. "The prophecies, which are in the

---

[1] Op. cit., p. 129.   [2] Op. cit., p. 132.   [3] Wellhausen, *Lucas*, p. 118.

process of fulfilment in Luke's own time, enhance the importance of his predictions for the future."[1] V. 28 ("lift up your heads") might be a temptation to self-righteous pride. But any such danger is counterbalanced by the threat in vv. 34–6. God's judgement is coming upon all the inhabitants of the earth. Not even the Christians are excluded (v. 35). But they have a chance to escape the final catastrophe, "and to stand before the Son of man" (v. 36).

We can now see why Luke treats the destruction of Jerusalem as an "eschatological" event. It is a symbolic embodiment of God's dealings with the world.[2] This is the sense of vv. 22f, where the "days of vengeance" for "these people" is expounded as the fulfilment of scripture—in other words, it is grounded in the will of God. But Luke's writing has many facets, and by no means excludes a "profane" aspect to the destruction of Jerusalem. As an event in universal history it is accessible to all. But it is a profane event in yet another sense. Through the guilt of the Jews Jerusalem ceases to be the bearer and guardian of the divine promises, and becomes no different from the rest of the world. The judgement over the city becomes a typical example of what will happen to the rest of this old, transitory world.[3]

(c) Jerusalem is thus reduced to a purely secular significance. But at the same time it acquires a universal significance. The history of the Jews after the crucifixion becomes typical for the whole trend of history in the old era. This enables Luke to interpret the whole history of the world as history under God, shaped and guided by the divine will.

The elaborate dating in Luke 3.1f brings this out clearly. The actual wording is modelled on Jeremiah 1.1 LXX. But the data given about the contemporary rulers are much more extensive. In

---

[1] Grundmann, Lukas, pp. 382f.

[2] Here the concept of the "eschatological" is to be seen in terms of the Lucan scheme of thought. It must not be projected on to a single conceptual level. It includes in the first place the earthly reality which is related to the heavenly glory, next the aspect of earthly history which is related to God's action at the time of the End and finally the empirical redemptive present in the sense of a realized eschatology (see on this below, pp. 135f).

[3] On the secular character of Israel cf. Conzelmann, op. cit., p. 134.

the prophetic books of the Old Testament it is usual to mention the reigns of the kings of Israel and Judah. In a similar way Luke puts the Roman emperor first, followed by the rulers in Palestine and the reigning high priests. The Baptist is dated by the year of the emperor's reign, which gives him a place in universal history. Luke achieves two things by this dating. First he places the event that is immediately to follow, the ministry of John the Baptist, and along with it that of Jesus as well[1]—in the context of the history of Israel. John the Baptist is introduced like an Old Testament prophet. This gives the Christ event a context in history linked with the Old Testament history. Just as God addressed his word to the prophets of Israel in the past, so now he speaks to John.

But the stage of God's action in history has been enlarged. The whole Roman empire is involved, the whole world as Luke saw it at the time, the οἰκουμένη (Luke 2.1). This is the limit of the horizon in Luke–Acts. "There is no trace of a 'theology of history' as a comprehensive view of world history."[2] The offer of salvation is made to the whole world. But the whole world awaits the divine judgement which will overtake it as it has already come upon the Jews. Hence Luke's view only touches the fringes of world history. The real history which shapes the future is the Church's history. That is where God's plan of salvation is really carried out.[3]

[1] See above, pp. 122f.   [2] Conzelmann, St. Luke, p. 168.

[3] See below, pp. 142ff. Conzelmann, op. cit., p. 178, says: "The deeds of God therefore are divided into two groups": his universal sovereignty and execution of his plan of salvation, "which He does alone and directly", and the activities which concern the life of the Church, which "He performs through Christ". The only evidence he cites for the first group is Acts 17.22ff. This reference to the Areopagus speech however is not convincing. In this speech the course of world history ends with the divine judgement (v. 31). As regards the saving work of God it would be more correct to distinguish *within the community* between the action of God in Christ and that through the Holy Spirit (on this see below, pp. 135f).

On the other hand it cannot be denied that Luke stands at a pre-eminent advantage in the development of an idea of "world history". In his essay, *Geschichtsanschauung und Geschichtsbewusstsein im NT*, 1938 (which unfortunately does not deal with Lucan writings), H. D. Wendland speaks of three profound contributions which the NT view of history "has made to the history of the Christian west"; its universalism, i.e. the rise of the notion of a single world history, the idea of "God's guidance and control of history" (the question of

(d) Once more then we have a twofold state of affairs. There is universal history under judgement, and there is the history inaugurated with Christ and shaped by the inexorable divine plan of salvation. Both aspects come out clearly in Gamaliel's famous argument from history in Acts 5.38f.[1] This speech serves as the climax to the apostles' dispute with the Sanhedrin, which has been going on since Acts 4.1. The scene has been well set by the allusion to fiascoes of Theudas and Judas (5.36f). Gamaliel appears as one who "has still not made up his mind about the religious character of the Christian movement".[2] The cat may jump either way. The Christian movement may be of men or it may come from God. Gamaliel shared the general Jewish belief that God was the Lord of history, and that come what may his truth will prevail. But Luke's readers, unlike Gamaliel, know how it all turned out. "Surely, history has already delivered its verdict. We Christians are ἐκ θεοῦ."[3] That this is what Luke thinks is shown by his careful choice of language. In speaking of the possibility that Christianity is of human origin he uses the subjunctive, but for the other alternative, that it comes from heaven, he uses the indicative (5.38b, 39a).[4] Behind this grammatical subtlety stands the happy certainty that the Christian faith has by now proved to be on the winning side. The future belongs to the Church, because the Church is ἐκ θεοῦ.

To sum up: by condemning their Messiah the Jews became a model of the world under divine judgement. The words Jesus addressed to his Jewish opponents now apply to "all" (Luke 13), even to the Christians in so far as they too belong to the fallen world. The judgement over Jerusalem is an anticipation of the last judgement. The whole world—with the Roman emperor as its figurehead—is affected by the Christ event. It must take sides,

meaning), and the belief in a "divinely appointed goal for all of history" (all the quotations are from pp. 32f). All these ideas are present in seminal form in the Lucan conception of history. But let us not overlook the fact that the Lucan understanding of Church history was later transferred to the Holy Roman Empire and its emperor Caesar (cf. Eger, op. cit., pp. 97ff). This in turn prepared the way for the development of our secular view of history.

[1] On Acts 4f see above, pp. 25ff.   [2] Zahn, *Apg.*, p. 218.
[3] Haenchen, *Apg.*, p. 211.   [4] H. J. Holtzmann, *Die Apg.*, 1901[3], p. 49.

for or against Jesus Christ and God as the Lord of history. The place in history where this decision for God is made is the Christian community, the true Israel.

3. The True Israel

(a) There is much to suggest that Luke's purpose in Acts was to portray Christianity as the legitimate successor to the Jewish religion.[1] Dibelius has shown that this is true so far as Paul's apologies in Acts are concerned (Acts 22ff).[2] In these speeches the doctrinal affinities between Christianity and Judaism are stressed. In fact, all that stands between them is the figure of Christ, crucified and risen. The two religions share a common hope in the resurrection, a point so strongly underlined in Acts 23.6ff that it leads to a split between the Pharisees and Saducees in the Sanhedrin. Again and again Paul complains that he has been accused of entertaining a hope which he shares with the Jews (Acts 24.15, 21; 26.6–8).[3] Paul himself is depicted in Acts as a model Jew.[4] He is a Pharisee, a member of the strictest sect of the Jewish religion (26.5). He serves the God of his fathers and believes everything "laid down by the law or written in the prophets" (24.14). He defends himself against the charge of having encouraged apostasy from Moses or the abandonment of circumcision by taking a vow like a law abiding Jew (21.18ff). All this goes to show Luke's great concern for the continuity between Israel and the Church. But the question needs looking into more closely. What place does this continuity have in his theology, and how does he understand it?[5]

---

[1] Cf. J. Weiss, *Earliest Christianity I*, 1959, p. 6 and the survey in Cadbury, *The Making*, pp. 306ff; Sahlin, op. cit., p. 339, explains the situation in terms of his proto-Luke theory, for Sahlin's proto-Luke Christianity is "the logical continuation and the divinely appointed completion of Judaism". Thus again he divides up between two different authors what Luke places in dialectical relationship (see above, p. 59, n. 4).

[2] *Studies*, pp. 170ff.   [3] Dibelius, *Studies*, p. 170.

[4] On this see Klein, *Die zwolf Apostel*, pp. 122ff.

[5] Cadbury, op. cit., p. 306, regards this as merely an apologetic tendency, whose purpose is to demonstrate the legitimacy of Christianity from the Jewish point of view.

I

(b) Let us start with the apostolate of the Twelve. The key text is the choice of Matthias (Acts 1.15–26).[1] This story interrupts the sequence consisting of the exaltation of Jesus and the outpouring of the Holy Spirit, two events which, according to Acts 2.33, belong together. In 1.13f the disciples are with one accord devoting themselves to prayer. This scene looks forward to Pentecost rather than to the election of an apostle. By waiting in seclusion they show that they have left everything in God's hands. Yet in 1.15ff Peter opens his mouth and initiates the proceedings. Added to this, there is a tension in the theology. In 1.8 Jesus charges them to go "to the ends of the earth".[2] But 1.15 reverts to an institution in Israel.[3]

This tension cannot be explained away from the previous history of the tradition. Its *Sitz im Leben*, as Rengstorf quite correctly points out, is "a highly particularistic form of Christian Messianism".[4] Hence it must be a very early tradition. Stauffer has shown that "the saying is riddled with terms, formulas, principles and usages derived from pre-Christian Jewish law".[5] Following him, Schweizer goes on to suggest that during the period between the earliest church at Jerusalem and Luke's own time certain functions of the Twelve which originally had a purely eschatological connotation came to be reinterpreted along the lines of the Jewish Colleges of Twelve.[6] The problem of early Church history need not concern us here. But to understand the text before us it is necessary to draw a clear distinction between the tradition and the redaction.[7] This brings us face to face with

---

[1] Klein, *Apostel*, p. 204, calls Acts 1.21f Luke's "Magna Charta of the office of the twelve apostles".

[2] Von Baer, *Der heilige Geist* p. 82, speaks of an "expansion of national hopes into the idea of a world wide mission".

[3] K. H. Rengstorf, "Die Zuwahl des Matthias (*Apg.* 1, 15ff)", *StTh* 15 (1961), p. 53.

[4] Ibid., p. 57.

[5] E. Stauffer, "Jüdisches Erbe im urchristlichen Kirchenrecht", *ThLZ* 77 (1952), cols. 201ff; the quotation is from col. 204.

[6] *Church Order*, p. 70, n. 265; on the institution of the "Twelve" cf. Rengstorf, *TWNT* II (E.T.), pp. 321ff; Bultmann, *Tradition*, p. 159; K. Lake, *Beginnings* V, pp. 37ff; H. von Campenhausen, "Der urchristliche Apostelbegriff", *StTh* I, (1947), pp. 96ff.

[7] This distinction is missing in B. Reicke, *Urgemeinde*, pp. 25f (on this see Haenchen, *Apg.*, p. 129). He treats Luke's narrative as a historical account, thus missing its theological point.

Rengstorf's question: what is a particularistic text like this doing in Luke, who was such a thoroughgoing universalist?[1]

We can answer this at once. Luke has utilized an ancient Jewish-Christian tradition to express the continuous existence of the Church in history. In his usual dialectical manner he has placed in juxtaposition the exaltation of Jesus to heaven and the mission of the apostles on earth. He draws a clear line between the Lord in heaven and his witnesses on earth. Only later, in the Pentecost story, do we hear about the distinction conferred upon the apostles by the gift of the Holy Spirit.

Here is the clue to what Peter does. He acts with complete human responsibility. But he does not think up the plan for himself. He acts in obedience to the word of the Lord, which cries out for fulfilment.[2] Note the precise timing of his action. One would have thought that the choice of Matthias, caused as it is by God and directed by his Spirit, would have come after the outpouring of the Spirit. How is it that Peter and the apostles can act like this even before Pentecost? Evidently, in choosing Matthias the community is back in the Old Testament stage, which is always prior to Pentecost.[3] The story describes how the Church lived and acted while waiting for the Holy Spirit. It brings out the quality of expectancy which always attaches to the Spirit.

Finally, note the contrast between the sobriety of the apostles in Acts 1.15ff and their ecstasy in 2.1ff. Rengstorf believes this contrast is deliberate.[4] The institutional side of the Church's work

[1] Op. cit., p. 57. Rengstorf himself sees in the Twelve an external sign of God's irrevocable Yes to the evangelization of Israel (p. 60).

[2] The manner of the election remains obscure. But the circumstance that it is God who makes the choice (v. 24), must not be regarded as an elimination of the human factor (Haenchen, *Apg.*, p. 127). That would make the choice a piece of magic.

[3] This is the point of the choice by lot, which stands in marked contrast to the later guidance of the community by the Spirit (von Baer, op. cit., p. 83). Cf. the Sunday after the Ascension in the Church's year. Originally "the church's great festal season" lasted for fifty days (G. Kretschmar, "Himmelfahrt und Pfingsten" *ZKG* 66 (1954–5), p. 212). In Acts, however, the ascension is placed upon the 40th day, thus creating a new period of expectation. The forty days in Acts 1.3 thus have a firm place of their own in the structure of Acts 1 (Menoud, "Pendant quarante jours", pp. 150f).

[4] Op. cit., p. 64.

must be carried out soberly. But the Spirit, the "power from on high" (Luke 24.49) surpasses anything that man can do. As a matter of fact the Twelve do not play a conspicuous rôle anywhere else in Acts. The real leader of the Church is the Holy Spirit.[1]

(c) A good clue to Luke's understanding of the apostleship will be found in Acts 1.21f. In the preceding verses the apostolate was shown to be an institution grounded in the will of God, independent of the personal qualifications of those who received it (vv. 16–20).[2] Now in vv. 21f the personal requirements of an apostle are spelled out. He must have accompanied Jesus from the baptism of John until the ascension, in other words, have been with him all through his ministry. And he must have been closely associated with the apostles. "No one outside the inner circle could qualify for the pre-eminent rank of apostleship."[3]

Klein claims that both verses come "entirely from Luke's own pen".[4] But against this it is to be noted that there are a number of discrepancies both in language and in substance between the two verses. These have been tabulated by Spitta.[5] The phrase, ἕνα τούτων, drags it feet. The word συνελθόντων must have referred originally to "the gathering together of the apostles at this very instant" (cf. Acts 1.6; 16.13; 25.17; 28.17). If it is intended to refer to "the journeyings of the apostles during the lifetime of Jesus" we should not expect an aorist participle. Spitta's conclusion is illuminating. It is only the clause ἐν παντί χρόνῳ . . . ἀνελήμφθη ἀφ᾽ ἡμῶν that is a redactional insertion into the original text.

Spitta's conclusion, arrived at on grounds of literary criticism, accords with our own observation. As we have seen, there is a discrepancy between the qualifications laid down for the apostolate and the commissioning of the apostles as witnesses. The call to the apostolate is based on association with Jesus

---

[1] Rengstorf is right in pointing this out (ibid., p. 40). But the significance of the Twelve for Luke must be seen in its proper place. Even the actual phrase occurs only at Acts 6.2; when he speaks of something done by the "apostles" he always means the "twelve apostles" (contra Rengstorf, ibid., p. 65).
[2] B. Reicke, op. cit., p. 24.   [3] Klein, op. cit., pp. 206f.
[4] Ibid., p. 205.
[5] F. Spitta, Die Apg., ihre Quellen und deren geschichtlicher Wert, 1891, p. 13.

throughout his ministry, whereas their witness is focused exclusively on the resurrection. Evidently Lucan redaction is at work. Here is a *double entendre* of the kind we find all the way through the Book of Acts.[1] On the one hand the apostle bears witness to the earthly life of Jesus (in addition to 1.15 see also 10.39, 41; 13.31). This requirement recalls the appointment of the apostles by Jesus in the Gospel (Luke 6.12ff). The parallel between this passage and the choice of Matthias in Acts 1.15ff is unmistakable. The selection made by Jesus during his life on earth points forward to the commissioning of the apostles by the exalted one (Luke 6.13b/Acts 1.8). The commission to bear witness is firmly anchored in the earthly life of Jesus.[2] Yet on the other hand it is equally noticeable how often the witness of the apostles is focused upon the resurrection (Acts 2.32; 3.15; 4.33; 13.31; Luke 24.48).[3] Side by side with the backward reference to the life of Jesus there is the preaching of salvation, the vital, forward looking message of the new life.[4] Asting brings out these two aspects of the apostolic witness in his careful way. He shows that the backward looking aspect "is entirely subordinated to the forward looking, vital and creative view of revelation".[5]

This completes the picture. The twelve apostles are for Luke the institutional agents of the Church as it takes shape in history. That is why they were called by the earthly Jesus—except Matthias, who was "elected" by the exalted Lord. Thus they are the embodiment of the true Israel, the place on earth where the Spirit is to be poured out "in the last days" (Acts 2.17). But they are also witnesses of the resurrection. In their person this foundational eschatological witness is riveted to a concrete place in history, namely the Church.[6]

[1] Cf. Asting, *Die Verkündigung des Wortes im Urchristentum*, pp. 599ff.

[2] Klein, ibid., pp. 203f.

[3] This argues for a formerly independent tradition, which Spitta, op. cit., p. 14, attributes to his source A.

[4] Asting, op. cit., pp. 605ff.

[5] Ibid., p. 614; Klein, op. cit., pp. 208f sees this tension in Luke's concept of witnesses as "primarily due to Luke's composition". According to Klein Luke was at pains to ensure the exclusive position of the apostles within a wider circle of Jesus' followers.

[6] On the presence of eschatological salvation in the community, see below, pp. 135f.

(d) The Church then has a human and historical aspect. In connection with this we must go back once more to John the Baptist. As we have seen, Luke connects him closely with Jesus, yet clearly distinguishes between the two figures.[1] Significant in this regard is the elaborate dating on Luke 3.1f and its relation to the ministry of Jesus. Luke "probably intends this dating to include the appearance of Jesus as well".[2] But although its connection with the beginning of Jesus' ministry is obvious,[3] it is significant that there is no direct mention of it, comprehensive and important though the dating is. The actual beginning of Jesus' ministry is marked in Luke 3.23 by the specific note on Jesus' age. If Luke really means to make a clear division between the period of John and the period of Jesus he could hardly merge the beginning of their respective ministries together. But the difficulty is solved if the difference between John and Jesus is one of quality rather than of time. Then they can work side by side, each with his own distinctive mission.[4]

John's mission remains within the old world. He is portrayed "just like an Old Testament prophet".[5] He sets the stage in history for the work of Jesus. Thus the eschatological activity of Jesus is given a place within the history of the world yet without "historizing" the Christ event. The separate dating in Luke 3.1f and 3.23 clearly marks off the old age from the new. But in the

[1] See above, pp. 21f.

[2] Conzelmann, RGG[3] III, col. 624 (cf. Klostermann, Lukas, p. 50); here, however, Conzelmann is inconsistent. Elsewhere he credits Luke with a pattern of redemptive history in which the period of John is sharply distinguished from that of Jesus (cf. St. Luke, p. 23). If the synchronism applies to the "period of Jesus", then John and Jesus are to be taken as contemporaneous.

[3] Cf. also Schlatter, Lukas, p. 29.

[4] Luke erases in 4.24 the temporal succession, which is strongly emphasized in Mark 1.14, by striking out μετὰ τὸ παραδοθῆναι τὸν Ἰωάννην from the text. On this see Zahn, Lukas, pp. 232f. This is exactly the same procedure as he followed in the apocalyptic discourse (cf. Mark 13.24 with Luke 21.25; see above, pp. 111ff). Because Mark includes the Baptist within the eschatological salvation event, he must clearly distinguish between the announcement of salvation by the Baptist and its fulfilment by Jesus (Mark 1.14). For Luke, on the contrary, the Baptist is the representative of the old age and stands outside the eschatological event of salvation. Since, however, for him the old age lasts into the present, the old and new ages overlap in the present as qualitative opposites.

[5] Friedrich, TWNT VI, p. 838, 13f. Originally the Baptist was undoubtedly a Messianic figure (Friedrich, ibid., p. 838, 35ff), but even for Q "John still stands outside the period of realized eschatology" (p. 842, 20ff).

person of John the Baptist the eschatological Christ event acquires historical continuity with Israel on the one hand and with the apostolate of the Twelve on the other. John comes before the twelve apostles, but like them he is an embodiment of the true Israel.[1]

(e) Luke 16.16 would seem to contradict what we have just said. There we read that the law and the prophets were until John. Since then the kingdom of God is preached and everyone enters into it violently. Conzelmann takes this passage as "the key to the topography of redemptive history".[2] There is a single redemptive history in which John and Jesus appear side by side. Yet they belong to different epochs, each clearly marked off from the other.[3] Now it is true that the temporal sequence in the text is unmistakable. By the omission of ἐπροφήτευσαν (Matthew 11.13) Luke 16.16a acquires a "clearly temporal meaning. The period of the law and the prophets last until John. Although John marks the shift of the aeons he belongs to the old age and forms its boundary line."[4]

But we must notice the level at which the point is made. Jesus is speaking to the Pharisees. He is talking about the external signs of the kingdom of God, the preaching of the kingdom by human agents. That this is the point is shown by the phrase ἀπὸ τότε, a very rare one in Luke.[5] Generally he uses ἀπὸ τοῦ νῦν to bring out the qualitative difference between two periods.[6] Luke 16.16 is an exception. Here two similar periods are placed side by side. The words ἀπὸ τότε separate them, but at the same time express the continuity between John the Baptist and the preaching of the kingdom of God.

---

[1] The OT framework in which the story of Jesus is couched comes out clearly, especially in the Lucan infancy narrative. Jesus grows up within the Jewish people "according to the law of Moses" (2.22), travels with his parents to the passover festival in Jerusalem (2.41ff), and goes "as his custom was" to the synagogue at Nazareth (4.26).

[2] St. Luke, p. 23. [3] St. Luke, p. 24.

[4] Friedrich, TWNT VI, p. 841, n. 367.

[5] In contrast to Matthew, who uses τότε ninety times (Jeremias, Parables, p. 82, n. 52); Bornkamm, Tradition, p. 47, speaks of Matthew's "beloved copula τότε".

[6] See above, pp. 98ff.

Let us look at these two periods more closely. The first is clearly the Old Testament period, which includes John the Baptist. But what is the second period marked by the preaching of the kingdom of God? There can be no doubt from Luke's usage elsewhere that it includes both the period of Jesus' ministry *and* the period of the Church. For the preaching of the kingdom of God is something that is done not only by Jesus (Luke 4.43; 8.1; 9.11, 60 etc.)[1] and the disciples (Luke 9.2), but later by the apostles as well (Acts 8.12; 20.25; 28.23, 31, etc.). The saying in Luke 16.16 thus places the old and the new periods side by side. Jesus marks the beginning of the kingdom of God which continues after he has left this earth. Thus the situation in the Old Testament is transcended. But it is not altogether abrogated. Rather, as is shown by the very next saying about the permanent validity of the law (v. 17), it is taken up into the new situation. The Church is continuous with "the law and the prophets", but it also transcends them through the preaching of the kingdom of God. Since it is under obedience to the will of God as recorded in the Old Testament it is the true Israel, able to take up the message of the kingdom and the new act of God in Christ.

It would seem therefore that we must divide Luke's pattern of redemptive history in a different way from Conzelmann.[2] He divides it into "three periods", of which the "central one" is that of Jesus.[3] But it is clear that Luke 16.16 only speaks of two periods, the old and the new. And the new period itself is again divided into two, at least from a historical point of view. There is also a major caesura within Luke–Acts. The Gospel describes the period of Jesus' earthly ministry, terminating with his departure from earth. Acts marks the period of the Church, characterized by the possession of the Spirit and the preaching of the kingdom of God, and lasting until Luke's own day (Acts 28.31). Here again there is further distinction between the earliest days of the Church, which are unique, and the later period.[4] But as I see it, there is a similar twofold division within

---

[1] But not by John. See above, p. 22, n. 1.
[2] Cf. *St. Luke*, *passim*, especially pp. 170ff.
[3] Conzelmann, ibid., p. 170.
[4] Conzelmann, ibid., pp. 14, 211, n. 1.

the ministry of Jesus itself. The caesura occurs at Luke 19.37. In their exaltant joy, the disciples look back on Jesus' mighty works, while Jesus goes up to Jerusalem to occupy the temple and to face his passion. The period of the mighty works is further divided by Luke 9.51 into the Galilean ministry and the journey to Jerusalem. Once more, the Jerusalem section can be divided into the teaching in the temple and the actual passion. Yet no precise division is apparent. What Luke is concerned about is that each period has its own distinctive character[1] and that one follows the other in time—a mark of genuine history.

The most important thing to notice is the way Luke distinguishes between a human history which is open to observation and that same history in its eschatological aspect, which eludes observation. Jesus is not the "centre of time" in any chronological sense. In his humanity he belongs to the new period marked by the preaching of the kingdom of God. In his divinity he stands outside of any chronological scheme, sharing God's contemporaneity with all human time. Conzelmann irons out Luke's distinctions and comes up with his dubious pattern of a redemptive history open to human observation. Such a view we have every reason to reject.

(f) In Luke 16.16 John the Baptist is the representative of the Old Testament period. He symbolizes the period in history which precedes the apostolic Church and its preaching of the kingdom of God. His period is a kind of ante-room, not only in the sense that he precedes the Church in time, but because the preceding period continues to be important for the period of the Church. This is illustrated in the two stories about Apollos and the disciples of John (Acts 18.24—19.7). Both passages deal with the baptism of John. His baptism is not enough to make a man a full Christian. Apollos has to be instructed by the Jewish couple, Priscilla and Aquila (18.26; cf. 18.2). The twelve disciples of John have to be baptized "in the name of the Lord Jesus" (19.5) and receive the Holy Spirit by the laying on of hands from Paul (vv. 6f). The disciples of John are very close to the Christian

---

[1] See above, pp. 30ff.

community, as is shown by the fact that they are actually called "disciples" (19.1)[1] implying that they are really Christians.[2] And all Apollos needed was to be "taught accurately the things concerning Jesus" (18.25).

Both Käsemann and Schweizer have insisted that these stories must not be taken historically. They have been written up by Luke. Käsemann says that the point of them is "the reception of ecclesiastical outsiders into the *Una sancta catholica*".[3] Schweizer thinks that they have something to do with the transformation of the Baptist tradition: "Just as the earlier tradition had transformed the eschatological preacher of repentance into the direct witness to Christ, so Luke transforms the disciples of John into forerunners of the Christian Church."[4] Käsemann interprets these stories in an "early catholic" direction. Luke, he maintains, was faced with the danger of gnosticism. That is why he wanted to picture the Church in the apostolic age as though it were free from divisions. Schweizer, however, interprets them along the lines of redemptive history. Luke, he contends, is anxious to show "the unbroken continuity of redemptive history from Judaism to the Christian Church".[5] Apollos and the disciples of John "represent an interim stage between Judaism and Christianity. But in the last resort they are Christians, and certainly not in competition with Christianity."[6] Schweizer is undoubtedly right against Käsemann in insisting that the *una sancta catholica* plays part anywhere else in Acts.[7] Rather, the whole movement of Acts 19.1–7 is "clearly towards the giving of the Spirit, marked by the outburst of glossolalia".[8]

Let us pursue the matter further along the lines suggested by Schweizer. In doing so we must bear in mind the clear distinction between the two levels, the human and historical, and the spiritual. The trouble with Käsemann is that he never gets beyond the

---

[1] μαθητής used in an absolute sense. [2] Haenchen, *Apg.*, p. 488.
[3] E. Käsemann, *Essays on N.T. Themes*, pp. 136ff; quotation, p. 141.
[4] E. Schweizer, "Die Bekehrung des Apollos, Apg. 18, 24–6", *EvTh* 15 (1955), pp. 247ff; the passage is on p. 248.
[5] Ibid., p. 253. [6] Ibid., p. 254.
[7] Not even Paul's collection is used as a demonstration of the *una sancta catholica* (op. cit., pp. 249f).
[8] Schweizer, op. cit., p. 249.

historical level. All he does is to shift the historical problem from Apollos and the disciples of John to Luke himself, whose ideas he simply places in their context in the history of religion. He ends up by making Luke a pragmatic ecclesiastical politician who uses an "ideological theology of history" to prove the legitimacy of his own claims.[1] He is thus blind to the theological import of the text, the truth behind which has a relevance beyond Luke's own immediate situation. True, the historical sequence of events in these passages is hard to decipher.[2] But this is due to Luke's reshaping of the tradition out of dogmatic interests, which points to a basic theological problem beginning in Luke's time but with a relevance beyond his day. This problem is the unity of the Church. But Luke is not advocating unity like some pragmatic ecclesiastical politician. He writes as he does because he knows that the divine revelation is bound to a particular place in history. This place is the apostolic Church, which has its beginnings in Jerusalem. Only there does the outpouring of the Holy Spirit take place.[3] Apollos and the disciples of John in their different ways occupy a position on the fringes of this Church, as the phrase "the baptism of John" indicates (18.25; 19.3). Apollos already knows about the Christian ὁδός (18.25). What he lacks is the vantage point in history designated by God. He must be brought into the Christian community by whose resources he is sustained. Hence the provision made by the "brethren" to enable the missionary to continue his journey (18.27). The disciples of John are in rather a different position. What they need is to be baptized in the name of Jesus and to receive the laying on of hands from an authorized representative of the apostolic Church to make them full Christians.

Once more John the Baptist, or in this case the Baptist community at Ephesus, appears as the embodiment of the old world in so far as it is open to the Christ event. Luke sees no contrariety between the Baptist's disciples and the Christian community. But

[1] Käsemann, op. cit., p. 148.
[2] Käsemann has brought out the point very clearly, ibid., pp. 136ff.
[3] Here Luke is not so far from Paul, who, as is well known, never broke off relations with Jerusalem (Bultmann, RGG² IV, col. 1025; G. Friedrich, "Die Gegner des Paulus im 2. Korintherbrief", Abraham unser Vater, 1963, pp. 213f).

neither are they on an equal level. The apostolic community enjoys the advantage of being the place where the Holy Spirit is outpoured. It embodies the unity of the Church in a common origin in history in the one Lord Jesus Christ.

(g) Thus far we have developed the Old Testament aspect of Luke's doctrine of the Church, its continuity with the history of Israel, and the unity of the Church based on a common origin in history. The acid test for this aspect of the Church is whether it is open for the eschatological—or, in Luke's language, heavenly —salvation. The apostolic community lived in a constant state of readiness to receive (Acts 1.13f) the Holy Spirit from heaven (Acts 2.1). The Church must show a similar openness towards those who are specially marked out by the Spirit of God. Apollos is just such a person, as we have seen, for he is described as being "fervent in Spirit" (18.25). We are told how he was accepted into the apostolic community. But we are also told of Stephen and Paul, two charismatics whose special relationship to the twelve apostles must now be shown.

The choice of the Seven (Acts 6.1–6), it seems to me, poses the question of an ordered ministry *vis à vis* a free, charismatic one. In a regularly ordered community there is always a danger of rigidity. When it succumbs to that danger it loses its capacity to meet the needs of the hour (in this instance, the "murmuring" of the Hellenists against the Hebrews, v. 1). So the community must be ready to accept new ministries raised up for it through charismatic endowments. But they in turn must become regular ministries in the community. That is why the Twelve take the initiative (vv. 2ff) in calling the seven pneumatics (v. 3) to a regular office in the Church.[1]

Among the Seven only Stephen stands out (Acts 6.8ff). There is a clear parallel between his martyrdom and the death of Jesus (7.59f). Indeed, Stephen's trial before the Sanhedrin (6.12–15) would seem to include material which Luke had omitted from the passion narrative, namely the prophecy about the destruction of

---

[1] Cf. this readiness on the part of the official Church in Luke to acknowledge charismatic gifts with the situation in 1 Clement.

the temple. The real charge against Stephen, his blasphemy against Moses and God (6.11), is introduced prior to his trial before the Sanhedrin, which makes the indictment there look like a doublet (vv. 13f).[1] In Stephen the reality of heaven becomes manifest. His face has the appearance of an angel (6.15; cf. Luke 20.36). He has a vision of the heavenly world (Acts 7.55f). Thus he is conformed to his Master "in suffering and glory". His death is the cause of unique turn of events, the transition to the mission outside of Palestine (Acts 8.4; 11.19ff). Thus Stephen plays a vital rôle in the apostolic community, which must find room for the charismatic. But his fate is strictly exceptional. No more than the death of Jesus does Stephen's martyrdom imply that all the disciples must become martyrs (Luke 22.35ff).[2]

(h) This tension between the two types of ministry, the regular and the extraordinary, comes out even more clearly in the way Luke portrays the relation between Paul and the twelve apostles. Klein is of the opinion that Luke's idea of the twelve apostles is a deliberate attempt to downgrade Paul and to put him in a kind of apostolic succession. Only so can Paul be saved for the Church at a time when gnostic circles were claiming him for themselves.[3] But, as Schmithals rightly argues, "Luke–Acts contains no traces of any opposition to gnosticism".[4] Now Klein is perfectly right when he maintains that the Paul of Acts is incorporated into the apostolic Church originating from Jerusalem.[5] Thus far we can go along with him, and the reader is referred to his discussion of this point.[6]

But Paul must now be considered from an entirely different point of view. It is only by his gnostic theory that Klein can explain the striking fact that this compromising type of Paul takes the leading part in the later chapters of Acts, while the Twelve

[1] Surkau, *Martyrien*, p. 108.
[2] The historical question of the relation of Hebrews and Hellenists in Jerusalem is not affected by this interpretation of the Lucan conception. On this see Friedrich, op. cit., pp. 181ff.
[3] Op. cit., pp. 162ff.
[4] W. Schmithals, *Das kirchliche Apostelamt*, 1961, p. 272.
[5] So too Schmithals, op. cit., p. 269.   [6] Op. cit., pp. 162ff.

fade into the background.[1] Luke's dialectical method enables him to incorporate Paul into ecclesiastical tradition and yet give him a unique place of his own. We will try to show this in detail.

First, let us see how Paul is put on the same level as the apostles. As a miracle worker he in no way is inferior to them. On the contrary, there is a striking "parallel between the exploits and adventures of Peter and the older apostles and those of Paul".[2] On the other hand Paul enjoys a certain superiority over the other apostles. The latter are "chosen" by the Lord (Luke 6.13; Acts 1.24), whereas Paul is a σκεῦος ἐκλογῆς for his Lord (Acts 9.15).[3] Furthermore, Paul is not only a "mediate" figure. He stands, to use Klein's language, "in a direct relation to the kingdom".[4] He has a dream and a vision in Troas (Acts 16.8f). At Corinth the Lord speaks to him by night (18.9f). In Jerusalem the Lord tells him about his impending journey to Rome (23.11). During the storm at sea the angel of God promises him that the whole of the ship's company will be saved (27.24). The three conversion stories oscillate between mediacy and direct relationship. In Acts 9.1ff Paul receives a direct call and mediated confirmation of it from Ananias. In Acts 22.1ff its mediate character comes out in the way Paul receives his commission in Jerusalem to preach to the Gentiles (vv. 17ff). In the third story the mediate aspect is completely lacking. There Paul is appointed by a "heavenly vision" from the Lord as a "servant and witness" (26.16, 19). This presentation of the two different aspects brings out clearly the dual position of Paul. While the second version connects his call to the history of Israel (Jerusalem, 22.17), the speech before Agrippa affirms his direct commission from heaven (26.16, "I have appeared to you" and v. 17, "I send you").

Finally, Paul is distinguished from the apostles because of his sufferings. Of course, the apostles also had to endure suffering

---

[1] Haenchen, *Apg.*, p. 103.

[2] Holtzmann, *Apg.*, p. 18, who marshals the parallels: the healing of the man born impotent (3.2ff/ 14.8ff); the raising of the dead (9.36ff/20.9ff); the miraculous deliverance from prison (12.7/16.26); miracles (5.15/19.12) etc.

[3] The expression is a *hapax legomenon* in the NT and with its fuller language brings out the election of Paul. Further, Paul is placed by the μοι in an intimate personal relationship with his Lord.

[4] Op. cit., *passim.* e.g., p. 158.

(Acts 5.40; 12.1ff). But for Paul, suffering is the hallmark of his life. He is promised suffering at the moment of his election (Acts 9.16, which stands in dialectical contrast with the full authority for his mission conferred at 26.16ff). The difficulties created by the "transition from Paul's call to be a missionary to his call to suffering in Christ's message to Ananias" are discussed in detail by Klein.[1] Some of Klein's observations are very acute. First, the promise of suffering in 9.16 is linked by the connecting particle γάρ (which has a slightly adversative meaning, "certainly"),[2] with the reference to his election in v. 15. Suffering and election are thus closely associated. Second, elsewhere in Luke πάσχειν "in the pregnant sense of suffering for one's faith" always applies to Jesus. Third, in Paul's letters apostolic service and apostolic suffering always go hand in hand (1 Corinthians 4.9ff; 15.30f; 11.24ff, etc.). But for Luke, "the combination of suffering with the ἐκλογή of Paul is a sort of *tour de force*", and in any case is quite exceptional. For Luke is otherwise very restrained in his use of the conventional language of martyrdom.

Klein's solution is not very convincing. His conclusion is that Paul's election is circumscribed by the suffering directly laid on him by Jesus ("I will show him . . ."). But there is a simpler solution. Paul's suffering makes him an apostolic (that is, a "regular") witness to Jesus. For through suffering he is conformed to Christ. Like his Master, he goes up to Jerusalem to suffer, with his eyes wide open, ready to die there like him.[3]

Here is another case of climactic parallelism. Paul's relation with the apostles corresponds exactly to that between the two

---

[1] Ibid., pp. 148ff; esp. n. 713.   [2] Arndt & Gingrich, *Lexicon*, p. 151.

[3] Acts 21.13. The journey of Paul to Jerusalem is shaped with this in mind. It is repeatedly emphasized in the text (19.21; 20.16; 21.15, 17). Paul goes up to Jerusalem "bound in the Spirit" (20.22), where, as the Holy Spirit testifies, "imprisonment and afflictions" await him (20.23; cf. 21.4, 10ff). The prophecy of Agabus (21.11) recalls the passion prediction in Mark 10.35. The exclamation of Paul's companions, "The will of the Lord be done" (21.14) agrees in substance with Jesus' prayer in Gethsemane (Matt. 26.42; Luke 22.42). Paul's willingness to die in Jerusalem takes the place (a very ingenious piece of authorship) of the fact that he was only arrested in Jerusalem (21.13). Perhaps this is the reason why Luke does not mention the collection, though he does so later (24.17). It would not have suited his intention of allowing Paul to go up to Jerusalem as Jesus went up to his passion

missionary charges in the Gospel.[1] The apostles embody the true Israel, the Church in history and in the world. As a member of this same Church, Paul is subordinated to the apostles. But primarily he is the symbol of the new act of God in Jesus Christ, which burst the old world wide open. Of course the apostles also serve in the same capacity, for they are also witnesses of the resurrection. But Paul stands in a special relationship to his Lord. The Lord acts directly through him and grants him the privilege of sharing in his (eschatological) suffering.[2]

(i) There is, then, in Luke's doctrine of the Church, a tension between historical continuity and receptivity for the eschatological salvation. Our last example of this tension will be Luke's use of $\lambda\alpha\acute{o}s$ and $\acute{o}\delta\acute{o}s$ (as a designation of the Christian community or its doctrine). There are thirty-six occurrences of $\lambda\alpha\acute{o}s$ in the Gospel and forty-eight in Acts. So it is undoubtedly one of "Luke's favourite words".[3] With few exceptions it is used exclusively of the Jewish people.[4] There is an important point of theology here. "The early Catholic point of view, which refuses to allow the name Israel to Judaism and regards the Church as the only true Israel, is therefore not yet reached."[5]

How does this general situation throughout Luke–Acts[6] square with passages like Acts 15.14 ($\lambda\alpha\grave{o}s$ $\acute{e}\xi$ $\acute{e}\theta\nu\hat{\omega}\nu$) and 18.10, which says that the exalted Lord has $\lambda\alpha\acute{o}s$ $\pi o\lambda\acute{u}s$ in Corinth? In both instances $\lambda\alpha\acute{o}s$ obviously means the Christian community. D. J. Dupont has tried to show that the Jewish term in Acts 15.14 has been widened so as to include the whole world.[7] N. A. Dahl, however, rejects this redemptive-historical type of exegesis, insisting that the two passages in question are exceptions to

[1] See above, pp. 23f.
[2] On the eschatological character of Jesus' sufferings see below. pp. 157ff.
[3] Strathmann, *TWNT* IV, p. 49, 56ff.   [4] Harnack, *Acts*, p. 50.
[5] Schweizer, *Church Order*, p. 63. Here Luke is following a tradition which must go back to Jesus. Jesus also "knows no church separate from all Israel", but lives "entirely within the national and religious associations of Israel" (Schweizer, ibid., p. 20; Cf. W. G. Kümmel, *Kirchenbegriff und Geschichtsbewusstsein in der Urgemeinde und bei Jesus*, 1943, p. 42).
[6] Cf. the parallel between $\lambda\alpha\acute{o}s$ and $\acute{o}\chi\lambda os$ in Luke. As Jesus journeys through Samaria the $\lambda\alpha\acute{o}s$ is conspicuous by its absence.
[7] D. J. Dupont, "$\Lambda A O\Sigma$ '$E\Xi$ '$E\Theta N\Omega N$ (Acts XV. 14)", *NTS* 3 (1956), pp. 47ff.

Luke's otherwise consistent usage. The point, he argues, is that
the Gentiles are now admitted to a share in the hope of Israel, as
was promised in Zechariah 2.15 LXX. The Church is the true
Israel, but cannot be identified with it.[1] In a similar vein, Goppelt
maintains that Luke sees "an organic development of the Church
from Judaism".[2] Yet, he continues, Luke's picture of Christianity
is not that of "a higher stage of historical development compared
with Judaism, but its eschatological antithesis".[3] But how can
Christianity be both the eschatological antithesis of Judaism and
its direct continuation? He does not explain.

The use of λαός in the message of the angel in Luke 2.10ff
may help us to answer this question. Originally vv. 10–12 referred
to the Jewish people, not to all peoples.[4] But Luke clearly intends
the joyous message to be for "all people", just as the ensuing
canticle of the heavenly host promises peace on earth to men of
good will. Luke widens the application but keeps it earthbound.
The community enjoys peace on earth (Acts 9.31), a counterpart
to the glory of God in heaven (Luke 2.14). Note carefully
the distinction between the two realms. On the historical level the
community is indeed the true Israel. It is a "people out of the
Gentiles", as in Acts 15.14. But the community is not a new Israel
in a historical sense. The adjective "new" applies to the eschatological or heavenly fulfilment of the Old Testament promises.
That which is new bursts open the confines of history. It is a
heavenly, not an earthly reality, and does not allow of absorption
into history. More will be said about this later on pp. 135ff.

The term λαός, then, expresses the historical continuity
between Israel and the Church. The uniqueness of the Christian
community, however, is expressed by another Greek word,
ὁδός.[5] What is implied by this curious use of the word? Michaelis
avers that this particular usage is "unparalleled anywhere else in
the New Testament, and cannot be explained from its derivation".[6] Bultmann translates it "direction" but proposes the

---

[1] N. A. Dahl "A People for His Name (Acts XV, 14)", NTS 4 (1947), pp. 319ff.
[2] L. Goppelt, Christentum und Judentum im 1. und 2. Jahrhundert, 1954, p. 228.
[3] Ibid., p. 233.   [4] Foerster, TWNT VII, p. 1015, 33.
[5] Acts 9.2; 19.9, 23; 22.4; 24.14, 22; cf. Bultmann, Theology II p. 116.
[6] Michaelis, TWNT V, p. 95, 1ff.

K

"Christian religion" as the best equivalent. He thinks it fore-shadows the later notion of the Christian as the "third kind".[1]

All the same, it makes good sense to translate it literally as "direction". This fits in exactly with Luke's use of the word λαός. The Christian community is not in competition with the Jewish people, but is still a "direction" within Judaism. In no sense does Luke regard it as a "new religion",[2] or he could not apply the word λαός so unambiguously to the Jews. It would make nonsense of Acts' description of the Church as the true Israel. But the term ὁδός expresses a clear dividing line within Judaism. Thus the use of ὁδός = way is perfectly justified. Christians are distinct from Jews because they follow the Master in his footsteps.[3] It is very much an earthly way on which the disciples[4] follow him. But along this way they share the victory of their Lord which marks the end of history.

So in Luke the historical λαός and the band of disciples who follow the ὁδός in personal decision (the brethren or believers) stand in dialectical contrast.[5] The only real difference between the Christian faith and Judaism is the confession of Jesus Christ. The new, eschatological reality is concentrated in the person of Jesus Christ, and this is what gives it its unique meaning.

Luke's doctrine of the Church is a complex one. He uses a variety of images to describe the Church as both "institution and

---

[1] Op. cit., p. 116.

[2] Thus, Grässer, *Parousieverzögerung*, following Bultmann, p. 212, and Schweizer, *Church Order*, p. 69, n. 258.

[3] See above, pp. 73ff.

[4] The absolute use of μαθητής in Luke (Acts 6.1f, 7; 9.10, 19, 26, 38; 11.26, 29; 13.52; 14.20, 22, 28; 15.10; 16.1; 18.23, 27; 19.1, 9, 30; 21.4, 16), underlines our thesis that Luke knows no form of the community going beyond the Jewish λαός. According to Schweizer, *Church Order*, "we can find in Luke no rigidly drawn outline of the idea of a Church". Along with the disciples Luke knows of "brethren" (Acts 1.15; 9.30; 10.23; 11.1, 29; 12.17; 14.2; 15.1, 3, 22; 23.32f etc.) and "believers" (2.44; 4.32; 18.27; 19.18; 21.20 = Jews; 21.25 = Gentiles; Schweizer, op. cit., pp. 66f). Always it is the individual that matters. Individuals stand in a special relation to Christ and thereby are bound to one another. Here is another Johannine "trait" in Luke. (On the similarity between Acts and John in their use of the term μαθητής cf. Rengstorf, *TWNT* IV, 463.)

[5] Cf. the distinction between people and disciples in the instructions of Jesus (see above, pp. 23f) and the thoroughgoing dialectic between the general-historical and eschatological aspects (see above, pp. 13–20).

event".[1] The Old Testament prototype remains basic for the continuing shape of the Church, but as the Church actually emerges it is its relation to Christ that really matters. The former of these truths is symbolized by the twelve apostles, who constitute the true Israel, by John the Baptist as the representative of the old world as God had willed it to be, and by the λαός, the people of God who live under his word. Their relationship to Christ in the narrower sense is described as a direct participation in his suffering and death. Stephen and Paul are examples of this. In a wider sense it means discipleship and belonging to the ὁδός. The apostles occupy a key position in this scheme. They are the agents of continuity in history, witnesses of the Risen Lord, and recipients of the Holy Spirit.

C. THE PRESENCE OF
SALVATION IN THE COMMUNITY

1. *Jesus Christ and the Holy Spirit*

In the Lucan writings the presence of salvation is secured in two ways—through the presence of Christ and through the gift of the Spirit. In the following pages our task will be to define their respective functions. We must at all costs free ourselves of the popular dogma that Christ is present in the community through the Spirit. For Luke the present Lord and the gift of the Spirit are parallel, but independent and complementary in operation.

This applies to the period of Christ's exaltation. During his life on earth Jesus was specially endowed with the Holy Spirit. We will take up this latter point first.[2]

[1] J. L. Leuba, *New Testament Pattern*, 1953, in discussing the institutional and the spiritual ways in which God works, always follows the "Lucan" line.

[2] On the significance of the Holy Spirit for Lucan theology cf. von Baer (see above, p. 43, n. 4); Barrett (ibid.); G. W. H. Lampe, "The Holy Spirit in the Writings of St. Luke", *Studies in the Gospels*, ed. D. E. Nineham, 1955, pp. 159ff; E. Ehrhardt, "The Construction and Purpose of the Acts of the Apostles", *StTh* 12 (1958), pp. 45ff. In the framework of our investigation we can only concern ourselves with the attempt to define the theological context of the language about the Holy Spirit in Luke's conception of redemptive history.

(a) The conception of Jesus through the Holy Spirit (Luke 1.35) and his baptism undoubtedly represent two parallel but competing traditions.[1] However, Luke connects them by the term $\pi\nu\epsilon\hat{v}\mu\alpha$ $\ddot{\alpha}\gamma\iota o\nu$.[2] This complementary tradition produces two different conceptions of the relation between Jesus and the Spirit. According to Luke 1.35 the human life of Christ proceeds from the creative power of God.[3] In his bodily existence Jesus is under the control of the $\delta\dot{v}\nu\alpha\mu\iota s$ of God. The Holy Spirit acts "*comme le principe de sa vie physique*".[4] Even in his earthly life Jesus is the new divine creation. He is not merely filled with the Holy Spirit from his mother's womb like John the Baptist (Luke 1.15). His human life as such is divinely created.[5]

The story of the baptism puts it in a different way. Here Jesus receives the Holy Spirit as a gift, "in bodily form" (3.21f). This happens to him while he is praying. Luke does not regard this simply as a doublet of 1.35. The baptism narrative serves to protect the story of the conception through the Holy Spirit from being misunderstood. It is not that Jesus was provided with a non-human, supernatural kind of body. In the baptism narrative Jesus is entirely man, "adopted" as the Son of God by being endowed with the Holy Spirit.[6] As Luke sees it, this is the realization in history of what Jesus had actually been from birth.[7]

[1] Klostermann, *Lukas*, pp. 55f.

[2] Mark 1.10 only speaks of the $\pi\nu\epsilon\hat{v}\mu\alpha$; Luke amplifies it in 3.22 to $\tau\grave{o}$ $\ddot{\alpha}\gamma\iota o\nu$; cf. Matt. 3.16, $\pi\nu\epsilon\hat{v}\mu\alpha$ $\theta\epsilon o\hat{v}$.

[3] The two clauses in v. 35 are parallel to one another and "in substance convey the same meaning" (Hauck, *Lukas*, p. 25).

[4] Loisy, *Luc*, pp. 89f.

[5] Here "physical" must not be taken in a naturalistic sense. This is a modern category and alien to Luke. The way the Spirit is received remains a mystery (this is rightly emphasized by von Baer, *Der heilige Geist*, p. 127ff, in his exposition of the word $\dot{\epsilon}\pi\iota\sigma\kappa\iota\dot{\alpha}\sigma\epsilon\iota$). The only important thing is that Jesus' corporeal and creaturely existence is created by the Spirit, i.e., by God.

[6] The D Text must be original. It well accords with the framework of Lucan theology (cf. Friedrich, "Hohepriestererwartung", p. 283); the contrary view is taken by Conzelmann, *St. Luke*, p. 21, n. 3.

[7] Hahn, *Hoheitstitel*, p. 318, quite rightly observes that $\kappa\lambda\eta\theta\dot{\eta}\sigma\epsilon\tau\alpha\iota$ $\upsilon\dot{\iota}\grave{o}s$ $\theta\epsilon o\hat{v}$ in 1.35 is connected in the total framework of the Lucan narrative with the event of the baptism. But the dialectical tension between a substantial endowment with the Spirit in the pneumatic conception and the actual impartation of the Spirit in the baptism must not be removed. Luke interprets Mark in such a way that the entry of the Spirit into Jesus, which Mark places at the baptism (1.10 = $\epsilon\dot{\iota}s$ $\alpha\dot{v}\tau\dot{o}\nu$;

Conversely, 1.35 serves to protect the baptism narrative from an "adoptionist" interpretation. It is not that Jesus was a devout human being who was elected to be the Son of God at his baptism. By means of this complementary parallelism the mystery of Jesus' person is kept intact.[1]

(b) Luke's idea of the matter is quite different from Mark's. In the incidents following the baptism the Holy Spirit continues to play a special part. Mark and Matthew seem to be not quite sure what to do with the gift of the Holy Spirit to Jesus in his baptism. But for Luke the Spirit is "a power which continues to work in the Saviour" (Luke 4.1, 14, 18).[2]

As the bearer of the Holy Spirit Jesus is at once unique and comparable to other men. In Luke 4.18 Jesus says: "The Spirit of the Lord is upon me because he has anointed me." Quite obviously, the anointing took place at his baptism[3] and implies that Jesus is unique (cf. Acts 10.38). But in Luke 4.1 it is different. Here Jesus returns "full of the Holy Spirit" from the Jordan River. This formula is used all the way through Luke–Acts. Not only Jesus, but other faithful men under both the old and new covenants are so designated.[4] Here Jesus is on a level with the apostles and the heroes of the old covenant. The statements about Jesus' endowment with the Holy Spirit thus serve both purposes. They distinguish Jesus as one who stands in a specially close relationship to God with a unique commission. But they also describe him as a man who like other men receives the Holy Spirit as a gift.[5]

Luke and Matthew = $\dot{\epsilon}\pi$' αὐτόν), is shifted backwards to the birth of Jesus. We have already noted a similar procedure in the eschatological discourses of Jesus (see above, pp. 13ff).

[1] Cf. the analogous statements about the Baptist; he is equipped with the Holy Spirit from his mother's womb (1.15), he will nevertheless receive a call like the OT prophets (3.1f; von Baer, op. cit., p. 49).

[2] E. Norden, Geburt, pp. 92–9. For von Baer, op. cit., p. 55, the Holy Spirit is "the bearer of the dominant motif of redemptive history".

[3] Friedrich, op. cit., p. 285.

[4] John (Luke 1.15), Elizabeth (1.41), Zacharias (2.35), Simeon (2.35), Peter (Acts 4.8), Stephen (7.55), Paul (9.17; 13.9), Barnabas (11.24), the Seven (6.3), "all" at Pentecost (2.4; cf. 4.31).

[5] This dialectic is unnoticed by Schweizer, TWNT VI, pp. 402f. Schweizer shows convincingly that Jesus in Luke is not a pneumatic in the common or garden sense. But, given the parallelism in expression, can it be denied that Jesus is also comparable to other instances of endowment with the Spirit?

(c) So much, then, for the Spirit in the earthly life of Jesus. But what of the Spirit's relation to the exalted Lord? What special function does he have in that connection? First, let us see how the Spirit is related to Christ. The Christ, who was conceived through the Holy Spirit and endowed with the Spirit at his baptism, is now exalted, and pours out the Spirit on the Church (Acts 2.33). The connection is surely not accidental. It probably has a previous history in Jewish sectarianism, with its doctrine of the triple creation of man through the Holy Spirit.[1] In any case, it results in a single, consistent interpretation of the Lucan doctrine of the Spirit, equating the latter with the fresh, creative power of God at work in the world.

Here we have the clue to the various operations which Luke ascribes to the Holy Spirit. This is obvious in the birth of Jesus. In the baptism narrative the insertion of σωματικῷ εἴδει (Luke 3.22) brings out the physical character of the Spirit's operation there. Then at Pentecost the Spirit releases ecstatic powers (Acts 2.4ff), chiefly the gift of prophecy (2.17f).[2] Similarly, the Spirit creates new life in the community. But the Holy Spirit has no soteriological functions. These are the prerogatives of the present Christ. The Spirit does not produce faith nor does he convey the forgiveness of sins. Rather, he follows conversion as the power of new life both in the individual and in the community.[3]

Thus the operation of the Spirit is parallel to, but independent of, the work of Christ. True, both are concerned with the one event of salvation,[4] but each in his respective sphere, which is

---

[1] Cf. O. Betz, "Die Geburt der Gemeinde durch den Lehrer", NTS 3 (1956–7), p. 325; Betz's suggestion is followed by Grundmann, Lukas, pp. 26f.

[2] According to Schweizer, Spirit of God, 1960, p. 41, "Luke regards prophesying, προφητεύειν, as the central and decisive activity of the Spirit". In Acts 2.18c "and they prophesy" is a Lucan interpolation in the quotation from Joel. The word γλῶσσαι in Acts 2 is consciously used by Luke in more senses than one. It includes ecstatic speech (v. 4), the reception of the Spirit (v. 3), and miraculous language (v. 11), and in the speech of Peter is interpreted as the gift of prophecy (vv. 17f; cf. 19.6; 10.46). Cf. Kretschmar, Himmelfahrt, pp. 234f; E. Lohse, "Die Bedeutung des Pfingstberichtes im Rahmen des lk. Geschichtswerkes", EvTh 13 (1953), pp. 422ff; Conzelmann, Apg., p. 27.

[3] Cf. Schweizer, Spirit, p. 49.

[4] The Spirit is poured out by the exalted Lord (Acts 2.33); cf. the unity in the manner in which both the Spirit and the exalted Lord act over the guidance of the community from heaven (see below, pp. 142ff).

quite distinct. That is why Luke draws no parallel between the baptism of Jesus at the Jordan and the Spirit-baptism of the disciples at Pentecost—a parallel which might easily have suggested itself by Acts 1.5, "You shall be baptized with the Holy Spirit."[1] The resurrection and the outpouring of the Spirit do not coincide as in John 20.19ff. In Acts if they are depicted as two distinct events, divided by a circumstantial account of the disciples and the women waiting in Jerusalem and the choice of Matthias to replace Judas. Moreover, the parallelism between Luke 9.51 and Acts 2.1 is remarkable: ἐν τῷ συμπληροῦσθαι τὰς (τὴν) ἡμέρας (-αν). The exaltation of Christ and the outpouring of the Spirit stand side by side, but are separated in time and place. Lastly, there is a parallelism to be noted between the Spirit and the "name of Jesus". The apostles heal (Acts 3.6, 16; 4.10, 30; 19.13) and preach (4.12, 17f; 5.28, 40) in the name of Jesus. They suffer for the sake of his name (5.41; 9.16; 21.13). Thus the exalted Christ is present to the community in virtue of his name.[2] This name has the power to save (Acts 2.21). But it is the Holy Spirit that fills the community with courage (4.31) and comfort (9.31), thus equipping it for its divine mission in the world (19.6; 20.28).

Hence there is a clear distinction of function between Christ and the Spirit. The Spirit-endowed Church remains the counterpart of its Lord, not merely the extension of his personality. Once again, we see how Luke averts the danger which was threatening the Church in his time. He might of course have simply carried on the Pauline kerygma, "The Lord is the Spirit" (2 Cor. 3.17). But that would have lent colour to false notions of a sacral history. Then—but only then—would we be entitled to treat him as a protagonist of "early catholicism".[3]

[1] Von Baer, op. cit., pp. 57f.

[2] On the name of Jesus cf. Bietenhard, *TWNT* V, pp. 272ff; Conzelmann, *St. Luke*, pp. 177f.

[3] Käsemann, "Paulus und der Frühkatholizismus", p. 81, rightly perceives that the Pauline doctrine of the Church as the body of Christ prepares the way for the early catholic view, which ties Christology and ecclesiology indissolubly together, thus making the Church the constitutive part of the redemptive event. If Käsemann then regards Paul as "a pioneer of early catholicism" (p. 77), Luke's strict differentiation between Christology and ecclesiology is all the more remarkable. The "heavenly affinities of the post-apostolic doctrine of the church"

The fact is, Luke more than any other New Testament theologian fought against this danger of a confusion between salvation and history. But the Spirit does not acquire any functions detached from Christ. The fresh, creative power which he brings is always dependent on the prior salvation of men effected by Christ himself.[1]

The way is now open for the next stage of our investigation. First, we will discuss the gift of the Holy Spirit to the community, then the presence of Christ in his Church.

2. *The Presence of Salvation in the Gift of the Holy Spirit*

(a) At Pentecost the Holy Spirit is poured out upon the Church (Acts 2.33; 2.1ff). Schweizer is quite right when he speaks of "the abiding of the Spirit in the Church".[2] Who is it who possesses the Spirit? According to the Pentecost story, "all" are filled with the Spirit (2.4; cf. 4.31). Yet it is the apostles who have the authority to pass on the Spirit through the laying on of hands (8.14–17). But the Pentecost narrative should not be read in the light of this later passage.[3] It was not only the apostles who received the Spirit at Pentecost. The word "all" in v. 4 comes from the prophecy of Joel cited in vv. 17f, where the whole community, including women and slaves, is promised the Spirit of prophecy.[4] This gift of the Spirit to the whole Church does not of course exclude a special power for its leaders (8.14ff; 19.6).[5]

It is curious that the outpouring of the Spirit is repeated more than once after Pentecost. Sometimes this can be explained on the ground that it happens "where a new step is taken into the

asserted by F.-H. Kettler, "Enderwartung und himmlischer Stufenbau im Kirchenbegriff des nachapostolischen Zeitalters", *ThLZ* 79 (1954), pp. 385ff (col. 392), is entirely absent from Luke (see above, p. 39, n. 3).

[1] Baptism in the name of Jesus follows the giving of the Spirit as a special act (Acts 2.38; 8.16; 19.5f). In exceptional cases (the commission of Gentiles, 10.44f) the procedure may be reversed.

[2] Op. cit., p. 39.   [3] So Schmithals, op. cit., p. 234.

[4] That all members of the community are called to prophecy is the salient difference between Christian and OT-Jewish prophecy (Friedrich, *TWNT* VI, p. 850, 25ff; cf. Schweizer, *Spirit*, p. 48.)

[5] Conzelmann, *St. Luke*, p. 108, n. 1.

world" (Acts 8.17; 10.44ff).[1] But in Acts 4.31 it is the same group of people who are involved as at Pentecost. The Church is filled with the Holy Spirit in answer to prayer. The point Luke wishes to make is that the Holy Spirit is never a possession which the Church can use at will. The Spirit was indeed given once for all and will abide with the Church until Christ returns. But the Church "possesses" the Spirit only by constantly receiving him anew. In Acts 4.31 Luke shows "the actualization of Pentecost".[2]

(b) All this throws some light on the question of whether the outpouring of the Spirit is an eschatological event or not. E. Lohse maintains that where the Church is living through the power of the Spirit there is realized eschatology. Yet Pentecost "inaugurates a new period in redemptive history, the last stage before the parousia and the end of the world".[3] Conzelmann[4] and Schweizer[5] regard redemptive history and eschatology as mutually exclusive. On this view Pentecost is "for Luke not the eschatological" event. "It introduces a, but not the, new age."[6]

Now it cannot be doubted that Luke regards the Spirit as the superhuman power of God.[7] It is not a power immanent within history. But the Spirit does produce new life in history. The fresh creative operation of the Spirit, as we have seen, is always given and received anew. It comes "down from heaven", from the world of God where the Spirit originates (Acts 2.2, 33). The fact that the Spirit is connected with the world of God suggests that both the exaltation of Christ and the outpouring of the Spirit

[1] Schweizer, *Spirit*, p. 48; cf. Acts 19.6.

[2] Conzelmann, *Apg.*, p. 38; a similar tension between possession of the Spirit and constantly renewed reception of the Spirit applies to the individual Christian (Schweizer, *Spirit*, p. 40).

[3] "Pfingstbericht", pp. 432f.   [4] *St. Luke*, p. 183.   [5] *Spirit*, p. 48.

[6] Schweizer, ibid.; cf. the discussion about the reading in Acts 2.17. Haenchen, "Schriftzitate und Textüberlieferung in der Apg.", *ZThK* 51 (1954), p. 162, deduces the originality of the B text μετὰ ταῦτα from his understanding of Lucan theology; similarly Schweizer, *Spirit*, p. 46, n. 2. Conversely F. Mussner argues for an eschatological understanding of the Pentecost speech of Peter (*BZ* NF 5 (1961), pp. 263ff), and therefore for the originality of ἐν ταῖς ἐσχάταις ἡμέραις (see above, p. 44, n. 2).

[7] Schweizer, *Spirit*, pp. 37ff; O. Glombitza, "Zur Charakterisierung des Stephanus in Act 6 and 7," *ZNW* 53 (1962), p. 240.

are really eschatological events. But for Luke this does not make the history of the Church equally eschatological. To understand redemptive history in this way would be to confound divine with human activity, which would be intolerable. When we speak of the Spirit as eschatological we mean that it is eschatology made present. Through the Spirit the new life which comes from God is constantly renewed in the community. The continuity of the Spirit's operation is undeniable. After all, the Spirit was "poured out" upon the Church. But this continuity is never institutional. It is not for men to do what they like with it. The abiding presence of the Spirit is still a superhuman gift, for which the faithful must wait, and which they must be ready to receive.

(c) The indwelling Spirit does not make man or his history divine in a Hellenistic sense. This is shown by the way the Spirit guides the community. Here the Spirit is personal power, distinct from the community or the individual leader and guiding them from outside. The Spirit tells Philip to join the eunuch in his carriage (Acts 8.29). The Spirit tells Peter to go with the messengers Cornelius had sent to fetch him (10.19f; 11.12). While the community is engaged in worship the Spirit orders the commissioning of Barnabas and Saul (13.2). As Paul journeys through Phrygia and Galatia it is the Spirit who hinders the preaching of the word and stops him from travelling on to Bithynia (16.6f).

The last of these passages speaks both of the Holy Spirit (v. 6) and of the Spirit of Jesus (v. 7). It looks as though Christ and the Spirit are interchangeable so far as the guidance of the community is concerned. In Acts 23.11 it is the Lord who sends Paul on his way to Rome. In 27.23f it is the angel of the Lord who appears to Paul, and tells him what to do, just as in the case of Philip (8.26). Since Acts refers to both God and Christ as κύριος,[1] the passage throughout would appear to imply an interaction between heaven and earth. It is the one divine Ego (10.20) that gives the community its directions from heaven.[2]

[1] Haenchen, *Apg.*, p. 82, n. 9.

[2] The gift of prophecy vouchsafed through the Holy Spirit is the bracket between the fresh creative and guiding functions of the Spirit. On the traditio-historical problem cf. Schweizer, *Erniedrigung*, pp. 83f.

Thus the history of the community acquires world-wide significance. For in the community, under the guidance of the Spirit the divine plan of salvation becomes a reality. This plan now calls for discussion.[1] The theologumenon is expressed in the following terms. The whole divine economy of salvation is designated by the term βουλή (Luke 7.30; Acts 20.27 and, in reference to Christ only, Acts 2.23; 4.28; 5.38).[2] It is also remarkable how many compounds occur with προ–. These may be divided into two groups. One group deals with divine predestination. Christ (Acts 3.20), the witnesses of the resurrection (10.41), Paul (22.14; 26.16), and even Jesus' opponents (4.28), are said to be predestined by God to do certain things. The other group refers to the word of God in scripture. This word is "prophesied" (1.16), seen beforehand in visions (2.31), proclaimed beforehand (3.18; 7.52; 13.24). From this it will be seen how the word of God in scripture is associated with divine predestination. The word of prophecy in the Old Testament is thus translated into the Hellenistic view of the world and time, and its meaning enlarged to embrace heaven and earth.[3]

The word δεῖ is also connected with this understanding of scripture. It is used with especial frequency in Luke.[4] It expresses submission to the will of God, which "personally summons men and which fashions history according to its plan".[5] Jesus himself submits to that will (Luke 4.43; 13.33; 22.37; 24.44, and,

[1] S. Schulz, ZNW 54 (1963), pp. 104ff, speaks of "divine providence in Luke". That is a correct rendering of Lucan usage, but must not be allowed to suggest that Luke is here concerned with the divine government of this world in a general way, in the sense in which the expression is used in dogmatics. Luke is also aware of such a "providence" in this sense, as part of the first article of the creed, but it remains peripheral to his main concern (Acts 14.17; 17.26). He always restricts realization of God's *redemptive* plan to the apostolic community.

[2] Cf. Schrenk, TWNT I [E.T.], pp. 635f.

[3] This broadening out of the OT promise as fulfilled by Christ to include the whole cosmos can be misread as a general doctrine of divine providence, in which the scriptural proof is reduced to a relative status (Schulz, op. cit., pp. 105f). The scriptural promise is, however, not limited, but transcended by the enthronement of Christ in heaven. "Redemptive history" now embraces the whole cosmos (see above, pp. 102ff).

[4] According to E. Fascher ("Theologische Beobachtungen zu δεῖ ", *Nt.liche Studien für R. Bultmann*, 1957[2], p. 246), it occurs 44 times in Luke, out of 102 times in the whole NT.

[5] Grundmann, TWNT II [E.T.], p. 22.

in the context of the passion, 9.22; 17.25; 24.7, 26). So too do his witnesses (Acts 5.29; 9.6, 16; 14.22, etc.).[1] We should also mention those passages which speak of the uselessness of trying to withstand God. Gamaliel warns the members of the Sanhedrin not to oppose God (Acts 5.39). Peter appears before the apostles in Jerusalem and defends his behaviour in Cornelius' house, saying: "Who was I that I could withstand God?" (11.17). Finally, the exalted Lord says to Paul: "It hurts you to kick against the goads" (26.14). Thus Paul proves to King Agrippa that he could not be disobedient to the heavenly vision (v. 19).

There can be no doubt that this last series of images is derived from Hellenistic thought.[2] But Luke does not take over the cyclical view of history, the view that history constantly repeated itself under fixed cosmic laws.[3] What happens in heaven has its counterpart on earth, but is not subject to the same laws of causation. Heavenly and earthly events are different in quality and cannot be reduced to a common denominator. Divine predestination stands in a paradoxical contrast with the contingency of earthly (that is, Church) history in its unique and purposeful character.[4] The timeless cosmic law of Greek thought is interpreted as divine contemporaneity with everything that happens on earth. Here too Hellenistic thought is taken up and

[1] Again, it is a disputed question whether this is an eschatological term (so Grundmann, TWNT II [E.T.], p. 23; Conzelmann, St. Luke, p. 153, n. 3, takes a different view). Here it all depends on the terminology, which must fit in generally with Lucan usage (see above, p. 114, n. 2). In any case it expresses that aspect of the event which is related to God's heavenly reality (on "must" used in connection with the suffering of Jesus see below, pp. 157ff).

[2] Cf. A. Vögeli, "Lukas und Euripides", ThZ 9 (1953), pp. 415ff; Schulz, op. cit., passim; on δεῖ see Grundmann, op. cit., pp. 22, 20ff.

[3] On the Hellenistic world picture cf. Schweizer, Erniedrigung p. 145. The use of the root ἀναγκ- in Luke is worth noting. In Luke 14.18 it means the power which separates a man from God. Acts 26.11 is also concerned with a reprehensible act. In Luke 17.1, where it is used of the dark side of the divine will, Luke replaces the ἀνάγκη in Matthew 18.7 with an ἀνένδεκτόν. Only once does Luke use the word in a context concerning redemptive history. According to Acts 13.46 it was necessary to speak the word of God to the Jews first. But this very passage brings out man's abiding freedom to decide, as seen in the way the Jews reject the Gospel. This necessity is in no way an eternal world law, but is temporally limited by the πρῶτον. Luke contains no "Ananke theologumenon" (Schulz, op. cit., p. 109).

[4] On Luke's familiarity with Old Testament historiography cf. Barrett, Luke the Historian, p. 19.

corrected, as we have seen exemplified in the Areopagus speech.

This, then, is a synthesis between Hellenistic thought and the Old Testament view of history. But this does not mean that there is a drama of salvation which is open to observation, and which denies man's freedom of choice.[1] The *dramatis personae*, as we can see from the case of the Jews, always have the possibility open to man of acting differently. But they allow themselves to be guided by the Spirit, or even persuaded to act otherwise than they would have done. Particularly at the crucial turning points in Acts it is obvious that the Spirit's guidance is an unforeseen miracle. Divine providence stands alongside of blindness to God's ways on the part of his witnesses. They must wait for the Spirit to show them the way (Acts 13.1f; 1.14). Peter objects three times to the Gentile mission, but the Spirit nevertheless guides him to it (10.9ff). Paul is guided to Europe, contrary to the itinerary he had planned for himself (16.6ff).[2] Thus the Spirit's action and the decisions of men stand in dialectical relation. Faith acknowledges the unity and continuity of history in the divine plan of salvation, but this does not mean that the contingency of history and the element of surprise are denied. Never does Luke project past experiences into the future like some modern philosopher of history. On the contrary, he bids us like the apostles to be open for the fresh, miraculous operation of the Spirit. Though in retrospect faith may detect with certainty the constancy of God's ways, it can never predict them in advance.

From this section on the Holy Spirit we have learned that Luke knows nothing of a "redemption history" in the sense of divine salvation extended into human history. He faces the task of bearing witness to the contingent revelation of God within a period of time which has become past history. He must express the presence of God in the past tense, yet prevent the observer from looking back at it and labelling it "sacred". The task Luke has before him is to preach the presence of God in a past event, and yet maintain the distinction between the divine and the

---

[1] Schulz, op. cit., p. 110.
[2] Haenchen, *Apg.*, 425, notices the parallel between the two texts. On Acts 16.9ff, cf. O. Glombitza, "Der Schritt nach Europa", *ZNW* 53 (1962), pp. 77ff.

human. As we have seen, Luke keeps a firm hold on the eschato-logical transcendence of the Spirit, although he is perfectly aware that the Spirit has been "poured out" upon the Church. He uses the concept of the Spirit to describe the acts of God in the on-going course of history. This enables him to affirm their continuity with the acts of God under the old covenant, and also to give them a concrete place in history, namely, the apostolic community endowed with the Spirit. Thus he prevents his Christology from being absorbed into the institutional forms of history. He avoids extending the sacramental conception of the "body of Christ" into on-going history. The exalted Christ can speak to the contemporary situation without becoming a tran-scendent figure out of touch with history altogether.

3. *The Presence of Salvation in the Encounter with the Exalted Christ*

As we have already mentioned, the presence of the exalted Lord in his Church is expressed by the "name" of Christ.[1] This is the mode of *description*. We turn now to the way his presence is expressed in *relevant preaching*. The Gospel of Luke is not merely a testimony to events of the past. It is also a witness which speaks directly to the reader in his contemporary situation.[2] It is the present Christ himself who encounters the reader in the Gospel narratives of the sayings and needs of Jesus. This may be illustrated from the sermon in the synagogue at Nazareth (Luke 4.17-30), and from the kerygmatic significance which Luke imparts to the cross and resurrection.[3]

(*a*) It is highly instructive to compare Luke 4.16ff with its Marcan parallel. The Lucan redaction is evident from the differences in

---

[1] See above, pp. 138ff.

[2] On this distinction, see R. Bultmann, *Das Evangelium des Johannes*, 1962[17], p. 298. In Luke, however, there is no alternative involved, for narration and address are dialectically related. In this way the Johannine approach is utilized and at the same time the historical corrections of the Christ message are brought out. On the common tradition of Luke and John cf. J. A. Bailley, *The Traditions Common to the Gospels of Luke and John*, 1963; P. Parker, "Luke and the Fourth Evangelist", *NTS* 9 (1963), pp. 317ff.

[3] We are here continuing the christological observations of pp. 37ff. In our earlier investigation we encountered a tension between historical narration and simul-taneous statements aimed at producing faith (see above, pp. 52ff).

the texts.[1] Mark 1.15 gives a brief résumé of Jesus' preaching without any particular situation. Luke turns this into an "inaugural sermon by Jesus in Nazareth". The theme of the fulfilment of salvation (πεπλήρωται, Mark 1.15 and Luke 4.21) is still there. But in place of Mark's bald announcement that "the kingdom of God is at hand", Luke tells us that "*To-day* is the acceptable year of the Lord" (Luke 4.21, 19). The present moment is the time of fulfilment. It is no longer qualified by the imminence of the kingdom of God, for the kingdom is already present in the word of proclamation.[2]

Such a notion of the kingdom could of course be construed in a purely timeless sense. But Luke avoids that danger by tying it down firmly to Old Testament prophecy (Isa. 61.1f). Hence it is not, as in Mark, the "time" that is fulfilled, but the scriptures. More than this, Luke transfers the Marcan narrative of the rejection of Jesus at Nazareth to this point (Mark 6.1ff), using it to provide Mark's résumé of the kerygma (1.15) with an historical setting. By this means he makes that story relevant to life. Jesus appears as a preacher in surroundings described in the minutest detail. The audience, which is not even mentioned in Mark 1.15, comes in for a detailed description. First, they are astonished at Jesus, and show a mistaken belief in miracles. Then they reject Christ's message, which is thus shown to be a free word of mercy for the "fall and rising of many" (Luke 2.34).[3]

Three points in this account are worth noting: Jesus as the Proclaimer who becomes the Proclaimed, Luke's use of "to-day", and the recipients of the message. We shall now discuss each of these three points in turn, drawing upon further texts to elucidate them.

---

[1] On Luke's dependence on the Mark cf. Dibelius, *Tradition*, pp. 110f; Bultmann, *Tradition*, p. 32; Conzelmann, *St. Luke*, pp. 31ff; A. R. C. Leaney, *The Gospel According to St. Luke*, 1958, pp. 50f.

[2] Conzelmann, *St. Luke*, op. cit., p. 40 (on Luke 4.43).

[3] The shift in the course of transmission is interesting. According to Bultmann, *Tradition*, p. 31, Mark 6.2 "was originally an account of some successful appearance of Jesus". This view of the matter was later reversed by the addition of the logion about the prophet (Mark 6.4). In Luke the amazement which *men* have for Jesus receives stronger emphasis (see below, pp. 152ff).

(b) First, we note that Jesus is proclaiming himself, "Jesus starts his sermon by immediately making himself its object."[1] Hence the paradox that Jesus is at once the proclaimer and the bringer of salvation. Each of these sides of the paradox must be considered separately.

The scene as a whole introduces us in remarkable detail to the ritual of the synagogue service, which Jesus attends "as his custom was on the Sabbath day" (v. 16). The reader stands up to read, and chooses a lesson from one of the prophets. The attendant hands him the scroll and receives it back again when he is finished. The teacher is seated on a raised platform.[2] The reader of Acts cannot fail to notice that this is how the apostles preached in the mission field. They too went to the synagogues (cf. especially Acts 13.14ff). No doubt Luke had seen it happen with his own eyes. It makes the reader feel at home. At any rate it is clear that Jesus is acting like a Christian preacher addressing the Church.

But this preacher is different from all others. He applies the word of salvation to himself. He is the anointed Messiah,[3] in whom the prophecy is fulfilled. In him the accepted year of the Lord has come. He has the power to deliver the captives, to give sight to the blind and to heal the sick—in short, to declare the new divine creation in his mighty acts (cf. 7.21f).

Luke describes Jesus here from two angles, which must be kept distinct. Jesus is the man who was reared at Nazareth, who lived in the religious traditions of his people and who preaches the word like any of the prophets and apostles. But he also claims to be the anointed one who accomplishes the divine salvation and who acts on earth with the authority of heaven. The vulnerable and ambiguous character of this claim becomes apparent when the people of Nazareth reject him.

This tension between historical narrative and preaching aimed at faith requires further examination. In this sermon Jesus proclaims his heavenly authority. Yet in the saying about the fall of Satan (Luke 10.18) he becomes the human spectator of his own heavenly work. In his three parables of the lost (Luke 15) Jesus is

---

[1] Wellhausen, *Lukas*, pp. 9f.   [2] Schlatter, *Lukas*, pp. 224f.
[3] For Luke this certainly implies a connection with Jesus' baptism (Friedrich, "Hohepriestererwartung", p. 285).

concerned to answer the charge of the Pharisees, "This man receives sinners and eats with them" (v. 2). He vindicates his conduct by pointing to the love of God who searches out the lost and brings them back to himself. He claims "to validate the will of God in exactly the same way as a man must if he were in God's place".[1] His word is meant to strike home as the authoritative word of God.

The careful way in which Luke distinguishes between the different aspects of the situation is made clear in the way he depicts Jesus' relation to the kingdom of God. First, we note the strong emphasis on the proclamation of the kingdom.[2] As the object of proclamation, the kingdom is for Luke a heavenly as well as a future reality. He uses phraseology which distinguishes clearly between the man Jesus and the heavenly kingdom.

But there is an entirely different relation between Jesus and the kingdom in such passages as Luke 10.9, 11; 11.20; 17.20f. These passages speak of the actual presence of the kingdom in Jesus. How is this to be understood? It is best to start with the phrase ἐφ᾽ ἡμᾶς, which, significantly, occurs both in 10.9 and in 11.20. In his second missionary charge Luke expands Mark's "the kingdom of God has drawn nigh" (Mark 1.15) by adding "upon you", thus giving an individualistic, existential twist to the statement. Now, in this very instant, the kingdom of God is about to become a present reality for the individual in the word of the witnesses. This means, he will encounter the presence of the exalted Lord.[3]

In Luke 11.20 Jesus says: "But if it is by the finger of God that I cast out demons, then the kingdom of God has come upon you." The kingdom is present in Jesus' exorcisms. His heavenly victory over Satan (10.18) marks the irruption of the kingdom of God in this world. It is realized in the miracles of Jesus, which are signs of the new divine creation. It is God who acts through Jesus (Acts 2.22). God is present and active in the miracles,[4] while

---

[1] E. Fuchs, *Studies of the Historical Jesus* (SBT 42), 1964, p. 21.
[2] See above, pp. 123ff.
[3] Conzelmann, *St. Luke*, p. 107; Grässer, *Parousieverzögerung*, pp. 140f.
[4] Cf. the emphasis on the suddenness of the miracle through the use of παραχρῆμα. This word is analogous to Luke's use of σήμερον about which we

Jesus as man acts with all the ambiguity of human action. As its setting shows, the movement of Luke 11.14–23 is towards the decision of faith. The astonished crowd (v. 14), the adversaries of Jesus who believe that the healing is the work of the devil (v. 15), and the "others" who ask for signs (v. 16), all witness in their various ways how Jesus' deed is open to various interpretations.

This fits in well with Luke 17.20f, where Jesus says that the kingdom of God does not come "with observation". He rejects the demand for a sign. All the same, signs of the new divine world are given, by Jesus "in your midst" (Acts 2.22). Why should not the much disputed ἐντὸς ὑμῶν in Luke 17.21 be taken in the same sense? This would fit in with the way Jesus' miracles are interpreted in Luke 4.18ff and 7.21f,[1] where they are manifestations of Jesus' heavenly authority, though in a hidden, ambiguous sort of way.[2] Mussner hits the nail on the head when he describes Jesus' answer as a "riddle". It conceals the mystery of Jesus' person from the blindness of his questioners. Only he "whose faith enables him to connect the kingdom of God with the appearance of the Messiah Jesus"[3] can penetrate that mystery.

(c) The dialectic between the revelation and concealment of the kingdom in the words and deeds of Jesus will help us to understand

shall speak below. On each occasion it is introduced into the Marcan source (Luke 4.39; 5.25; 8.47). It can replace Mark's smoother εὐθύς (Luke 8.44, 55; 18.43) and is otherwise usual in Lucan miracle stories (13.13; Acts 3.7). Luke 19.11 proves it to be an eschatological term. On the synoptic comparison see H. J. Held in Bornkamm, *Tradition*, pp. 177f, n. 3.

[1] Cf. also Luke 19.37, where the disciples praise God for the mighty work they have seen.

[2] Conzelmann, *St. Luke*, p. 117, distinguishes between the presence of the kingdom and its preliminary signs. He rightly guards against spiritualizing interpretations. No one will assert that Jesus proclaimed a completely realized eschatology. When God acts through Jesus (Acts 2.22), it must be assumed that he is really present in the works of Jesus. The kingdom of God is not susceptible of formal definition; it must be defined in accordance with christological statement.

[3] F. Mussner, "Wann kommt das Reich Gottes?" *BZ* NF 6 (1962), p. 110. In the exposition of ἐντὸς ὑμῶν from Origen onwards (cf. B. Noack, *Das Reich Gottes bei Lukas*, 1948, pp. 3ff) it is possible to study how each expositor in the last analysis is guided by his dogmatic presuppositions. That is true even of the interpretations proposed by A. Rüstow, *ZNW* 51 (1960), pp. 197ff, who suggests an ethical solution (p. 216), and by Vielhauer, "Gottesreich", pp. 54f, who considers that in 17.21 Luke equates the kingdom of God with the Christian religion.

why Luke places so much emphasis on "to-day" in the sermon at Nazareth (Luke 4.21).[1] He uses it to make three points. First, it rivets the Christ event to history, to a past attested by scripture. "To-day" the prophecies of the Old Testament are being fulfilled. Now, as men listen to Jesus, Old Testament history reaches its goal. It is the "to-day" of God's grace (vv. 18f), offered to the reader of the Gospel no less than to the people of Nazareth. This "to-day" is no will-o'-the-wisp, ready to vanish in the mists of timelessness. It remains the "to-day" of fulfilment, riveted to the history of God's dealings with Israel. But that does not mean that the "to-day" of Luke 4.21 is past history.[2] It only becomes so when we deny to Luke's gospel any quality of witness. Even the Old Testament recognizes the "to-day" which brings the past into the present.[3]

But the "to-day" of the gospel witness means more than it did in the Old Testament level. It is not just a recalling of the past so as to make it present. It is, in the second place, the actualization of the divine presence from heaven. That is because it is connected with the presence of the kingdom, of which we spoke above. In the message of the angels (Luke 2.11) the heavenly glory shines round about the shepherds as a sign of the divine presence (v. 9). The presence is there "to-day," in the announcement of salvation. Because of its eschatological overtones, the "to-day" of the divine presence cannot be projected indefinitely into time. Luke does of course regard the period of the Spirit-endowed Church as a time of fulfilment. But that fulfilment is never actually visible in history. Since it is the presence of the Spirit, as well as of Christ himself speaking directly in the "to-day" of the preaching, it is constantly given anew, yet always future.[4]

[1] Cf. Luke 2.11; 3.22 D (cf. Acts 13.23); 19.5, 9; 23.43; the word has a pre-eminent place in the Lucan presentation: all the passages quoted are concerned with the salvation promised from heaven or from the lips of Jesus.

[2] Conzelmann, *St. Luke*, pp. 36, etc. Cf. Vielhauer, "Paulinism", *Studies in Luke-Acts*, pp. 48f; Grässer, op. cit., p. 188.

[3] Cf. Ps. 95.7b; Deut. 4.39f etc. (Fuchs, *TWNT* VII, pp. 269f); on the present significance of decisive events in the distant past in OT history see Boman, *Hebrew Thought*, pp. 137ff.

[4] This qualification is lacking in H. Schürmann, *Evangelienschrift und kirchliche Unterweisung* (Erfurter theolog. Stud. 12), 1962, pp. 68f. For Schürmann the

Our exegesis is confirmed, in the third place, by the way in which the "to-day" of which Jesus speaks in his sermon actually occurs in the ears of his audience (4.21). Each one present is individually gripped by the word and compelled to make a decision. The word is aimed directly, and hits the target here and now. It is addressed to the shepherds abiding in the fields (2.11, "you"). It is addressed to the house of Zacchaeus (19.9). So it is tied not only to past history (of which it is the fulfilment) or to the Lord who speaks from heaven. It is tied to those who hear it as well. It cannot be objectivized in a general sort of way.[1] The people to whom the message is addressed are not ciphers, which can be exchanged for one another. They are not to be separated from the message. That this is how people behave when they hear the word of the present Lord can be shown, once more, from the sermon in the synagogue at Nazareth.

(d) How did the people at Nazareth react to Jesus' sermon? The question has been variously answered. V. 22 suggests that they were pleased and astonished and that their question was not meant in a malicious sense.[2] The use of the word μαρτυρεῖν in Luke supports this interpretation. He never uses the word in a negative sense.[3] But to suppose that the audience reacted in a positive way poses a problem for the overall understanding of the scene. This is because of the "sudden and completely motiveless change of attitude on the part of his listeners". First, they are enthusiastic. But they at once break out into "the bitterest criticism and rejection, finally reaching a murderous pitch".[4] To get over these difficulties, Jeremias adverts to the text of Isaiah

eschatological period lasts beyond the time of Christ into the time of the Church (he refers to Acts 3.24, all the prophets proclaimed "these days"). The salvation events "as eschatological facts" retain their present eschatological reference and continue to be present for us in the Church. Must not such a conception lead inevitably to the sacralization of Church history, which is just what Luke is so careful to avoid? Marxsen, "Exegese", p. 25, also sees in Luke "a fulfilment projected in stages into redemptive history".

[1] Fuchs, TWNT VII, p. 273, 15ff, reduces the "to-day" to the moment of encounter with Jesus as a historical person.
   [2] Wellhausen, Lukas, p. 10.   [3] Cf. Strathmann, TWNT IV, p. 50.
   [4] J. Jeremias, Jesus' Promise to the Nations, 1958, p. 44.

61.2.[1] After the part quoted by Jesus, the passage goes on to speak of the "day of vengeance". Jeremias renders the ambiguous words μαρτυρεῖν and θαυμάζειν thus: "They protest with one voice . . . and were furious . . . because he only spoke about God's year of mercy (and omitted the words about the Messianic vengeance)."[2] So he reaches the conclusion that "Luke 4.22 exhibits no break in the attitude of his audience towards Jesus. On the contrary, it records that from the outset unanimous rage was their response to the message of Jesus."[3]

Unfortunately, this exegesis is highly artificial, and does not explain how Luke himself understood the reaction of the people of Nazareth. To reconstruct the scene historically bars the way to a true understanding of the pericope.[4] As Zahn correctly observes at v. 22, the approval and astonishment of the audience is caused more by the graciousness of the preacher than by what he actually said.[5] This is a helpful observation. Their astonishment is for the externals, for "the gracious words which proceeded out of his mouth". They pay attention to Jesus, but see only the human aspect of his person, the gifted orator, the infant prodigy from their own town, the local carpenter's son.

Much depends here on the way we take the phrase λόγοι τῆς χάριτος. Following Zahn, we would translate it in the Hellenistic sense of "winsome words".[6] This rendering commends itself because the whole emphasis is on the external side of the picture. The eyes of all are fastened on Jesus and they hear the words "which proceeded out of his mouth". But their observation is superficial. As Luke shows by the way he uses the term elsewhere (Acts 14.3; 20.24, 32), we have here a technical term with the unequivocal meaning of "message of grace".[7] The ambiguity must be deliberate on Luke's part. It serves to underline the

[1] Following K. Bornhäuser, *Das Wirken des Christus durch Taten und Worte*, 1921, p. 59.
[2] *Jesus' Promise*, p. 45.   [3] *Ibid.*
[4] Cf. the similar attempt in B. Violet, "Zum rechten Verständnis der Nazareth-Perikope", *ZNW* 37 (1938), pp. 251ff; Klostermann and Grundmann ad loc. also infer from the context that by v. 22 the audience had already rejected Jesus.
[5] *Lukas*, p. 239.   [6] Cf. also Arndt & Gringrich, *Lexicon*, p. 885.
[7] Hence Klostermann, *Lukas*, ad loc. leaves both interpretations side by side without choosing between them.

provocative character of God's word, which challenges man to a decision. You can take it as a purely human word—or as God's word of grace. The people of Nazareth only appreciate the winsome words of the preacher. But the reader of the gospel is challenged to hear "in their ears" the message of divine salvation (v. 21b) and to accept it.

Luke keeps up the tension through verse 22.[1] The decision is still an open matter. The astonishment of the congregation should turn from a mere hankering after sensation into an adoration of God for his miracles, the winsome words into the word of grace. "Is he not (the) son?" ask the people of Nazareth. "Yes, the Son of God" the reader would tacitly add. But they see in him only the man, the son of Joseph.

This exegesis is confirmed by an examination of Luke's use of the words "to see" and "to be astonished". "Go see"[2] is another deliberate *double entendre* on Luke's part. In the first place, it has eschatological associations. The future glory of Jesus (Luke 21.27) is rendered visible by his deeds on earth (7.22).[3] In Luke 10.23 the eyes which *see* what the disciples see are pronounced blessed. Conversely, the disciples will later long to *see* one of the days of the Son of Man (17.22). Simeon can die in peace because his eyes have *seen* the divine salvation (2.29; cf. v. 26).

Yet there is an entirely human aspect to this seeing. One can see without perceiving (Luke 8.10). One may see merely outward occurrences and not the thing intended. One may look for miracles rather than for salvation. This kind of seeing is characteristic of Herod (9.9; 23.8) and of Jesus' family (8.19–21), which Luke deliberately contrasts with the disciples in 8.9f.[4] The people of Nazareth fall into the same category, as we see from Luke 4.23.

---

[1] The word ἀτενίζειν expresses tension (Acts 6.15; 1.10; 10.4 and more frequently), Klostermann, *Lukas*, ad loc.

[2] Since "seeing" here has a figurative meaning (cf. Michaelis, *TWNT* V, p. 378), the various words (ἰδεῖν, ὁρᾶν, βλέπειν, θεωρεῖν or "to lift up one's eyes to") can be taken together. In this passage "all eyes were fastened upon him" corresponds to "but now they are hid from your eyes" (Luke 19.42). The people of Nazareth could now "see". For the inhabitants of Jerusalem on the other hand, the time of their visitation passes unnoticed (19.44).

[3] Conzelmann, *St. Luke*, p. 192; on the significance of "seeing" cf. p. 105.

[4] Conzelmann, *St. Luke*, p. 51.

Note that the verses just quoted come by and large from the special Lucan material.[1] The matter was one of particular concern in Luke's time. The first problem is, whether the generation of eye-witnesses had any special advantage over those who came to believe later. The answer is no. Even those who were closest to Jesus, his own fellow-countrymen and relatives, were blind to him. The other problem is that the life of Jesus had become a matter of past history. It has ceased to speak directly to the present and can be contemplated ("seen") as an objective, completed thing. Luke clings firmly to the fact that the life of Jesus is now indeed a thing of the past. He does not try to escape the danger of historical positivism by denying the past dimension in the story of Jesus merely in order to give it present relevance. But he sees this past dimension as only one aspect, to be held together with the "to-day" of which Jesus speaks. The past as such remains ambiguous, but by accepting the present word of Jesus the mystery concealed in the past can be penetrated.

The idea of "seeing" brings out the either/or nature of the challenge. The verb $\theta\alpha\upsilon\mu\acute{\alpha}\zeta\epsilon\iota\nu$ suggests a suspension of judgement. They have still not made up their minds.[2] Luke gets the term from his tradition. For Mark likewise speaks of the astonishment of the people (Mark 5.20), meaning by it the momentary excitement let loose by the miraculous powers of Jesus. We can see this from the parallel use of the verb $\dot{\epsilon}\kappa\pi\lambda\acute{\eta}\sigma\sigma\epsilon\sigma\theta\alpha\iota$ (Mark 1.22; cf. Mark 7.37 with Matthew 15.31). Luke takes up this notion but gives it a different place in his overall scheme. He uses $\theta\alpha\upsilon\mu\alpha\zeta\epsilon\iota\nu$ for an attitude still prior to the decision of faith, one of being merely impressed by an extraordinary event (Luke 11.14). But it can also express a pre-Easter faith in the miraculous though still hidden ways of God[3] (2.18, 33; 1.63; 24.41). Here the word

---

[1] In Luke 8.20 there is an alteration of Mark 3.32 ($\zeta\eta\tau\epsilon\hat{\iota}\nu$). Mark also uses "seeing" in a figurative sense. It enables him to speak of the vision of future glory (Mark 9.1; 14.62). Mark 9.1 is changed so as to make the vision present in Luke 9.27 (Conzelmann, St. Luke, p. 104). Luke here comes close to the Johannine use of "seeing" (Bultmann, Joh.-Ev., pp. 44ff; Michaelis, op. cit., pp. 362ff; cf. also O. Cullmann, "Der joh. Gebrauch doppeldeutiger Ausdrücke als Schlüssel zum Verständnis des vierten Evangeliums", ThZ, 1948, pp. 360ff (cf. idem, Early Christian Worship, 1953, p. 41).

[2] Cf. Bertram TWNT III [E.T.], pp. 27ff.   [3] Bertram, op. cit., p. 31, 4f.

has a neutral or even positive sound. But this is somewhat modified in the contrasting attitudes in Luke 9.43b. "All" are amazed, but the disciples are told to let the word about Jesus' impending suffering "sink into their ears". What Jesus is looking for is not merely a general attitude of wonder, but a concrete, concerned hearing that does not founder on the scandal of his suffering (7.23). The verbal echoes in Luke 4.22a ("all") and 4.21 ("in your ears") show how close the two passages are. With the people of Nazareth amazement passes into rejection, with the disciples it should lead to a recognition of the glory of Jesus which lies hidden beneath his suffering.[1]

To return to the sermon at Nazareth. This much is certain: by "giving testimony" and by their "astonishment" Jesus' audience registers its outward approval. So they are faced with a decision. But since all they can see in Jesus is the "son of Joseph", they have decided against him.

In v. 22 they have not yet rejected Jesus. But it must be noted that Luke omits Mark's statement, "they took offence at him" (Mark 6.3b). It is only Jesus' reply in v. 23 that exposes their unbelief. So preoccupied are they with the human aspect of his person, that Jesus anticipates their demand for signs specifically related to his person.[2] He thus actually provokes the rejection of his countrymen. He does not oblige them as they would like. Consequently they expel him from their midst as a foreign body (vv. 28f).

So our interpretation of Luke 4.16–30 is quite consistent all the way through. On any other interpretation ἐμαρτύρουν in v. 22 would have to be taken in a negative sense, contrary to normal Lucan usage. To be sure, we have taken the story entirely in its contemporary relevance for Luke and his readers. The result is a pattern we have discovered all the way through the Lucan writings. The first reaction evoked by the preaching of the gospel is that ordinary human curiosity is aroused. Then the

---

[1] Cf. Bultmann's distinction between unbelief, which has already rejected the proclamation, and existence prior to faith, "which has not yet been encountered by the proclamation" (Glauben und Verstehen I, 1954², p. 298).

[2] The πάντως is—with Klostermann's alternative suggestion, ad loc.—to be translated: "in any case" (you will now demand of me a miracle); cf. Acts 21.22.

extraordinary quality in Jesus' words and deeds challenges his audience to a decision of faith. Either they accept in faith the heavenly power of Jesus as the disciples accept it, or they remain open-minded like the crowds or the Pharisees in Acts, or they reject Jesus' claim like the Sadducees (Acts 5.33, 40), the relatives of Jesus, and in the present case, the people of Nazareth.

(e) The individual thus has an existential encounter with the "to-day" of the proclamation. This leads us once more to the meaning of the cross and resurrection. Several times already we have touched on the way Luke regards Jesus' suffering. Now it is time to draw some definite conclusions.[1]

It is a much debated point whether Luke attaches any saving significance to the death of Jesus.[2] If it is denied that he does so, it follows that the cross is merely due to the Jews' misunderstanding, their failure to grasp the meaning of the Old Testament prophecies.[3] There is some truth in this, for, as we have already noted, the crucifixion is linked with the destruction of Jerusalem, which is the Jews' punishment for killing Jesus. In other words, the meaning of the cross in redemptive history is played down.[4] Again, in the speeches in Acts there is a stereotyped contrast between the Jewish crime of murder and the saving act of God in the resurrection of Jesus. This would seem to support the theory that for Luke the cross was simply an act of judicial murder committed by the Jews.[5]

But that is only one side of the picture, the human and historical side. There is another side too. Luke regards the suffering of Jesus most definitely as a mystery, even more so than Mark does

---

[1] See above, pp. 17f; pp. 30ff; pp. 52ff; pp. 73ff; pp. 128–32.

[2] For this Acts 20.28 is quoted (G. Sevenster, *RGG*³ I, cols. 1757f: E. Lohmeyer, "Vom christlichen Abendmahl", *ThR* NF 9 (1937), p. 181; Lohse, *Martyrer*, p. 181). Against this it is to be noted that Luke does not take over Mark 10.45 and, according to Conzelmann, *St. Luke*, p. 201, "The idea of the Cross plays no part in the proclamation" (cf. Vielhauer, *RGG*³ II, col. 583). According to the mediating position adopted by Lohse, *Martyrer*, pp. 189f, Luke relegates the atoning significance of the cross to the background.

[3] So Käsemann, *Essays on N.T. Themes*, p. 29; followed by Wilckens, *Missionsreden*, p. 216.

[4] See above, pp. 17f.

[5] Acts 2.23f, 26; 3.15; 4.10; 5.30f; 10.40; 13.28–30; cf. E. Stauffer, *The Theology of the New Testament*, 1955, pp. 339ff.

(Luke 9.45; 18.34). He traces it back to the saving purpose of God. Jesus "must" suffer according to the divine plan.[1] Hence his suffering is not only a human crime permitted by God, but was planned by his living, active will. It is part of the divine plan of salvation.[2]

The meaning of the cross must therefore not be considered in isolation, but must be understood in the light of the whole drama of salvation.[3] Like the fourth evangelist (John 1.11,14) Luke speaks of the (saving) visit of God to his people.[4] It is a visitation which betokens salvation and judgement for the whole world. In his own language, Luke describes the path of Jesus through suffering to his exaltation in heaven.[5] The intimate connection between cross and glory safeguards two important truths. The statements about the glory are preserved from a false *theologia gloriae* by the references to suffering, while the affirmation of his suffering does not remain in isolation. That might have suggested a mysticism of passion and death, as well as a denial of the character of the world as the divine creation. Instead, it is tied up with the announcement of the glory of Jesus.

It is this connection with the heavenly consummation that preserves the distinctive significance of the cross. Though Luke draws a sharp distinction between the path of Jesus to the cross and the fate of the disciples (Luke 22.35ff), he does recognize the place of suffering and the cross in the life of discipleship (9.23ff; 23.26ff; cf. 21.17; Acts 9.16).[6] Through the promise of salvation contained in the kerygma of the cross the Christian is drawn into the suffering of Christ (Luke 12.49ff). As his Master trod the path

[1] Luke 9.22; 17.25; 24.7, 26; let it be recalled that Paul and Stephen are conformed to their Lord in their suffering (and so exceptionally marked out, see above, pp. 128–32).

[2] R. Otto, *Kingdom*, pp. 246f.

[3] Otherwise Luke is forced into Pauline categories, and justice is not done to his position. You cannot blame Luke for being silent on the redemptive significance of the cross and at the same time attack his view of redemptive history. For this minimized emphasis on the cross as an event of redemptive history shows that Luke is particular concerned not to prolong salvation into history. For him salvation is given by the exalted Lord from heaven (Acts 5.31).

[4] Grundmann, *Lukas*, p. 28; cf. Luke 1.68, 78; 7.16; for the Jews the rejection of this visitation becomes their judgement (19.44); Beyer, *TWNT* II [E.T.], 603ff; see above, pp. 8of.

[5] See above, pp. 30ff.   [6] See above, n. 1.

of death, so the Christian at the end of his tether is promised eternal salvation, like the penitent thief (Luke 23.43). By individualizing the passion in his own peculiar way[1] Luke guards the saving mystery of the cross from being treated as an objective event of the past. The cross is not now the absolute end of the world. It is the preliminary end for the individual Christian who hears its message in the word of preaching.

So we arrive at the conclusion that Luke regards the cross as an eschatological event (in the realized sense of the word). Its saving significance can only be comprehended in the context of the whole drama of salvation. A man must be brought to the end of his tether by the cross of Christ before he can receive salvation.[2]

(f) The same holds good for Luke's testimony to the resurrection, which receives such striking emphasis in the Book of Acts.[3] And yet its effects are strictly limited. As we have seen, it no longer marks the shift of the aeons. Its cosmic significance has been transferred to the exaltation.[4] Instead, the resurrection of Jesus to life in the new world becomes the first of all resurrections.[5] The question thus arises as to the place of the witness to the resurrection in the overall Lucan scheme. Here a distinction must be drawn between two different aspects of the resurrection event. From one angle, the resurrection is viewed in the context of the Jewish doctrine of the general resurrection of the dead (Acts 23.6; 24.15, 21). This imparts to it a factual character, which can only be known indirectly through "those who were chosen as witnesses" (Acts 10.41a). These witnesses "vouch for the factual character of the event" (Acts 1.21f).[6] They insure the historical

---

[1] See above, pp. 17f.

[2] The πρῶτον in Luke 17.25 applies by analogy to the individual Christian.

[3] Acts 2.24, 31f; 3.15; 4.10, 33; 10.40f; 13.30, 33f, 37 etc. cf. H. Braun, "Zur Terminologie der Acta von der Auferstehung Jesu", ThLZ 77 (1952), pp. 533ff; Wilckens, Missionsreden, pp. 137ff.

[4] See above, pp. 18ff; cf. the parallel with the death of Jesus on the cross. Also the suffering of Jesus is on the one hand strongly emphasized (note the increased number of passion predictions, compared with Mark), yet on the other hand limited in its historical significance.

[5] Wilckens, op. cit., p. 139, n. 3.   [6] Braun, op. cit., p. 534.

continuity of the testimony and at the same time tie it down to a particular point of history, namely, the apostolic Church. Jesus did not appear before "all the people", but specifically to the apostles (Acts 10.41).[1]

But still, there is another side to the resurrection.[2] It is not only an historical event to be proved by argument. It is also an eschatological event marking the beginning of the divine new world. This side of it cannot be stated in objective language, but must be made kerygmatically as an offer to the individual believer. Though the new age is still in the future so far as he is concerned, he can win life with the risen Christ even now. Christ is the ἀρχηγὸς τῆς ζωῆς (Acts 3.15), the "first to rise from the dead" (26. 23).

We are now in a position to see the point of that long quotation from Psalm 16 in Peter's speech at Pentecost (Acts 2.14ff; for the quotation, see vv. 25–8, 31 and cf. Acts 13.35). Wilckens considers it "quite possible that it was Luke himself who found this quotation and used it as a proof of the resurrection".[3] The repetition in v. 31 reinforces the point that the σάρξ of Jesus is incorruptible,[4] and this is attributed to the resurrection. It is a new creaturely existence that God has created in the resurrection of Jesus, anticipating the time of the restoration of all things (Acts 3.21.)[5]

In a similar way Luke rewrites the Marcan–Matthean version of the resurrection narrative (Luke 24.1–11). The interpretive word spoken by the two angels, "Why do you seek the living among the dead?", shifts the accent to the affirmation that Jesus

---

[1] According to Braun, op. cit., suggestions already perceptible in Paul (1 Cor. 15) are raised to the level of a theological programme.

[2] Cf. Acts 10.41b and the shape of the resurrection stories in Luke. "Nowhere does the risen Christ bear so few traits of one already exalted to heavenly glory as in Luke": he walks for a whole hour with two of his disciples, men touch his flesh and bones, he bids them farewell as in his lifetime (H. Grass, *Ostergeschehen und Osterberichte*, 1962², p. 45).

[3] Op. cit., p. 141.

[4] In Acts 2.31 ἡ σάρξ αὐτοῦ is inserted into the LXX text (Braun, op. cit., p. 526).

[5] Jesus' resurrection is to be viewed in analogy to his miracles. It is from a human angle the demonstrable return of a man from death into this life (see above, n. 2. Faith, however, takes this event as the beginning of the *new* creation of God, in which God makes man participate in his heavenly glory.

is alive (cf. Acts 1.3). He is the living one in the midst of a world in bondage to death. The faithful acceptance of this testimony brings salvation and life (Acts 2.39f).

The double aspect of the resurrection comes out very clearly at the end of the Areopagus speech. After the apologetic argument[1] in the first part of the speech comes the challenge to decide for God. God has overlooked the former times of ignorance, but is now calling everywhere for repentance (Acts 17.30). The reason for this is the coming divine judgement by the agency of a specially chosen man. V. 31 continues: πίστιν παρασχὼν πᾶσιν, ἀναστήσας αὐτὸν ἐκ νεκρῶν. Since Dibelius[2] the phrase πίστιν παρασχών has generally been translated "furnish a proof".[3] This is in accord with contemporary usage, and reproduces the popular meaning of the phrase. The resurrection is attested by trustworthy witnesses. Thus the apologetic motif of the speech is carried right through to the end.

Now there is here a remarkable affinity with Acts 20.31. In his farewell speech at Ephesus Paul says he has preached "repentance toward God and faith in our Lord Jesus Christ" both to Jews and to Greeks. Should the word πίστις, which Luke couples with repentance, be translated (even if Luke was here drawing on tradition)[4] quite differently from where it occurs at the end of the Areopagus speech? The reader could hardly be expected to think so. The problem is solved if 17.30 is another deliberate *double entendre*. By calling attention to the proof of the resurrection, a simultaneous offer is made of (invisible) faith in the risen one.[5] The reaction of the audience bears out this exegesis, for several people become believers as a result of Paul's speech (v. 34).

Thus this passage shows how Luke can weld together straightforward narrative and kerygmatic appeal to faith into a single dialectical whole. By describing the historical aspect of the redemptive event he prevents his kerygmatic offer of salvation

[1] See above, p. 71, n. 2.   [2] *Studies*, p. 57.

[3] Cf. Haenchen and Conzelmann, ad loc.; Zahn, *Apg.*, p. 626: "providing a universally acceptable guarantee".

[4] According to Conzelmann, *Apg.*, ad loc., 20.21 is a "good Lucan summary of the doctrine, following a community pattern".

[5] Cf.Luke 4.22 the double meaning of "words of grace" (see above, pp. 152ff), and Acts 17.18 the *double entendre*, ἀ(Α)νάστασις.

in Christ as a present reality from being merged into history and thus becoming a purely human word. Living as he does in linear time, man cannot help objectifying the past. He cannot bear unadulterated kerygmatic relevance. Luke is fully aware of this, but keeps it within clearly defined bounds. He combines objective narration of the earthly life of Jesus with testimony to the eschatological salvation which he came to bring, the mystery of which is only discernible to faith.

To sum up, in Chapter 3 we have seen that Luke considers salvation to be consummated with the exaltation of Jesus. The Old Testament prophecies are proleptically fulfilled in heaven and transcended by acquiring universal dimensions. Luke has no notion of any redemptive history extending in time. True, God works through the Holy Spirit for renewal in history. Yet the plan of salvation never becomes a series of observable redemptive facts and so a purely human thing. The Holy Spirit remains the superhuman reality of God. As such he binds together the history of Israel, Jesus, and the Church. In Israel the Spirit was imparted only to individuals. But now, as the creative intervention of God, the Spirit is the agent of Jesus' conception, and is poured out upon the whole apostolic community. While the Holy Spirit witnesses to God's creative activity in the old world, the risen and exalted Christ represents the new world of God. In the word of grace (Acts 14.3; 20.32) and salvation (13.26) he is personally present. In the "to-day" which marks the fulfilment of salvation he speaks to his own. As the crucified one he calls them to renounce the world and as the risen one he calls them to new life, begun in him. What are the implications of this for the world and its ongoing history? To this we must turn in the concluding chapter.

Conclusion

At the beginning of this century W. Wrede branded the conflict in theology at that time as one involving the alternatives "Jesus or Paul". After exposing the contrasts between the religion of Jesus and the faith of Paul he went on to call the apostle the second founder of Christianity.[1] In answer to Wrede, Bultmann argued the difference between Jesus and Paul as not one of "ideas or terminology".[2] It lies in the fact that for Paul a shift of the aeons has taken place, whereas for Jesus it still lies in the future.[3] That is why "the transmission of Jesus' proclamation could not simply take the form of reproducing his thought. . . . The Proclaimer had to become the Proclaimed."[4]

Today we have a similar alternative between Paul and Luke. But again it is necessary to take into account the difference between the periods to which they belonged. Luke could not simply reproduce the theology of the apostolic age. Since he was post-apostolic, he was obliged to make a new theological assessment of the situation. Whereas for Paul the shift of the aeons caused by the resurrection meant that the Proclaimer had to become the Proclaimed, Mark, and still more Luke, sees Jesus once more during his earthly lifetime as the Proclaimer. This is because in some sense the old aeon still continues. The post-apostolic Church shares the basically changed situation brought about by the fact of Jesus,[5] while at the same time it is still moving with Jesus towards the final renewal of the world.

It is this two-sided truth which forms the theme of Lucan

[1] W. Wrede, *Paulus*, 1904, p. 204f.
[2] R. Bultmann, "Die Bedeuting des geschichtlichen Jesus für die Theologie des Paulus", *Glauben und Verstehen* I, 1954[2], p. 201.
[3] Op. cit., p. 200.   [4] Op. cit., p. 205.   [5] Op. cit., p. 202.

theology. Luke's treatment of it is quite different from that of Paul and John. Both of the latter recognize the problem posed by the simultaneity of eschatology and history, and solve it by insisting that "the eschatological occurrence is already taking place in the present".[1] Each has his own way of arriving at this solution. Paul views it as a salvation event transforming the whole cosmos. It is even "now" in process, and is making the continuation of the old world meaningless.[2] His proclamation of the presence of the eschaton is a consequence of his awareness of the transformation of the world, which inevitably brings the end of the old world in its train.

In contrast to the cosmic and sacramental categories in which Paul views the world in its totality, John takes a more individualistic line. He is concerned with the individual's experience of the eschaton in faith, when he decides "against the world for God".[3] The world in its totality, whose ongoing history both John and Luke recognize, remains unaffected by all this. Note the difference between Paul and John. For Paul the continuation of history is meaningless because the new aeon has begun and the end of the world is imminent. John by contrast knows all about the continuation of history, but pays no attention to it because he concentrates entirely on personal decision.

This is what makes Luke an independent theologian in his own right, alongside of Paul and John. The problem which Luke tackles is that of relating the ongoing history of the world, in which the Christ event was staged, with the new world of God which Christ brought. In doing so he presupposes certain theologumena of Paul and the Johannine tradition. Paul's theology of redemptive history and the individualistic propen-

---

[1] Bultmann, *Theology* II, p. 10. Bultmann then continues: "though John was the first to carry the idea radically through". Here is Bultmann's foreshortening. The beginnings of a theology of redemptive history in Paul, which are taken up by Luke, are in Bultmann removed by an interpretation in line with Johannine thought. Cf. the very different view in E. Käsemann's instructive discussion, "Zum Thema der urchristlichen Apokalyptik", *ZThK* 59 (1962), pp. 257ff, where the apocalyptic horizon of Pauline theology is demonstrated (pp. 278ff).

[2] 2 Cor. 5.17; 6.2; further the ἔπειτα in 1 Corinthians. 15.23 for the continuation of history from the resurrection of Christ until his return (Vielhauer, "Paulinism", p. 46).

[3] Bultmann, *Theology* II, p. 76.

sities of the Johannine tradition are held together in dialectical tension. Thus Luke constructs a theology which maintains the created character of the world, while at the same time providing a theological answer to the problem posed by the fact that the redemptive event now lies in the past. In conclusion, let us summarize the main points of Lucan theology.

1. The created character of the world is made visible through the revelation of Christ. This makes it possible for Luke to present the world as open for the action of God. In Jesus Christ the true Adam has appeared, man as God willed him to be (Luke 3.23, 38). In a similar vein the Areopagus speech takes issue with Hellenistic thought, and seeks to present the structures of the world as God's creation. The pattern of question and answer likewise serves to relate the old world and the new. The old world expresses itself in the questions addressed to Jesus, while his answers correct it. The Christian message penetrates the social structures of the old world, transforming them so as to make them receptive to the word.

Thus the life of the world is recognized up to a point. But it is not canonized. It is still the fallen world under divine judgement. And this judgement has already been proleptically executed on the Jews. The Christians are exhorted to patience in suffering (Luke 21.19). The need for this kind of other-worldliness comes out clearly in Luke's treatment of riches. The dangers they are fraught with are exposed and remorsely condemned (Luke 12.13–34; 16.14f, 19ff; 6.20f). But affluence is not evil in itself. God and Christ are frequently symbolized in the parables by wealthy lords (15.11ff; 16.1; 19.12ff). Wealth demands responsible stewardship (19.3; 16.9; 14.13f; 6.34f).[1] There is no place for a Hellenistic attitude of contempt for the world. Jesus' miracles and the creative powers of the Holy Spirit in the community are signs of the presence of the divine new world towards which the Church is moving. The old world is already being transcended by virtue of the new, saving act of God. Its created character is

[1] Cf. R. Koch, "Die Wertung des Besitzes im Lk.-Ev.", *Bibl.* 38(1957), pp. 151ff; Rengstorf, *Lukas*, pp. 4f.

M

acknowledged, but transcended by that greater thing which has come with Christ.

2. There is a similar dialectic in Luke's treatment of the form of the Church on earth. The Church is the place where the exalted one manifests his presence and where the Holy Spirit creates anew. In other words, it is the place in this world which is open to the divine work of salvation. It is a place with definite local associations, for it originates at Jerusalem, and is made up of a particular group of men, the twelve apostles. But this apostolic Church is open on both sides. The leaders of the community are constantly being corrected by the transcendent operation of the Holy Spirit (Acts 11.17f; 16.6ff), and are ready to welcome Christians with special gifts of grace, like Paul and Stephen. But the community is also open to the outside world (Luke 12.41). Alongside of the disciples stand the people ("all" as Luke prefers to call them). They ask questions, react with astonishment or have still not made up their minds about the mystery of Christ. So Luke takes the earthly form of the Church seriously. But it is at the same time defined and superseded by the "heavenly" Christ event, an event which is wholly transcendent and supernatural.

3. The redemptive event belongs to the past. As such it is the precondition of salvation in the present. Its importance is limited, but essential. The redemptive history effected by God in the past is fulfilled in the "to-day" of Christ's presence. In the social structure, i.e. in the tradition—meaning, for Luke, the Old Testament-Jewish history—the past extends into the present and indeed beyond it. It imparts historical continuity to the process of salvation in the present. Here two points must be borne in mind. First, Luke never treats the past as though it were objectified history in the modern sense of the word. The Christ event, belonging though it does to the past, is always ambiguous. That is what lies behind Luke's dialectical treatment. One instance of this we have noted in his use of the verb "to see". Even the visible events of the past are always open to the decision of faith.

The facticity of the redemptive event, which Luke also sees (cf. the Prologue), is only one aspect of the past. It is never absolutized in a positivistic way. It is this open character of the past that Luke manages to portray by means of his dialectic between earthly and heavenly events. The exaltation of Jesus into heaven, for instance, is not only palpably effective in the present, but is also contemporary with the past. Thus the Christ event can be presented as a biography in ordinary secular terms. Indeed, it is essential to do so if it is not to become "sacred" and hence mythical. But the biography of Jesus is open to faith. It is the heavenly—or in modern language, the eschatological—act of God in Jesus which is thus open to faith.[1] In other words, the redemptive event corrects and opens up the structures of this world, though it can never be found within them. It comes direct from heaven, and becomes present for the individual in the moment of confrontation. Anyone can see the divine judgement upon the Jews which took place in the destruction of Jerusalem. For it was an earthly event. But the shift of the aeons is hidden in heaven until "the restoration of all things" (Acts 3.21).

This is how Luke solves the theological problem posed by the fact that redemption has become an event in the past. He discovers a *via media* between the gnostic denial and the early catholic canonization of history. His solution is to give simultaneous expression to the supernatural mystery and the earthly visibility of Christ and his history.

---

[1] For Käsemann, *Essays*, p. 29, the history of Jesus in Luke is "something absolutely in the past, namely, *initium Christianismi*". But Käsemann is identifying the modern immanent view of history with that of Luke, which is open for heaven, Cf. *per contra*, C. H. Ratschow, "Anmerkungen zur theologischen Auffassung des Zeitproblems, *ZThK* 51 (1954), pp. 360ff. Ratchow warns us not to dissolve the objective-historical conception of time in favour of the existential ("time for"). Otherwise the acts of God which are the ground of faith become unessential, "belonging irretrievably to the past" (pp. 383f).

Index of Authors

Althaus, P., 5
Arndt, W. F., and Gingrich, F. W., 81, 131, 153
Asting, R., 22, 121

Baer, H. v., 118, 119, 135, 136, 137, 139
Bailey, J. A., 146
Baltensweiler, H., 99
Barrett, C. K., 11, 43, 135, 144
Barth, K., 10, 40
Bartsch, H. W., 10, 22, 25, 51, 52, 93, 101
Bauer, J., 64
Bauernfeind, O., 18, 96, 97
Behm, J., 21
Bertram, G., 74, 155
Betz, O., 138
Beyer, H.W., 158
Bieneck, J., 45
Bietenhard, H., 37, 139
Billerbeck, P., and Strack, H. L., 94
Blass, F., 48
Blinzler, J., 32, 73, 109
Boman, T., 64, 151
Bornhäuser, K., 153
Bornkamm, G., 2, 10, 40, 41, 71, 100, 106, 123
Bousset, W., 44, 53, 58, 99
Braumann, G., 17, 51
Braun, H., 18, 159, 160
Brun, L., 8, 24, 28, 31, 51
Bultmann, R., 2, 3, 4, 5, 20, 22, 31, 39, 41, 45, 52, 53, 63, 67, 75, 77, 79, 87, 97, 118, 127, 133, 143, 146, 147, 155, 156, 163, 164
Busch, F., 13
Bussmann, W., 9

Cadbury, H. J., 1, 10, 63, 64, 65, 117
Campenhausen, H. v., 118
Conzelmann, H., 1, 3, 6, 8, 9, 11, 13, 15, 16, 17, 18, 19, 22, 23, 24, 28, 30, 31, 32, 33, 36, 40, 44, 45, 47, 48, 49, 51, 55, 56, 60, 61, 62, 73, 74, 83, 84, 91, 93, 94, 95, 96, 100, 106, 107, 108, 111, 112, 114, 115, 122, 123, 124, 136, 138, 139, 140, 141, 144, 147, 149, 150, 151, 154, 155, 157, 161
Cranfield, C. E. B., 80
Cullmann, O., 40, 44, 45, 53, 59, 90, 109, 155

Dahl, N. A., 133
Dalman, G., 33
Davies, J. G., 92
Delling, G., 19, 33, 94
Dibelius, M., 13, 15–18, 33, 43, 54, 58, 59, 62, 63, 67, 69, 70, 79, 81, 84, 110, 117, 147, 161
Dobschütz, E. v., 30
Dodd, C. H., 15, 95
Dupont, D. J., 132

Ebeling, H. J., 47
Eger, H., 78, 116
Ehrhardt, A., 135
Eltester, W., 68

Fascher, E., 143
Feuillet, A., 55
Foakes, F. J., 96
Foerster, W., 52, 58, 76, 77, 105, 133
Friedrich, G., 22, 37, 40, 49, 50, 58, 122, 123, 127, 129, 136, 137, 140, 148
Fuchs, E., 10, 90, 149, 151, 152

Gärtner, B., 70
Glombitza, O., 141, 145
Goltz, E. v.d., 53
Goppelt, L., 133
Grass, H., 160
Grässer, E., 3, 11, 13, 40, 60, 76, 80, 94, 99, 101, 102, 134, 149, 151, 153, 158
Greeven, H., 53
Gressmann, H., 58
Grundmann, W., 13, 14, 21, 23, 31, 33, 54, 57, 81, 82, 83, 84, 86, 87, 114, 143, 144

Index of Scriptural References